Cutting Your Test Development Time with HP Vee

Hewlett-Packard Professional Books

Helsel	Cutting Your Test Development Time with HP VEE: An Iconic Programming Language
Madell, Parsons, Abegg	Developing and Localizing International Software
Poniatowski	The HP-UX System Administrator's "How To" Book

Cutting Your Test Development Time with HP Vee

An Iconic Programming Language

Robert Helsel
Hewlett-Packard Company

P T R Prentice Hall
Englewood Cliffs, New Jersey 07632

Library of Congress Cataloging-In-Publication Data

Helsel, Robert.
    Cutting your test development time with HP Vee : an iconic programming language / Robert Helsel.
      p.   cm.
    ISBN 0-13-099987-3
    1. Visual programming languages (Computer science). 2. HP VEE (Computer program language). 3. Computer software--Testing.
I. Title.
QA76.65.H45   1994
006--dc20   93-4503
                                                                                       CIP

Editorial/production supervision: *Harriet Tellem*
Cover design: *Tommyboy Graphics*
Manufacturing Manager: *Alexis R. Heydt*
Acquisitions editor: *Karen Gettman*
Editorial assistant: *Barbara Alfieri*

©1994 by Hewlett-Packard Company

Published by P T R Prentice Hall
Prentice-Hall, Inc.
A Paramount Communications Company
Englewood Cliffs, New Jersey 07632

All rights reserved. No part of this book may be reproduced, in any form or by any means, without permission in writing from the publisher.

The publisher offers discounts on this book when ordered in bulk quantities.
For more information, contact: Corporate Sales Department
                                              PTR Prentice Hall
                                              113 Sylvan Avenue
                                              Englewood Cliffs, NJ 07632
                                              Phone: 201-592-2863,
                                              FAX: 201-592-2249

Printed in the United States of America
10 9 8 7 6 5 4 3 2 1

IBSN 0-13-099987-3

Prentice-Hall International (UK) Limited, *London*
Prentice-Hall of Australia Pty. Limited, *Sydney*
Prentice-Hall Canada Inc., *Toronto*
Prentice-Hall Hispanoamericana, S.A., *Mexico*
Prentice-Hall of India Private Limited, *New Delhi*
Prentice-Hall of Japan, Inc., *Tokyo*
Simon & Schuster Asia Pte. Ltd., *Singapore*
Editora Prentice-Hall do Brasil, Ltda., *Rio de Janeiro*

Microsoft, Word, and Excel are registered trademarks of the Microsoft Corporation.

Lotus and 1-2-3 are registered trademarks of Lotus Development Corporation.

HP-UX is Hewlett-Packard's implementation of the UNIX operating system. UNIX is a registered trademark of UNIX System Laboratories, Inc.

DT VEE is a registered trademark of Data Translation, Inc.

SunOS, SPARCstations, and Open Windows are registered trademarks of Sun Computers, Inc.

Image Alchemy is a registered trademark of Handmade Software, Inc.

Paintbrush is a trademark of Zsoft Corporation.

Acknowledgments

I would like to thank all the people who offered suggestions on this book: Sue Wolber, Scott Turner, Donna Trinko, Mike Toney, Jeanie Sumrall-Ajero, Rob Saffer, Debbie Rhoades, Miles Porter, Vicki Pompea, Mark Papineau, Ken Koehn, Doug Kennedy, Jay Johannes, Bill Hunt, Chuck Heller, Karen Helt, Bill Heinzman, Gary Goodale, Grant Drenkow, Ken Colasuonno, John Bidwell, Alan Bell, Doug Beethe, Randy Bailey, and Jim Bachman.

Special thanks go to Karen Champagne from Data Translation for supplying the material on DT VEE, to Bruce Hebert for the material on Dynamic Link Libraries, to John Dumais for the information on compiled functions, and to Jim Armentrout and Van Walther for examples and material from the current HP VEE class.

Without the continuing support of management, this book could not have been completed. Special thanks go to the managers who provided the time and resources to finish this book: Bill Bush, Wayne Willis, Doug Collins, Roger Muller, Brad Miller, and George Sparks.

Finally, I'd like to thank Karen Gettman, Senior Editor from Prentice Hall, and Pat Pekary, HP Press Editor for making the process of publishing smooth and enjoyable.

Contents

Preface

Part I: HP VEE Fundamentals

1. Using the HP VEE Development Environment
   Overview   1-1
   The Development Environment Components   1-4
   Using Menus   1-5
   Saving Your Work, Exiting HP VEE,
      and Restarting Your Program   1-8
   Helping Yourself   1-10
   Using Objects   1-11
   Object Pins and Terminals   1-18
   Connecting Objects to Make Programs   1-20
      Lab 1-1: Display Random Number   1-20
      Lab 1-2: Display Waveform   1-22
      Lab 1-3: Set and Get a Global Variable   1-24
   Conserving Screen Space   1-26
      Lab 1-4: Noisy Cosine Program   1-27
   Chapter 1 Checklist   1-30

2. Creating a Simple Test Program
   Overview   2-1
      Lab 2-1: The Pulse Program   2-2
   Easy Text Documentation of Your Program   2-13
   Using Online Help and Debugging Tools   2-16
   Chapter 2 Checklist   2-29

3. Two Easy Ways To Control Instruments
   Overview   3-1
      Lab 3-1: Configuring an HP-IB Instrument   3-5
      Lab 3-2: Configuring a Function Generator
               for Direct I/O   3-10
   Using an Instrument Driver   3-13

Using Direct I/O	3-17
Chapter 3 Checklist	3-28

4. Analyzing and Displaying Test Data

Overview	4-1
HP VEE Data Types	4-2
HP VEE Analysis Capabilities	4-5
Using Math Objects	4-10
Lab 4-1: Calculating Standard Deviation	4-10
Using the Formula Object	4-12
Display Capabilities	4-16
Customizing Displays	4-18
Chapter 4 Checklist	4-22

5. Storing and Retrieving Test Results

Overview	5-1
Using Arrays to Store Test Results	5-2
Using the To/From File Objects	5-5
Lab 5-1: Using the To/From File Objects	5-9
Using Records to Store Mixed Data Types	5-16
Lab 5-2: Using Records	5-16
Using DataSets to Store and Retrieve Records	5-24
Lab 5-3: Using DataSets	5-24
Customizing a Simple Test Database	5-28
Lab 5-4: Using Search and Sort Operations With DataSets	5-28
Chapter 5 Checklist	5-37

Part II: Common Tasks Using HP VEE

6. Generating Reports Easily

Overview	6-1
Lab 6-1: Generating a Simple Report	6-2
Using Spreadsheets With HP VEE	6-20
Lab 6-2: Generating a Report With MS Excel	6-21
Chapter 6 Checklist	6-29

7. Integrating Programs In Other Languages

Overview	7-1
Understanding the Execute Program Object	7-2
Lab 7-1: Using a System Command (PC)	7-5
Lab 7-2: Using a System Command (UNIX)	7-7
Lab 7-3: Using Compiled Programs	7-10
Chapter 7 Checklist	7-14

8. Leveraging Your HP VEE Test Programs

Overview	8-1
Merging HP VEE Programs	8-2
Lab 8-1: Merging a Bar Chart Display Program	8-2
Using Functions	8-4
Lab 8-2: User Function Operations	8-5
Using Libraries With HP VEE User Functions	8-11
Lab 8-3: Creating and Merging a Library of User Functions	8-12
Lab 8-4: Importing and Deleting Libraries	8-16
Chapter 8 Checklist	8-19

9. Test Sequencing

Overview	9-1
Using the Sequencer Object	9-2
Lab 9-1: Creating a Test Execution Order	9-3
Lab 9-2: Passing Data in the Sequencer	9-12
Lab 9-3: Analyzing Data from the Sequencer	9-23
Lab 9-4: Storing and Retrieving Logged Data	9-26
Chapter 9 Checklist	9-29

10. Using Operator Interfaces

Overview	10-1
Key Points Concerning Operator Interfaces	10-2
Common Tasks In Creating Operator Interfaces	10-4
Lab 10-1: Using Menus	10-4
Lab 10-2: Importing Bitmaps for Panel Backgrounds	10-9
Lab 10-3: Creating a High Impact Warning	10-11
Chapter 10 Checklist	10-16

11. Optimizing HP VEE Programs

Overview	11-1
Basic Techniques for Optimizing Programs	11-2
Optimizing With Compiled Functions (HP-UX and SunOS)	11-8
Chapter 11 Checklist	11-25

12. Writing Instrument Drivers

Overview	12-1
Lab 12-1: Creating a Simple Customized Driver	12-9
Chapter 12 Checklist	12-17

13. Using HP VEE Features Unique To MS Windows

Overview	13-1
Differences Between HP VEE for Windows and HP VEE for UNIX	13-2
Using Dynamic Data Exchange (DDE)	13-6
Lab 13 - 1: Building a Simple DDE Object	13-7
Using Dynamic Link Libraries (DLLs)	13-12
Chapter 13 Checklist	13-21

14. Using HP VEE Features Unique to HP-UX

Overview	14-1
Communicating with HP BASIC/UX Programs	14-2
Lab 14-1: Communicating with HP BASIC, Case #1	14-5
Lab 14-2: Communicating with HP BASIC, Case #2	14-7
Using Remote Test Capabilities	14-10
Chapter 14 Checklist	14-14

15. Data Acquisition With PC Plug-in Cards

Overview	15-1
Data Acquisition Using DT VEE	15-2
Using the Data Acquisition Objects	15-5
Lab 15-1: Configuring a Subsystem	15-8
Lab 15-2: Using the D/A Config Object	15-14
Lab 15-3: Stopping After an Error	15-20
Lab 15-4: Using the Config Objects with the D/A Subsystem	15-24
Lab 15-5: External Clocks and the A/D Subsystem	15-27

Lab 15-6: Using One Subsystem to Clock
    Another Subsystem   15-29
Example Application: Brain Wave Analysis   15-33
Chapter 15 Checklist   15-37

Appendixes

Appendix A: Ordering and Configuration Information
HP VEE for Windows   A-1
HP VEE-Test for HP-UX   A-1
HP VEE for Sun   A-2
DT VEE for Windows   A-2
Where to Order HP VEE   A-3
Where to Order DT VEE   A-6

Appendix B: Additional Lab Exercises
General Programming Techniques   B-1
Using Masks   B-11
Using Strings and Globals   B-14
Optimizing Techniques   B-16
UserObjects   B-18
HP VEE User Functions   B-20
Operator Panels   B-27
Working with Files   B-32
Moving Data To and From Files   B-32
Records   B-34
Test Sequencing   B-40
Instrument Drivers   B-47
Compiled Functions (HP-UX)   B-50

PREFACE

Why Learn HP VEE?

Hewlett-Packard Visual Engineering Environment (HP VEE) is an iconic programming language optimized for instrument control. Customers report reducing their test development time up to 80% compared to conventional programming techniques. Furthermore, you can leverage your current software investment, because HP VEE integrates with textual languages including C, C++, Pascal, Fortran, and HP BASIC/UX. HP VEE is supported on popular test platforms such as PCs running MS Windows, Hewlett-Packard workstations, and Sun SPARCstations, so it's a portable and flexible language. HP VEE is being used in a wide range of test applications including design characterization and verification, functional test in manufacturing, test executives, and incoming inspection.

This book is the fastest and easiest way to learn HP VEE. If you can afford the time, take HP's customer class or hire an HP Systems Engineer to teach HP VEE onsite. But if you need to learn HP VEE on your own, then this book was designed for you. You can grasp the fundamentals in a day by studying the first five chapters. Then you can go directly to the chapters in Part II that are relevant to your application. You can complete the entire book in a week. Your key benefit in doing so would be to double your productivity. That, in turn, can reduce costs and time to market.

Iconic vs. Textual Programming Languages

With HP VEE you create programs by connecting icons together using the mouse; with a textual language you use keywords following rules of syntax. The result in HP VEE resembles a data-flow diagram, which is easier to use and understand than traditional lines of code.

There is no laborious edit-compile-link-execute cycle using HP VEE.

CUTTING YOUR TEST DEVELOPMENT TIME WITH HP VEE

The following two figures compare a simple function programmed first in a textual language (ANSI C, in this case), and then in HP VEE. The function creates an array of 10 random numbers, finds the maximum value, and displays the results.

/* Program to find maximum element in array */

```c
#include <math.h>
main( )
{
  double num[10], max;
  int i;

  for (i=0; i<10; i++){
    num[i]=(double) rand( )/pow(2.0,15.0);
    printf("%f\n",num[i]);
  }
  max=num[0];
  for (i=1; i<10; i++){
    if (num[i] > max) max=num[i];
  }
  printf("\nmax: %f\n",max);
}
```

Figure 1: ANSI C Program

Preface

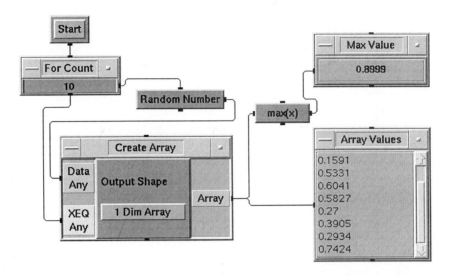

Fig. 2. HP VEE Program

You can see that each icon performs a specific function. For example, there are icons to create arrays or to obtain the maximum value from an array. Time-consuming tasks such as controlling instruments, creating customized data displays, or developing operator interfaces become very easy using HP VEE. This method of test development leads to productivity gains up to five times greater than conventional techniques.

Leverage Your Existing Test Software

HP VEE runs on PCs running MS Windows, HP-UX and SunOS workstations. There is also a special version of HP VEE sold by Data Translation called DT VEE, which runs on MS Windows and allows communication with PC plug-in cards. On each of these platforms HP VEE provides mechanisms for linking conventional test programs as well as commercial applications. For example, you could use HP VEE to sequence existing tests in HP BASIC/UX, C, C++, Fortran, or Pascal on an HP-UX workstation. HP VEE also provides a number of interprocess communication features to share data with commercial applications such as relational databases.

Maintain a Flexible I/O Strategy Based on Standards

HP VEE I/O Capabilities:

- Instrument drivers for over 300 instruments

- Driver writer's tool

- Direct I/O icon to send instrument command strings over standard interfaces such as HP-IB (IEEE488), GPIO, RS 232

- Direct VXI backplane control using the HP's V/382 instrument controller

- Support of PC Plug-in Instruments using DT VEE (see Appendix A)

Exploit HP VEE Manufacturing Test Capabilities

- Reduced development and maintenance time with iconic programming

- Powerful test sequencing

- Integration with conventional languages like C, C++, Pascal, Fortran, and HP BASIC/UX

- Convenient and flexible operator interface capabilities

- Platform support for HP and SUN workstations as well as PCs

- Remote test capabilities

- Interprocess communication tools to link with other applications such as relational databases or statistical analysis packages

- HP's excellent array of support options

- Less expensive "run only" version available

The Best Way to Use This Book

This book provides a tutorial for the test system developer in two parts. Part I teaches the fundamentals of HP VEE in a single day. Each chapter will take approximately two hours to complete. Part II is task-oriented, so you can go directly to the chapters that suit your application. If you work through the entire book, it will take you about a week to complete. To teach you HP VEE as quickly as possible, we have used guided examples for the most part. If you can spare the time, you should also work through the examples in Appendix B, which challenge you to solve problems on your own. Solutions are provided with explanations.

You can use the HP VEE software on any of the supported platforms for the purposes of this tutorial. See Appendix A for ordering and configuration information. Although you don't need HP VEE documentation for this course, we encourage you to consult it for more information on any given topic. The goal of this tutorial is to enable you to program your applications with HP VEE as soon as possible. It covers the same material as the HP VEE customer class. If you want to achieve expert capability, you may want to continue your study with the product documentation after this book.

Let's get started.

Bob Helsel

VXI Systems Division

Hewlett-Packard

Part I: HP VEE Fundamentals

1

Using the HP VEE Development Environment

Average time to complete: 1.5 hrs.

In this chapter you'll learn about:

Overview

HP VEE (Hewlett-Packard Visual Engineering Environment) is an iconic programming language that produces dramatic reductions in test development time. Programs are constructed by connecting icons together on the screen. The resulting HP VEE program -- which resembles a block diagram -- may be run like a program in a textual language such as C or HP BASIC. The exercises in this chapter will introduce you to a style of program development that is not only efficient but intuitive and fun as well.

(Please refer to the Preface for a more detailed discussion of HP VEE features and benefits.)

- Environment components

- Selecting menu items

- Saving programs, exiting and restarting HP VEE

- Getting help

- Using HP VEE objects

- Input and output pins

- Connecting objects to make programs

- Creating HP VEE UserObjects

CUTTING YOUR TEST DEVELOPMENT TIME WITH HP VEE

An HP VEE Program

You can see an example of an HP VEE program in the figure below.

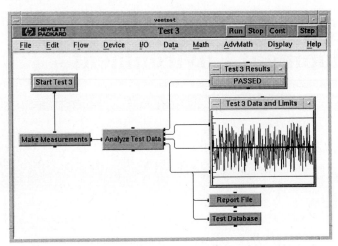

Fig. 1-1. An HP VEE Program (Detail View)

This is the "Detail" view of the program, which shows all the connections between icons ("objects") and is analogous to source code in a textual language. The objects perform various functions such as I/O operations, analysis, and display. All objects use their input and output pins in a consistent way: data input pins on the left, data output pins on the right, operational sequence pins on the top and bottom. Each object may be displayed as an icon or in its "open view". For example, in Fig. 1-1 the object labeled Analyze Test Data is shown as an icon; the object labeled Test 3 Data and Limits is shown using an open view. The open view is larger and more detailed. An object might also contain a subprogram, which can be viewed and changed. You start this program by clicking Start Test 3. This object triggers the Make Measurements object, which gathers test data and passes it to the next object for analysis. Analyze Test Data not only analyzes the test data, but also puts out a pass/fail message, sends the data and test limits to a display, and copies a record of the test data to a report file and a database. You can see how easy it is to follow the flow of the program. Make Measurements and Analyze Test Data are objects you can create and label yourself. HP VEE programs are modular and practically document themselves. You save the program to a file, which you can open, change, and run in HP VEE.

An additional benefit of programming in HP VEE is that it only takes a few seconds to create an operator interface (the one below took about 30 seconds to create). The figure below shows the "Panel" view of the program in Fig. 1-1. Only the start object and displays are presented to the operator making the test extremely easy to use. The panel view can also be stored in a way that secures it from any unwanted alterations.

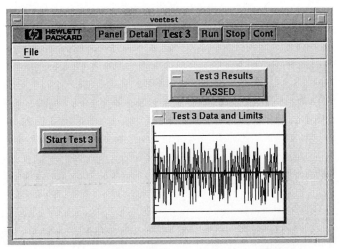

Fig. 1-2. An HP VEE Program (Panel View)

This chapter will teach you how to start and stop HP VEE, how to help yourself while you're learning, and the basic mechanics of getting objects from the menus and connecting them together to create programs. First, let's look at the basic components of the HP VEE development environment.

CUTTING YOUR TEST DEVELOPMENT TIME WITH HP VEE

The Development Environment Components

After you've followed the installation instructions, you will see the HP VEE development environment. (Configuration and ordering information are located in Appendix A.) Figure 1-3 shows the PC version; Figure 1-4, the UNIX version. The two are essentially the same, except the positions of the tool bar and menu bar are reversed.

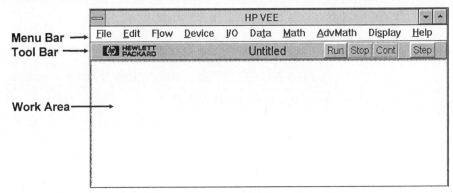

Fig. 1-3. The HP VEE Development Environment (PC)

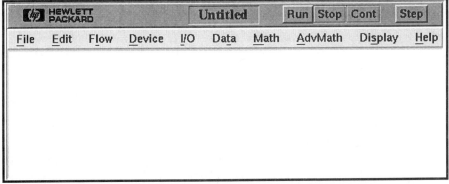

Fig. 1-4. The HP VEE Development Environment (UNIX)

1 - 4

Using the HP VEE Development Environment

- The *Menu Bar* provides menus holding the commands and icons used to build your programs.

- The *Tool Bar* displays the title of your program and provides buttons to control execution.

- The *Work Area* is where you construct your program with icons.

    Note: *This book focuses on the B.02.00 version of HP VEE. Slight differences in earlier versions will be annotated as we go along. You can identify your version by selecting Help => On Version... .*

Using Menus

Let's use a specific example to explain how menus work. The process will be the same for all menus. First, you'll open the Device menu, select an object from the Virtual Source submenu, and place it in the work area. Next, you'll open the "object menu" and select Help to find out how the object operates.

Note: *"Click and hold" means that you should press the left mouse button, and hold it down, until you move the mouse pointer to a new location. "Click" means to quickly press and release the left mouse button. If you need to use the right mouse button, we will say so in the instructions. If you have a mouse with three buttons, you won't need the middle button using HP VEE.*

1. Click and hold **Device** to open the menu.

    A pull-down menu appears.

2. Move the mouse pointer down to the **Virtual Source** submenu, then right to **Function Generator,** and then release the mouse button.

    An outline of the Function Generator object appears.

CUTTING YOUR TEST DEVELOPMENT TIME WITH HP VEE

3. Move the **Function Generator** to the center of the work area, and click to place the object.

The object appears where you placed it.

*Note: In future exercises instructions similar to those above will be condensed into the following format: Select **Device => Virtual Source => Function Generator**, and place it in the center of the work area.*

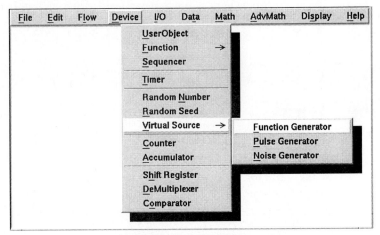

Fig. 1-5. The Device => Virtual Source Submenu

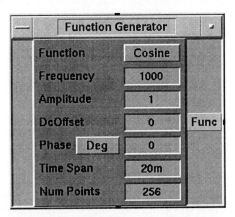

Figure 1-6. The Function Generator Object

Using the HP VEE Development Environment

The arrow to the right of Virtual Source indicates a submenu. Three dots after a menu item indicate that one or more dialog boxes will follow. For example, File => Save As ... operates this way.

4. Now open the **Function Generator** object menu by clicking the horizontal bar in the upper left-hand corner of the object.

    You can see the object menu bar and the open menu in the following figure. Most object menus open the same way.

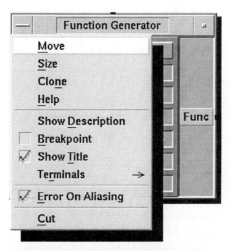

Fig. 1-7. The Function Generator Object Menu

Tip: Often a more convenient way to open an object menu is to simply place the mouse pointer over the object and click the right mouse button. Try this using the Flow => Start object. The menu will "pop up" at the location of the pointer.

The Function Generator object is used to simulate test data. You can use it to generate waveforms such as sine, cosine, triangle, square, ramp as well as DC only. If you want to know more about it, just open its object menu and click Help.

Saving Your Work, Exiting HP VEE, and Restarting Your Program

To Save Your Work and Exit HP VEE

1. Select **File => Save As ...** and complete the dialog box.

   A dialog box entitled Save File appears. The following two figures show the PC and UNIX formats for this box.

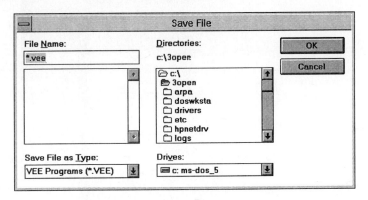

Fig. 1-8. The Save File Dialog Box (PC)

In the PC dialog box, if the default selections for a drive, directory, and file type are suitable, you can just type in a file name and click **OK**. Otherwise, double-click a directory in the **Directories** menu to open it. Select a drive by opening the **Drives** menu and clicking on your choice. Open the menu labeled **Save File as Type**, and make a selection. (The default extension is **.VEE**.) Finally, double-click in the **File Name** field, type in a file name, and click **OK**. HP VEE will automatically add the **.VEE** extension.

Using the HP VEE Development Environment

For the UNIX version of the Save File dialog box, see the figure below.

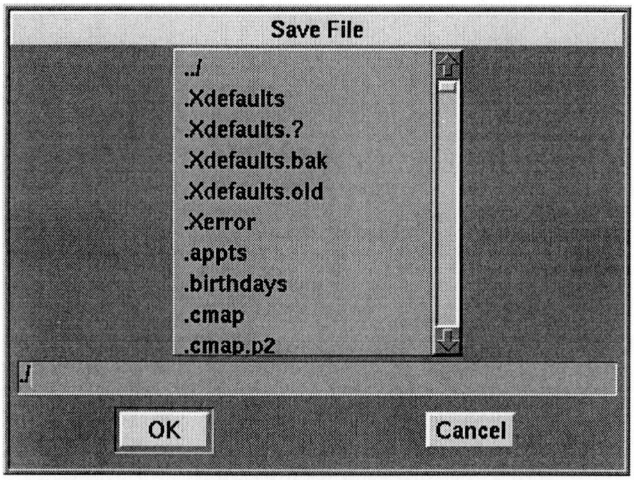

```
                    Save File
    ../
    .Xdefaults
    .Xdefaults.?
    .Xdefaults.bak
    .Xdefaults.old
    .Xerror
    .appts
    .birthdays
    .cmap
    .cmap.p2

    ./

       [  OK  ]              [ Cancel ]
```

Fig. 1-9. The Save File Dialog Box (UNIX)

In the UNIX dialog box, just type the file name and click **OK**. Your home directory is the default. If you'd like to save the file in another directory, use the **Backspace** key to delete the characters **./**, then type the file name with the complete path and click **OK**. In UNIX you need to add the **.vee** extension.

> *Tip:* *A handy way to replace a typed entry (version B.02.00 or later) in a dialog box is to click and drag the mouse pointer over the entry to highlight it. Or you can highlight the entry by double-clicking the input field. Then you can simply type your correction and click OK.*

2. Select **File => Exit** to close the HP VEE application window.

   Shortcut: Press Ctrl-e to exit HP VEE.

CUTTING YOUR TEST DEVELOPMENT TIME WITH HP VEE

To Restart HP VEE and Run Your Program

1. **PC:** Double-click the **HP VEE for Windows** icon.

   UNIX: From your home directory, enter **veetest**. (If the HP VEE directory is not in your path, enter the whole path: **/usr/lib/veetest**. Check with your system administrator if any problems arise.)

2. Select **File => Open** and complete the **Open File** dialog box.

   The PC and UNIX formats are the same as for the Save File dialog box. Note that in HP VEE for Windows, the default directory for user programs is the VEE_USER directory, unless you specified something else during installation.

   HP VEE will read your program into the work area.

   Tip: *In UNIX versions, the command, veetest -r <filename>, will start HP VEE and the program specified by <filename>. (Again, if the HP VEE directory is not in your path, you need to enter the complete path, /usr/lib/veetest -r <filename>.)*

Helping Yourself

- Click Help in an object menu to get specific information on that object.

- Click Help on the main menu bar to access the online help facility for HP VEE, which will give you information on features, instruments drivers, common tasks, short cuts, the version you're running, how to use the help facility, and release notes.

- Although you will not need to use HP VEE documentation to complete this self-paced training, consult the product documentation for more detailed information on any particular feature or concept.

To Stop HP VEE by Brute Force

Most of the time you can just select File => Exit to stop HP VEE. You probably will never need to use the following techniques, but occasionally you might do something very creative, and HP VEE stops responding to the mouse or keyboard.

In UNIX you need to "kill" the process (UNIX terminology is not very polite about these things):

1. Enter **ps -ef | grep vee** in HP-UX (or **ps -aux|grep vee** in SunOS) at a prompt to identify the process identification number. You will see a line with **veetest** on the end. The number following your login is the process number you want. In my case it's **bobh <number> ... veetest**.

2. Ente**r kill -9 <number>** to stop the HP VEE application. Then you can simply start HP VEE over again.

In MS Windows:

1. Press **Ctrl-Alt-Delete** and a window pops up giving you various options. Usually you want to simply stop HP VEE and return to Windows, where you can start over again. Just follow the instructions in the window.

Using Objects

To Delete an Object from the Work Area

You've already learned how to select an object from a menu and place it in the work area. Let's cover deleting an object using the Function Generator for this exercise. Get that object from the Device menu and put it in the work area. Here are two ways to delete an object from the work area. We'll give the faster way first.

1. Place the mouse cursor over the object and press **Ctrl-d**.

   - OR -

1. Open the object menu (by clicking on the horizontal bar in the upper left-hand corner), and select **Cut**..

Practice getting various objects from the menus and deleting them. If you want to know how they work, just access Help in any object menu.

To Duplicate an Object

The Clone operation duplicates an object exactly including any changes you've made such as sizing or renaming.

1. Open the object menu and select **Clone**.

   An outline of the duplicated object appears.

2. Move the outline to the desired location, and click to place the object.

To Move an Object

   Note: Select File => New to open a new file and clear your work area before starting a new exercise, if necessary. If an exercise builds on a former one that you need to retain, we'll say so.

Let's use one of the display objects for an example. Select Display => Waveform(Time) and place it on the right side of the work area.

1. Open the object menu and select **Move**.

   The mouse pointer becomes a small rectangle with cross hairs.

Using the HP VEE Development Environment

2. Place the mouse pointer over the object, press and hold the left mouse button (called "dragging"), while you move the object to the desired location.

3. Click again to place the object.

   Shortcut: *You can also click and drag the title bar of the object.*

To Edit the Name of an Object

1. Open the object menu and select **Change Title...** .

   A Change Title dialog box appears with the current title highlighted.

2. Type the new title and click **OK**.

   Note: If you have a version of HP VEE prior to B.02.00, you edit the name of an object by clicking on the name to get a cursor, then entering the new name.

To Switch an Object Between Iconic and Open Views

HP VEE displays objects either in an iconic or "open view,." as shown in the figure below.

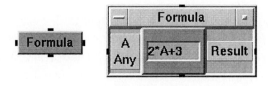

Fig. 1-10. Object in Iconic and Open Views

1 - 13

CUTTING YOUR TEST DEVELOPMENT TIME WITH HP VEE

Note: *The A in the formula refers to the input terminal, "A Any". The "Any" means any HP VEE datatype. You could double-click the terminal to get more detailed information on what type of data the terminal is receiving.*

The iconic view conserves space in the work area and makes your programs more readable. The open view provides more detail and allows you to edit the internals of an object.

1. To switch from an open to iconic view, click the dot on the right end of the object's title bar. To return to an open view, double-click the icon.

To Size an Object

1. Open the object menu and click **Size**.

   You will see a small right angle on the cursor.

2. Move the right angle to desired position of the lower-right corner and click.

   Note: *You can also size an object when you first select it from a menu. After you've placed the object outline, just click and drag with the right mouse button to indicate the desired position of the lower-right corner of the object.*

To Select or Deselect an Object

1. An object is selected when you click it; HP VEE puts a shadow behind it (see Fig. 1-11). To deselect it, just move the mouse pointer over the work area and click.

Using the HP VEE Development Environment

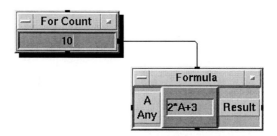

Fig. 1-11. Selected and Deselected Objects

Note: *We will also use the word "select" to indicate choosing a menu item, but the context will make the meaning obvious.*

You select an object to let HP VEE know that you want to do something to that object in particular. For example, if you select an object, then click Edit => Cut, that object alone will be deleted.

To Select Several Objects

You'd want to do this when performing an operation on multiple objects such as *Edit => Cut* or *Edit => Move Objects*.

1. Click **Edit => Select Objects**.

2. Click on the desired objects.

   Shortcut: *You can select several objects more quickly by pressing Ctrl and clicking the desired objects.*

To Deselect All Objects

1. Click anywhere on the HP VEE work area.

1 - 15

To Edit Objects

1. Click **Edit** on the menu bar and select the operation you want.

   - OR -

1. Place the mouse pointer anywhere on blank work area space and click the right mouse button.

   A pop-up Edit menu appears.

   Note: *Any menu items that are inactive appear in a different shade than active items. For instance, the Cut, Copy, and Clone operations in the Edit menu appear in a different shade from active menu items, until at least one object is highlighted in the work area.*

To Move the Work Area

1. (Make sure there is at least one icon in the work area.) Place the mouse pointer anywhere on the background of the work area, press and hold the left mouse button, and move the work area in any direction.

   Note: *Scroll bars appear if your program is too big for the work area. To use the bars just place the mouse pointer over the vertical or horizontal scroll bar and drag it in the desired direction. See the figure on the next page.*

Using the HP VEE Development Environment

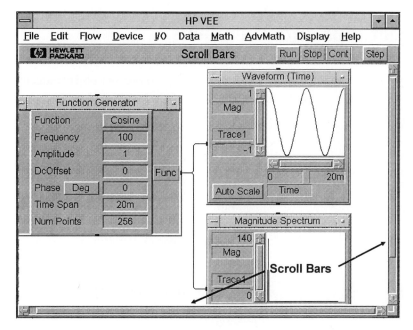

Fig. 1-12. Scroll Bars Appearing in Work Area

To Clear the Work Area

1. Select **File => New**.

To Delete Lines

1. Press **Shift-Ctrl** and click the line you want to delete.

    - OR -

1. Select **Edit => Delete Line** and click the line you want to delete.

CUTTING YOUR TEST DEVELOPMENT TIME WITH HP VEE

Object Pins and Terminals

You create an HP VEE program by connecting objects together with data lines. These lines are attached to "pins" on the objects.

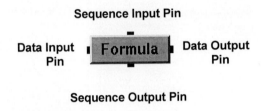

Fig. 1-13. Input and Output Pins

You connect the data input and output pins to carry data between objects. The sequence pin connections are optional. If connected, they will dictate an execution order flowing from the top of the work area to the bottom.

Terminals are simply the open view representation of the data pins. They carry detailed information such as the name of the terminal, the type and value of the data being transmitted.

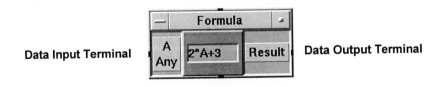

Fig. 1-14. Input and Output Terminals

To Add Data Input Terminals to an Object

1. Open the object menu and select **Terminals => Add Data Input**.

   The terminals will automatically be named A, B, C, ..., but you can rename them.

   Shortcut: *Just place the mouse pointer over the terminal input area and press CTRL-a.*

To Delete Data Input or Output Terminals from an Object

1. Open the object menu and select **Terminals => Delete Data Input**.

   Shortcut: *Just place the mouse pointer over the terminal input area and press CTRL-d.*

To Examine or Alter Terminals

You'd want to do this to see what type of data is passing through a terminal, to specify what type of data it will accept, or to rename it.

1. Double-click on the terminal. Change any of the fields, if appropriate, then click **OK**.

To Edit the Terminal Name

1. Double-click the terminal. The **Name** input field is highlighted.

2. Type the new name and click **OK**.

Connecting Objects to Make Programs

Let's work through a few simple examples. The principles will be the same for all programs. This program simply generates and displays a random number. It will give you practice in connecting objects and documentation.

> *Note: The exercises are designed to teach certain programming principles, and the programs themselves may serve no practical purpose.*

Lab 1-1. Display Random Number

1. Document your program:

   a. Select **File => Change Title ...**, type **Display Random Number**, then click **OK**. (In versions before B.02.00 you edit the title bar directly.)

   b. Select **Display => Note Pad** and place it at the top center of the work area. Click on the editing area to get a cursor, then enter:

   Display Random Number generates a real number between 0 and 1, then prints it to a display box.

2. Select **Device => Random Number** and place it on the left side of the work area.

3. Select **Display => AlphaNumeric** and place it to the right of the **Random Number** object.

4. Open the object menus and select **Help** to understand the objects better. Double-click on **Random Number** to get the open view.

Using the HP VEE Development Environment

5. Connect the objects by clicking outside but near the **Random Number** data output pin. Move the mouse pointer near the **Alphanumeric** data input pin and click.

   You should get a data line connecting the two objects.

   Note: *When connecting objects with lines, notice that you click near a pin to start a line, not directly on it. As you move the mouse pointer with the line attached near the target pin, a box highlights the pin. Then you click again to complete the connection.*

   Note: *If for some reason you want to terminate the line-connecting operation before you've completed the link, just double-click the mouse on the work area (away from any terminal) and the line will disappear.*

6. Click **Run** and you will see a random number displayed, as shown below.

   Select **File => Save As ...**, type **DISPRAND.VEE**, and click **OK**.

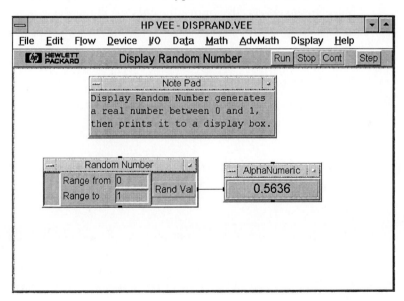

Figure 1-15. Display Random Number

1 - 21

Lab 1-2 : Display Waveform

This program gives you additional practice in the basic mechanics of constructing an HP VEE program. You'll generate a cosine waveform and display it.

> *Note:* *We will assume that you select File => New to clear your work area before all lab exercises. If you need to revise a former program, we will say so.*

1. First, let's document the program. Select **Display => Note Pad** and place it at the top-center of the work area. Click on the editing area to get a cursor, then enter:

   Display Waveform generates a cosine waveform and prints it to a real time display.

   You may have to size the **Note Pad** depending on your screen. (Open the object menu, select **Size**, move the cursor-- in the shape of a right angle -- to the desired position of the lower-right corner of the object, then click.)

2. Select **Device => Virtual Source => Function Generator** and place it on the left side of the work area.

3. Select **Display => Waveform (Time)** and place it on the right side of the work area.

4. Click near the **Function Generator** data output pin, move the mouse pointer to the data input pin of the **Waveform (Time)** object, and click again.

5. Click **Run** on the tool bar. Your program should look like the figure below.

6. Select **File => Save As ...**, type in **DISPWAVE.VEE**, then click **OK**.

Using the HP VEE Development Environment

Note: To conserve space we will just print the program without the surrounding HP VEE environment.

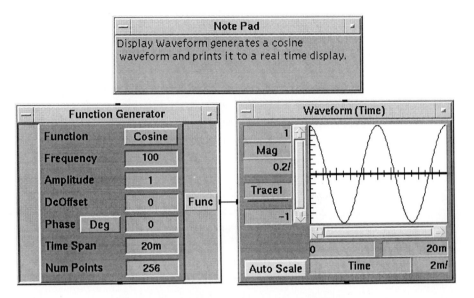

Fig. 1-16. The Display Wave Program

CUTTING YOUR TEST DEVELOPMENT TIME WITH HP VEE

Lab 1-3: Set and Get a Global Variable

This program gives you more practice in the basic mechanics of building an HP VEE program while introducing global variables. You can use the Set and Get Global objects to set any HP VEE data type to a global variable that can then be referenced at any point later in your program. This example uses a number of type Real. We'll discuss all of the HP data types in Chapter 4.

1. Select **Display => Note Pad** and place it at the top-center of the work area. Click on the upper left-hand corner of the editing area to get a cursor, then enter:

    Set and Get a Global Variable prompts the user to enter a real number. The variable, num, is set to this real number. Then the variable, num, is recalled and displayed.

2. Select **Data => Constant => Real** and place it on the left side of the work area. Open the object menu and examine the **Help** entry.

3. Open the **Real** object menu and select **Change Title...** . Type the prompt **Enter a Real Number:**, then click **OK**. (Before version B.02.00 you edit the title directly on the title bar.)

    Note: We're using one of the Constant objects for an input dialog box by simply changing its title to a prompt. This is a common technique for getting user input.

4. Select **Data => Globals => Set Global** and place it to the right of the **Real** object. Click and drag over **globalA** to highlight it, then enter **num**.

    This means that the user will enter a real number in the Real object. When they click Run, that number will be set to the global variable, num.

5. Connect the data output pin of the **Real** object to the data input pin of the **Set Global** object.

6. Select **Data => Globals => Get Global** and place it below the **Set Global** object. Change the variable name to **num**.

Using the HP VEE Development Environment

7. Connect the **Set Global** sequence output pin to the **Get Global** sequence input pin.

   Note: *A global variable has to be set, before you can use it; therefore, we need to use the sequence pins in this case to make sure that the variable num has been set, before you retrieve it with Get Global.*

8. Select **Display** => **AlphaNumeric** and place it to the right of the **Get Global** object.

9. Connect the **Get Global** data output pin to the **Alphanumeric** data input pin.

10. Enter a real number and click **Run** on the tool bar. Your program should look like the one below.

11. Select **File** => **Save As ...** and name your program **GLOBAL.VEE**.

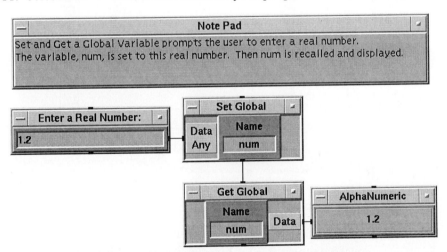

Figure 1-17. Set and Get a Global Variable

1 - 25

Conserving Screen Space

There is an object in the Device menu called a UserObject, which is essentially another HP VEE environment inside the main work area. Think of it as a subroutine or your own customized object that you use like any other object HP VEE provides. See the figure below.

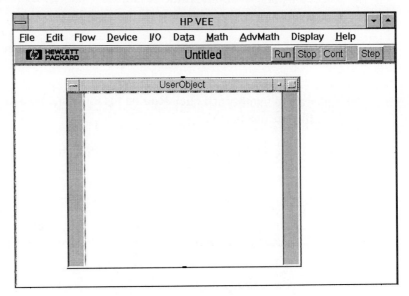

Figure 1-18. A UserObject

If you put parts of your program into UserObjects, they can be iconized to conserve screen space. You can also label that UserObject in a way that describes its functionality. Let's try a simple example.

Using the HP VEE Development Environment

Lab 1-4: Noisy Cosine Program

This lab shows how a userobject can conserve your screen space. You'll add a cosine waveform to a noisy waveform inside a UserObject named Noisy Cos. The resultant wave will then be displayed.

1. Select **Device => UserObject** and place it to the left side of the work area. Open the **UserObject** object menu and click **Change Title....** Type **Noisy Cos** and click **OK**. Open the object menu again and select **Terminals => Add Data Output**.

   (Before version B.02.00 you edit the title bar directly. From now on we will just instruct you to change the title, which you can do in the manner that suits your version of HP VEE.)

   The UserObject is now named Noisy Cos, and it has a data output pin with the default label X.

2. Select **Device => Virtual Source => Function Generator** and place it in the **UserObject**. Highlight the **1000** in the **Frequency** input field and type **100** instead. Iconize the **Function Generator** by clicking on the iconize button in the upper right corner of the object.

3. Select **Device => Virtual Source => Noise Generator** and place it below the **Function Generator** in the **UserObject**. Open its **Help** entry to find out what it does. Iconize the **Noise Generator**.

4. Select **Math => + - * / => +** and place it to the right of the generators in the **UserObject**. Consult the **Help** entry for +. Connect the data output pins of both generators to the two input pins on the + object.

   HP VEE will now add the two waveforms. You want to send this resultant wave to the UserObject data output pin.

5. Connect the data output pin of the + object to the **UserObject** data output **X**.

1 - 27

6. Select **Display => Waveform (Time)** and place it to the right of the **Noisy Cos UserObject.** Connect the **Noisy Cos** data output to the **Waveform (Time)** data input. Open the **Waveform (Time)** object menu and select **Panel Layout => Graph Only**.

7. Click **Run** on the tool bar. Your program should look like Figure 1-19.

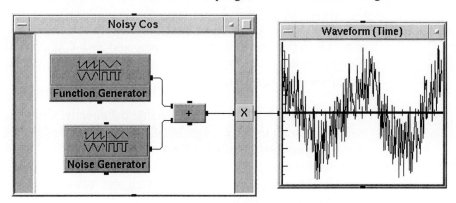

Fig. 1-19. The Noisy Cosine Program

8. Iconize **Noisy Cos** now. You have the same functionality, but you've conserved a lot of work space and simplified your program. See Figure 1-20.

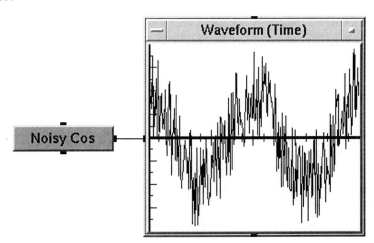

Fig. 1-20. The Noisy Cosine Program After Iconizing

Using the HP VEE Development Environment

This completes Chapter 1, which gives you a basic understanding of the HP VEE development environment and how to use it. The next chapter will unify the methods you've learned by building a simple program. The last page of each chapter provides a checklist of tasks covered. Use it to give yourself a quick test.

Chapter 1 Checklist

You should now be able to do any of the following tasks. Review topics as needed, before going on to Chapter 2.

- Identify the main menu bar, program execution buttons, and work area.

- Select menu items from the main menu and object menus.

- Simulate waveform data.

- Look up on-line help documentation from the main menu bar and from the object menus.

- Open an object menu in two different ways.

- Save your work, exit HP VEE, and restart your program.

- Perform the following operations on an object: moving, renaming, iconizing, expanding, sizing, selecting, deselecting.

- Identify data and sequence pins on an object and explain their purpose.

- Examine terminals and change their names.

- Move the work area; clear the work area.

- Explain a UserObject and its purpose.

- Write a small program within a UserObject.

- Maximize a UserObject.

- Run and save a program.

Creating a Simple Test Program

2

Average time to complete: 2 hrs.

Overview

In this chapter you'll create an HP VEE program that generates a pulse waveform, adds noise to it, then stores and displays the results. The user will be able to select the frequency of the pulses and the amount of noise added from a simple operator interface. You'll encapsulate this simulated test within a UserObject, so that it can be iconized and easily exported to another program. This lab exercise will also incorporate HP VEE debugging and documentation tools.

How long would it take you to create this program in a textual language like C? It should take you about an hour in HP VEE -- even the first time. After that, it would take approximately 10 minutes.

In this chapter you'll learn about:

- Creating modular tests

- Getting user inputs

- Simulating test data

- Storing and displaying results

- Documenting your program

- Creating an operator interface

- Using debugging tools

- Using HP VEE online help

CUTTING YOUR TEST DEVELOPMENT TIME WITH HP VEE

Lab 2-1: The Pulse Program

We'll partition the instructions under task headings to make it easier to apply the procedures to other programs.

To Edit the HP VEE Title Bar

1. Change the title of your program to **Pulse Program**. (Refer to Chapter 1 if you need more detail on how to do this.)

To Make a Test Procedure Modular

By storing your test procedure inside a UserObject, you can iconize the entire test to conserve screen space. Also, you can merge this program with another more easily, because it is an easily identifiable module. Finally, the UserObject could easily be converted to a function at a later date, which you could then call from any number of points in your program.

1. Select **Device => UserObject** and place it in the middle of the work area.

2. Maximize the **UserObject** by clicking on the maximize button at the upper right-hand corner of the object. (If you click on the iconize button by mistake, just double-click the icon to enlarge it again.)

To Document Your Program

HP VEE provides a documentation utility called "veedoc", that will extract all object titles, entries from the Display => Note Pad object, and entries from the Show Description dialog box, and stores them in a file. All objects have a Show Description item in their object menus, which provides a dialog box to accept documentation on that particular object. The veedoc file also shows nesting levels, and provides a way to correlate the documentation with

Creating a Simple Test Program

screen dumps. Now, you'll make entries in the Show Description dialog box. Later in this chapter you'll get to use the documentation utility.

1. Change the **UserObject** title to **PulseNoise**.

   There should be no spaces or unusual characters in the name, since you might want to convert this UserObject to a function in the future. (Versions B.02.00 and later allow underscores in a function name.)

2. Open the object menu and click **Show Description**.

3. Click on the dialog box input field to get a cursor and type the following:

   Purpose:

   The PulseNoise UserObject generates a pulse waveform, adds noise, stores the results, and displays the noisy pulse. The user inputs the desired frequency and amount of noise each time the program runs. An operator interface will only show the user input dialog boxes and the waveform display. A data output pin will also hold the resultant waveform.

   Input Pins :

   None

   Output Pins:

   A data output pin labeled X will hold the resultant waveform.

   Click **OK**, when you're done.

   Note: Your entries in the Show Description dialog box will not be visible to a user unless they access them through the object menu for information; however, the veedoc utility will print them out.

2 - 3

CUTTING YOUR TEST DEVELOPMENT TIME WITH HP VEE

To Create a Dialog Box for User Input

In the Data => Constant submenu are various HP VEE datatypes that provide dialog boxes for the user to assign constant values. You can also use these objects to request user input. You simply change the name of the constant object to a user prompt. The following exercise should make the process clear. You'll ask the user to input the Frequency setting for the Pulse Generator.

1. Select **Data => Constant => Integer** and place it in the upper-left work area of the **UserObject**.

2. Change the title on the **Integer** object to **Freq?**. Click and drag over the default number **0** to highlight it, then enter **100**.

   Reminder: You can also double-click the input field to highlight an entry from version B.02.00 on.

To Set Up the Pulse Generator

We'll use a "virtual source" called a pulse generator to simulate data from an instrument. In chapter 3, we'll cover communication with real instruments. You'll need to add a data input pin to receive the frequency setting from the Integer object.

1. Select **Device => Virtual Source => Pulse Generator**, and place it to the right of the input box.

   You may need to use the Size command in the Pulse Generator object menu to conserve work area space.

2. Open the Pulse Generator object menu and click **Terminals => Add Data Input**.

Creating a Simple Test Program

A list box appears with the possible data input pins you may add to change the different functions on the Pulse Generator. **Frequency** is already highlighted, so just click **OK**. HP VEE adds the terminal.

Shortcut: *You could also place the mouse pointer over the data input pin area and press Ctrl-a to get the list box.*

3. Connect the data output pin of the **Integer** object (labeled **Freq?**) to the **Pulse Generator** data input pin.

   Notice that Frequency can only be changed through the input pin now; you can no longer edit the Frequency input field.

4. Enter different numbers in your input box and run this section of the program. See Figure 2-1.

   Tip: *You will get an error box, if you enter frequencies above 193 unless you reduce the Pulse Width. If you get a red error box, just click OK and correct the error before running the program again. Clicking Stop removes the red error outline. (Clicking Stop once pauses the program; clicking twice stops the program.)*

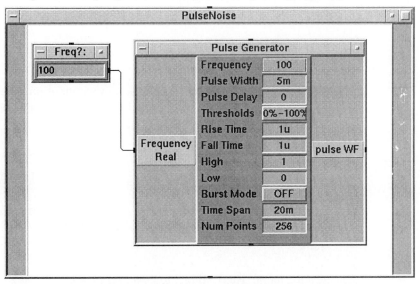

Fig. 2-1. The PulseNoise UserObject at an Early Stage

2 - 5

CUTTING YOUR TEST DEVELOPMENT TIME WITH HP VEE

5. Iconize the **Pulse Generator** and move it closer to the input box to simplify the screen.

To Set Up the Noise Generator

HP VEE also includes a virtual instrument to generate a noise waveform, which you can add to other waves. The amount of noise is controlled by adjusting the amplitude.

1. Select **Device => Virtual Source => Noise Generator** and place it to the right of the noise input box.

2. Open the object menu and select **Terminals => Add Data Input.**

3. Select **Amplitude**.

You can see that the default values for Time Span and Num Points are the same for both of the generators.

To Create a Noise Input Box

Now that the Noise Generator has an amplitude input pin, you can input this data as a real number. HP VEE provides an object that makes this easy, a Real Slider, which is located in the Data menu.

1. Select **Data => Real Slider** and place it to the left of the **Noise Generator**.

    To select a value, just click and drag the slider bar up or down. The value chosen displays at the top. You can also change the range limits, if you want.

2. Edit the name, **Real Slider**, to be a user prompt: **Noise?**.

Creating a Simple Test Program

3. Access **Help** in the object menu, if you have any questions about the object.

4. Connect the **Real Slider** data output pin to the **Noise Generator Amplitude** input pin.

5. Iconize the **Noise Generator** and move it closer to the input box.

   You can move an icon by simply clicking and dragging with the mouse.

To Add Two Waveforms

The addition object signified by a + symbol can be used to add waveforms as well as scalar numbers. If both inputs are arrays, the data must have the same size and shape. Size means the number of elements in an array. In this case, we know both waveforms have 256 points. Shape refers to the structure holding the data: a scalar, a one-dimensional array (ARRAY 1D), a two-dimensional array (ARRAY 2D), and so on. Waveforms from the generator objects are stored as one-dimensional arrays, which you can verify by opening the output terminal to examine the Shape field.

1. Select **Math** => + - * / => + and place it to the lower-right of the **Pulse Generator**.

   Examine the **Help** entry for + in the object menu.

2. Connect the **Pulse Generator** data output pin to the upper-left data input pin of the + object.

   A data line should be left between the two objects.

3. Connect the data output pin from the **Noise Generator** to the lower data input pin of the + object.

   So far your program should look like the one in Figure 2 - 2.

CUTTING YOUR TEST DEVELOPMENT TIME WITH HP VEE

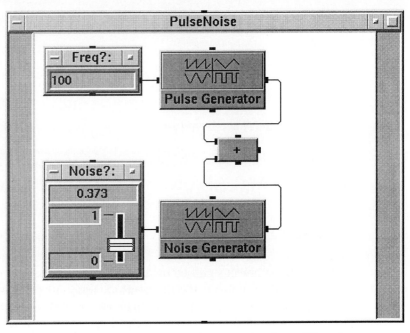

Fig. 2-2. Pulse Program After Adding Two Waveforms

To Display a Waveform in the Time Domain

1. Select **Display => Waveform (Time)** and place it to the right of the addition object. (You may need to use Size in the object menu.)

2. Connect the data output pin of the + object to the data input pin of the **Waveform (Time)** display.

   Check the connections by clicking **Run** on the HP VEE tool bar. You should see a pulse displayed. Try entering different frequencies and moving the slider bar for the amount of noise you want before running the program again. Click **Auto Scale** on the **Waveform (Time)** object to scale the display quickly.

To Put the Program Results in a File

1. Select **I/O => To => File** and place it in the lower-right work area.

   It doesn't matter if you overlap other objects, because you'll iconize the To File object in a moment.

2. Change the default filename, **myFile**, to **pulsnois.dat**.

3. If there is no check mark to the left of **Clear File At PreRun & Open**, then click on the small input box.

   To File defaults to appending data to the existing file. In this case, however, you want to clear the file each time you run the program.

4. Examine **Help** in the object menu. You can use the default settings, but click on **WRITE TEXT a EOL** anyway to examine the different choices you have. We'll go over this in detail in Chapter 5.

5. Iconize the **To File** object by clicking the iconize button at the upper right-hand corner of the object.

6. Connect the data output pin of the + object to the data input pin of **To File**.

   Note: You can connect one data output pin to several data input pins.

7. Click **Run** again to test your program.

   Double-click the **To File** object to get the open view, then double-click the input terminal **A Any** to examine its contents. You should see an array of 256 points.

To Add a Data Output Pin to the UserObject

You do this the same way you would for any HP VEE object.

1. Open the UserObject object menu by placing the mouse pointer on the title bar or input/output areas and clicking the right mouse button. Select **Terminals => Add Data Output**. HP VEE adds an output named **X**.

    Shortcut: *You can add a data output pin by placing the mouse pointer on the output terminal area and pressing Ctrl-a.*

2. Connect the data output pin of the + object to **X**.

3. Run your program, then double-click on **X** to examine the contents.

The **PulseNoise UserObject** should look like the figure below.

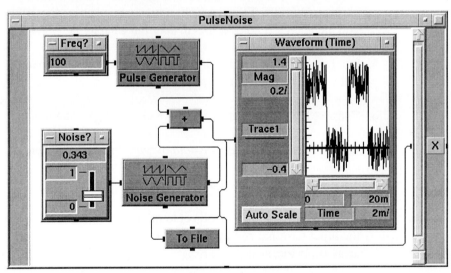

Fig. 2-3. The PulseNoise UserObject (Detail View)

To Create an Operator Interface

First, you're going to select the objects that you want to appear in the Panel view, which acts as your operator interface. Then simply selecting Edit => Add To Panel will create the panel.

1. Press and hold **Ctrl** while clicking on all of the objects you want to select. Click on both user input boxes and the **Waveform (Time)** object. Each will now have a shadow to indicate your selection. Click anywhere on the background to indicate that you're done selecting objects.

   Note: You can also select Edit => Select Objects, click on the objects you want to select, then click on the background to stop.

2. Pop up the **PulseNoise Edit** menu by placing the mouse pointer over the background and clicking on the right mouse button. Click **Add to Panel**.

   Note: You can also pop up an Edit menu by placing the mouse pointer over the work area background and pressing the right mouse button.

   The selected objects will appear in the panel view, as shown in Figure 2-4.

   Your program is still intact. Just click **Detail** on the left side of the PulseNoise title bar to return to the detailed view. Click **Panel** to return to the panel view. You may need to select **Size** in the object menu to enlarge the window.

   Shortcut: Press the "maximize" button (the large square button in the upper right-hand corner of the UserObject) from the Detail view to go to full screen size.

3. Go to the **Panel** view.

   You can move objects easily by dragging them to different locations. Experiment with different arrangements of objects such as the one in Figure 2-4.

CUTTING YOUR TEST DEVELOPMENT TIME WITH HP VEE

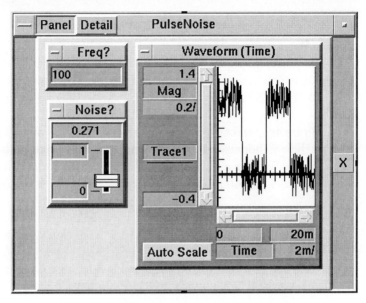

Fig. 2-4. The Panel View of PulseNoise

5. Enter various inputs for frequency and noise and run your program.

   Notice that your program operates the same way in the detail or panel view.

To Save Your Program

1. Select **File => Save As...** and complete the dialog box, as you did in Chapter 1. Name the program **pulsnois.vee**.

Creating a Simple Test Program

To Print a Copy of Your Program

The following instructions presume that you configured a printer during installation.

1. Go to the detail view of the program.

2. Click the maximize button to expand the window.

3. Open the **UserObject** object menu and click **Edit => Clean Up Lines** in case the lines got messy in the development stage.

4. Select **File => Print Screen...** , edit the dialog box presented to suit your preferences, then click **OK**.

Easy Text Documentation of Your Program

HP VEE has a utility called veedoc that resides in your main directory. Veedoc will list all objects, their names, their Show Description entries, and their "nesting". For example, objects within a UserObject are nested one level from the main VEE environment, and these levels are indicated by numbers. The following exercises will clarify what we mean.

To Generate Documentation Automatically

Using MS Windows:

1. Go to a DOS window.

2. Enter **cd \vee** at the prompt to change to the HP VEE home directory.

3. To print to the screen:

CUTTING YOUR TEST DEVELOPMENT TIME WITH HP VEE

Enter **veedoc** *filename*, where *filename* is the name of the file that holds your program -- pulsnois.vee, for example.

To save the veedoc output:

Enter **veedoc** *program_filename > program_filename.doc* .

To print the veedoc output file:

Enter **print** *filename.doc*.

Using UNIX:

1. Click a window with a UNIX prompt.

2. To print veedoc output to the screen:

    Enter **/usr/bin/veedoc** *filename*. (Or just type **veedoc** *filename*, if the **/usr/bin** directory is in your PATH.) For example, to use **veedoc** with this last program enter **veedoc pulsnois.vee**.

    To save the veedoc output:

    Enter **veedoc pulsnois.vee > pulsnois.doc** to save the **veedoc** output in a file called **pulsnois.doc**.

    To print the veedoc output:

    Enter **veedoc pulsnois.vee | lp** to print to a printer.

Veedoc pulsnois.vee should yield the file shown in Figure 2-5.

Creating a Simple Test Program

Source: pulsnois.vee
Revision: B.00.00
Date: Thu 19/Aug/1993

Title: Pulse Program

0: PulseNoise
 Description:
  The PulseNoise UserObject generates a pulse waveform, adds noise, stores the results, and displays the noisy pulse. The user inputs the desired frequency and amount of noise each time the program runs. An operator interface will only show the user input dialog boxes and the waveform display. A UserObject data output pin will also hold resultant waveform.
 Input Pins: None
 Output Pins: A data output pin labeled "X" will hold the resultant waveform.

0:0: Freq?
0:1: Pulse Generator
0:2: Noise Generator
0:3: Noise?
0:4: +
0:5: Waveform (Time)
0.6: To File

Fig. 2-5. Documentation Utility Output

Notice the source, HP VEE revision of the veedoc utility, date, and program title at the top. The numbers before the decimal points indicate levels of nesting. Since there was only one level in this program, all numbers start with a **0**. The number after the decimal point indicates the order in which the objects were programmed. The title of the object follows the identification number plus a Show Description entry, if there was one.

> ***Note:*** *After running veedoc on a program a File => Print All command will put the identification numbers on the objects, so you can match the text documentation to your printer output.*

CUTTING YOUR TEST DEVELOPMENT TIME WITH HP VEE

Using Online Help and Debugging Tools

Now that you've created a simple program, we'd like to show you how to teach yourself HP VEE.

One of the best ways to learn about HP VEE is to examine the Help entries in the object menus, and then experiment with the objects until you understand how they work. These entries should be consulted first when something goes wrong.

If this doesn't solve the problem, and you would like to explore related topics, you should consult the Help facility on the main menu bar.

Using the Help Facility

Regardless of what operating system you're using, the help facility will provide information on the following topics:

- All menu items

- Instrument driver information

- Frequently performed tasks

- Definition of HP VEE terms

- Short cuts

- Using the help facility

- HP VEE version

Exercises Using the Help Facility

- Find the help screen for the **For Count** object and read it.

Creating a Simple Test Program

- Do the same thing for the **Start** object.

- Look up the short-cut way to delete an object.

- Find detailed information on the HP 3325B Function Generator.

- Look up the word "terminal".

- Look up your HP VEE version number, and find out if there is any information specific to that version that's not covered in the manuals.

> *Note:* *HP VEE will give you two types of dialog boxes, when it doesn't understand what you're doing: a yellow-titled Caution box or a red-titled Error box. The error number given may be referenced in Error Codes in the Help menu along with the message, cause, and recovery action.*

Debugging Programs in HP VEE

Let's use the Pulse Program to demonstrate debugging methods, so select **File => Open**, highlight **pulsnois.vee**, and click **OK**.

To Show Data Flow

1. Select **Edit => Show Data Flow**.

CUTTING YOUR TEST DEVELOPMENT TIME WITH HP VEE

(To turn it off, you just select it again.) When you run your program you will see small boxes moving along the data lines to indicate the flow of data in your programs.

Note: *You can create your programs in most cases by connecting data input/output pins alone without using any sequence pins. Notice that data moves from left to right in an HP VEE program, as shown below.*

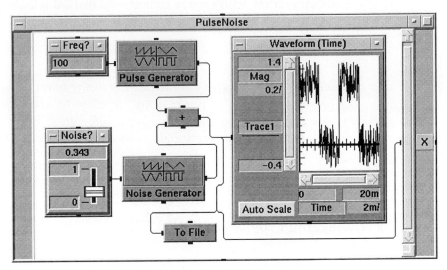

Fig. 2-6. The Pulse Program

Data moves from the input boxes to the Pulse and Noise Generators to the + object. Finally, it moves to the Waveform (Time) display, the output pin X, and the To File object.

To Show Execution Flow

1. Select **Edit => Show Execution Flow**.

2 - 18

When you run the program, you will see a colored outline around the objects as they execute.

Use Show Data Flow and Show Exec Flow to understand how your program is operating, but turn them off to get higher performance. Combining these features with debugging tools such as breakpoints will help you understand how a VEE program works and where possible errors lie.

To Examine Data on a Line

Checking the data at different points in your program confirms whether or not you're getting the results you expect. You already know how to double-click on terminals to examine the data. The Line Probe is a way to view the data on a given line.

1. Select **Edit => Line Probe**. The pointer becomes a small plus sign, which you place over a line and click to examine the data.

   A dialog box will present the datatype and value(s).

   Shortcut: *Hold down Shift and click on the line to get the dialog box.*

2. Click **OK** when you're done viewing the data.

Using the Alphanumeric Displays for Debugging

You can add the Alphanumeric or Logging Alphanumeric displays at certain points in your program to track the flow of data. When things are working correctly, just delete them. Remember that AlphaNumeric displays a single data container (a Scalar value, an Array 1D, or Array 2D); whereas, Logging AlphaNumeric (either a Scalar or Array 1D) displays consecutive input as a history of previous values.

2 - 19

CUTTING YOUR TEST DEVELOPMENT TIME WITH HP VEE

To Set a Breakpoint on a Single Object

You set breakpoints in a program before a particular object operates to examine the data.

1. Open the object menu and click **Breakpoint**.

To Set Breakpoints on Several Objects

1. Select the objects. (Press Ctrl and click on each object.)

2. Select **Edit => Breakpoints => Set Breakpoints**.

    An arrow will indicate the next object to operate when you hit a breakpoint.

3. Click **Cont** on the tool bar to continue the program execution.

To Clear a Breakpoint on a Single Object

1. Deselect **Breakpoint** from the object menu.

To Clear Breakpoints on Several Objects

1. Select the objects.

2. Select **Edit => Breakpoints => Clear Breakpoints**.

Creating a Simple Test Program

To Clear All Breakpoints

1. Select **Edit => Breakpoints => Clear All Breakpoints** .

To find out the order of execution of the objects one at a time and to be able to investigate the data as you go along, you should step through the program. An arrow will appear on the upper left-hand corner of an object just before it executes.

To Step Through a Program

1. Just click **Step** on the tool bar.

    A small arrow will point to the next object about to execute.

To Continue a Program

1. Just click **Cont** on the tool bar and the program will complete execution.

To Pause or Stop a Program

1. Click **Stop** once on the tool bar to pause a program. To completely stop a program, click **Stop** twice.

CUTTING YOUR TEST DEVELOPMENT TIME WITH HP VEE

The Order of Events Inside an Object

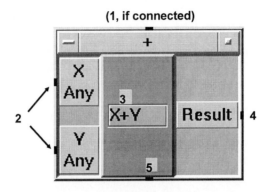

Fig. 2-7. The Order of Events in an Object

1. If the sequence pin is connected, the object will not operate until it receives a message to execute (a "ping" in HP VEE terms). However, the sequence pin does not have to be connected.

2. All data input pins *must* have data before the object operates. (Most objects may add data input/output pins. Explore the Terminals cascading menu in any object menu to find out what pins can be added.)

3. The object performs its task. In this case, **X** is added to **Y**.

4. The data output pin fires. The object waits for a signal that the data is received, before its operation is completed.

   Therefore, a given object does not fire its sequence output pin until all objects connected to its data output pin have executed.

5. The sequence output pin fires.

There are two exceptions to this sequence of events:

First, control input pins may be added to some objects, which may cause an immediate execution of an object sub-function such as a Clear or Autoscale operation in the Waveform (Time) display. Control lines to an object are dashed lines. Note that the object is not required to have data on a control pin to execute. See the figure below.

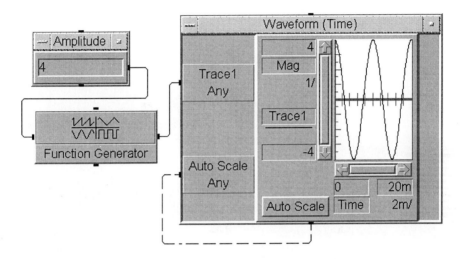

Fig. 2-8. Control Line Used to Execute Autoscale

Secondly, error output pins may be added to trap errors inside an object. They will override standard object behavior. If an error occurs during object execution, the error pin will send out a message, and the data output pins will not fire.

CUTTING YOUR TEST DEVELOPMENT TIME WITH HP VEE

The Execution Order of Objects in a Program

1. Start objects operate first.

    Note: Device => Start is used to operate individual threads, as shown below. A thread is a set of objects connected by solid lines in an HP VEE program.

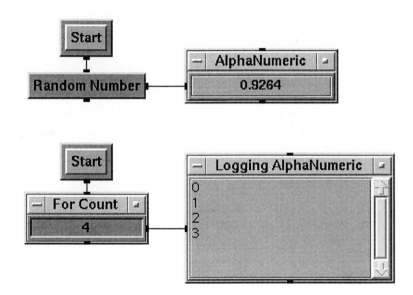

Fig. 2-9. Start Objects Executing Separate Threads

2. Objects with no data or sequence pins operate next. Data => Constant objects are often in this category.

3. Objects with input pins operate when *all* connected inputs are satisfied. Recall that connecting sequence inputs is optional.

Stepping Through the Pulse Program

1. Get the **Pulse** program on your screen.

2. Click **Step** on the right of the tool bar.

3. As you keep clicking **Step**, an arrow appearing at the upper left-hand corner of the object about to execute guides you through the program sequentially.

Since there is no Start object, the first object with no inputs is the UserObject, so it executes first. Within the PulseNoise UserObject the input boxes have no input pins, so they execute first in no defined order. If you wanted them to execute in a particular order, you could control this by connecting their sequence pins. Data flows left to right, so you will see the data generators executing next in no particular order. The addition (+) object cannot execute until both inputs are satisfied. Then the Waveform (Time) and To File objects execute in no particular order. Again, you could mandate execution order anywhere in the program by using the sequence pins or the or the Edit => Do object. (To learn more about the Do object consult Help.)

CUTTING YOUR TEST DEVELOPMENT TIME WITH HP VEE

On Your Own

Generate a sine wave. Add noise to it. The user should be able to control the amplitude of the wave as well as the amount of noise to add. Display the results graphically using a red trace. Add a control input pin to your display for AutoScale and connect it to the sequence output pin. (After the display has gathered the data, the sequence out pin fires, which triggers the AutoScale control pin.)

Store the results in a file called sinenois.dat. Put your test procedure in a module named SineNoise. Create a user interface that shows the user input boxes and the display. Save your program as sinenois.vee. Print hardcopy of the detailed view of your program. Save textual documentation of your program in sinenois.doc and print a copy of this file.

EXTRA CREDIT!

Figure out how you would retrieve the program data from the sinenois.dat file and display it in a Alphanumeric display. You'll have to enlarge the display with Size in the object menu.

(HINT: You'll need to use sequence pins. When retrieving the data you'll be looking for an array, not a scalar.)

Creating a Simple Test Program

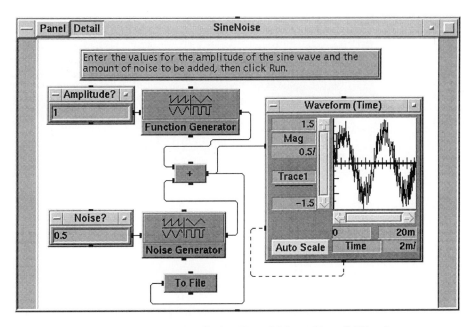

Fig. 2-11. The SineNoise UserObject (Detail View)

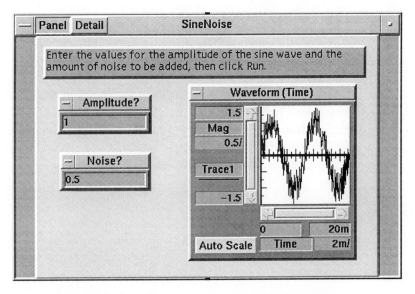

Fig. 2-10. The SineNoise UserObject (Panel View)

2 - 27

CUTTING YOUR TEST DEVELOPMENT TIME WITH HP VEE

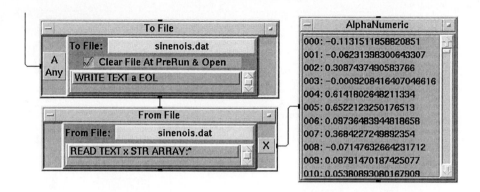

Fig. 2-12. Extra Credit Part of Sinenois Program

Notes on Different Versions of HP VEE

This book focuses on the B.02.00 version of HP VEE. (You can find your version in the Help menu.) If you have earlier versions such as B.00.01 on HP-UX or B.01.00 on SunOS, there are a few slight differences in some of the screens. HP intends to synchronize these different B.xx.xx versions in late 1994. We will annotate these differences when they arise in the instructions. They do not affect the way a program runs or its portability. For example, prior to B.02.00 you renamed an object by editing the title bar directly; with B.02.00 you selected the *Change Title...* option in the object menu. Before B.02.00 most default files were named *myDataFile*; with B.02.00 most default files are named *myFile*. As you can see, the differences are minor, and we will point them out as we go along.

Chapter 2 Checklist

You should now be able to perform the following tasks. Review topics, if necessary, before proceeding to Chapter 3.

- Create a modular test program.

- Document your work.

- Use the veedoc utility.

- Set up dialog boxes for user inputs.

- Simulate test data for prototyping.

- Add inputs to objects.

- Add inputs to control functions on the Pulse and Noise Generators.

- Use math operators.

- Store test results in a file.

- Create a UserObject that outputs a single result.

- Create an operator interface for a program.

- Save and print a program.

- Use online help.

- Show data and execution flow.

- Use the line probe to examine data.

- Use Alphanumeric displays for debugging.

CUTTING YOUR TEST DEVELOPMENT TIME WITH HP VEE

- Use breakpoints.

- Step through a program.

- Explain the order of events inside an object.

- Explain the execution order of objects in a program.

Two Easy Ways To Control Instruments

3

Average time to complete: 1 hr.

Overview

HP VEE provides two easy ways to control instruments: instrument panels and the "Direct I/O" object. Instrument panels give you a simple user interface to control an instrument from your computer screen. With a panel you don't need to know the unique software commands that control a particular instrument. Once you've set up the instrument using menu selections and dialog boxes, the driver will automatically send the right command strings over the bus.

With the Direct I/O object, on the other hand, you do have to know the instrument command strings. HP VEE provides you with a convenient method of transmitting commands and receiving data. Using Direct I/O you can communicate with any instrument that connects to one of the supported interfaces.

In this chapter you'll learn about:

- Configuring an HP-IB instrument

- Using an instrument driver

- Using the Direct I/O object

This chapter is designed to give you the fundamentals of controlling instruments to cover most situations using HP-IB, RS-232, or GPIO interfaces. For more information on communication with the VXI backplane, consult HP VEE documentation. Data acquisition with PC plug-in cards is covered in Chapter 15 using DT VEE (sold by Data Translation).

To better understand the methods being discussed in this chapter, let's take a look at an example of an instrument panel and a Direct I/O object.

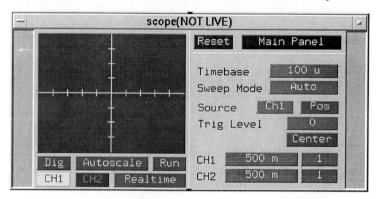

Fig. 3-1. The HP54504A Scope Instrument Panel

Fig. 3-2. A Function Generator Direct I/O Object

An instrument panel gives you maximum ease-of-use and saves the most development time. You get over 300 instrument drivers from different instrument vendors with HP VEE. If you need drivers for instruments not currently supported, you have a number of options:

Two Easy Ways To Control Instruments

- Use the Direct I/O object instead of an instrument driver.

- Use the Driver Writer's Tool supplied with HP VEE to create your own customized driver (see Chapter 12).

- Use the Instrument Driver Language to write your own driver (see Chapter 12).

- Ask HP to add the driver to the queue of drivers under development.

- Ask HP to recommend contractors that could write the driver.

With Direct I/O you can communicate with any instrument. Although it requires slightly more effort than an instrument driver, it's still very easy to use. Also, Direct I/O yields faster execution speeds. Choosing the best method of instrument control will depend on driver availability, the need for fast test development, and your performance requirements.

Whether you use drivers or Direct I/O, you need to configure your instrument before you can talk to it from a program, so the first lab exercise covers configuration.

> *Note: Prior to version B.02.00 the first dialog box for configuring instruments was different, which will be explained in various notes in the following instructions. If you have version B.02.00 or greater, just disregard these notes and continue with the lab.*

Lab 3 - 1: Configuring an HP-IB Instrument

With HP VEE you can develop your programs without the instruments present. For the purposes of this exercise, let's configure a multimeter (HP 3478A) for use with an instrument panel. Then we'll show you how easy it would be to add the physical instrument to the configuration.

CUTTING YOUR TEST DEVELOPMENT TIME WITH HP VEE

To Configure a Multimeter Without the Instrument Present

1. If you have version B.02.00 or greater, select **I/O => Instrument...** and place it in the center of the work area. Move the dialog box to the upper-left work area (click and drag its title bar). See the figure below.

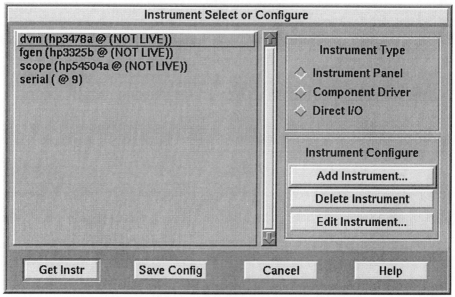

Fig. 3-3. The Instrument Select or Configure Box

The instruments on the left have already been configured to run with HP VEE examples. Please do not delete them. To configure an instrument, you first choose the Instrument Type in the upper-right area of the box. We've already described the differences between an Instrument Panel and a Direct I/O object. A Component Driver simply uses a subset of the functions provided by an instrument panel. (Consult HP VEE documentation for more information on Component Drivers.) After you've chosen an instrument type, you click Add Instrument... under Instrument Configure in the lower-right area of the box to get a Device Configuration dialog box.

Note for Versions Prior to B.02.00: Earlier versions of HP VEE had a slightly different process for getting to the Device Configuration

Two Easy Ways To Control Instruments

dialog box. You first selected I/O => Configure I/O to get the Configure I/O Devices dialog box, as shown below.

Fig. 3-4. Configure I/O Devices Box (Before B.02.00)

In this earlier version of HP VEE, you click Add... to get to the Device Configuration box. (Now let's get back to B.02.00.)

2. Click **Add Instrument....**

The entries in the **Device Configuration** dialog box mean:

Name: Any unique name you'd like to call the instrument in your program. (You can't call two instruments by the same name.)

Interface: Choose one from HP-IB, Serial, VXI. (GPIO available on the HP 9000, Series 300 workstations).

Address: The select code of the interface (HP-IB is usually 7) plus the local bus address of the instrument (the default on the multimeter is 23).

CUTTING YOUR TEST DEVELOPMENT TIME WITH HP VEE

If you leave the address at 0, it means that you're developing without an instrument present.

Device Type: This will be the name of the driver file for the instrument. HP VEE will enter this for you, as you will see in a moment.

Timeout: The maximum number of seconds allowed without an instrument response, before you get an error message.

Byte Ordering: Specifies the order the device uses for reading and writing binary data. You can toggle between Most Significant Byte first or Least Significant Byte first. All IEEE488.2-compliant devices must default to MSB order. (This entry does not appear before B.02.00.)

Live Mode: This will be set to the **OFF** position, unless you have an instrument present. If you've specified an address, HP VEE defaults to the **ON** setting, which signifies live communication with the instrument.

Direct I/O Config ... and **Instrument Driver Config ...** will present additional dialog boxes.

3. Edit **newDevice** to **Multimeter** making sure to use the **Tab** key instead of the **Enter** key. (If you hit the **Enter** key by mistake, just click **Edit Instrument...** and continue.)

   Tip: *Pressing the* **Tab** *key after typing in a field will move you to the next field;* **Shift-Tab** *moves you to the previous field. Pressing* **Enter** *is equivalent to clicking* **OK***, and HP VEE will close your dialog box.*

4. Leave all the other defaults as they are, and click **Instrument Driver Config ....** Your screen should look similar to Figure 3-5, except we've already selected an **ID Filename**.

Two Easy Ways To Control Instruments

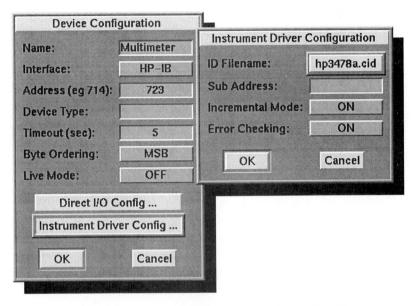

Fig. 3-5. The Instrument Driver Configuration Box

5. Click the field to the right of **ID Filename** to obtain a list box entitled **Read from what Instrument Description file?**. This list includes all of the instrument driver files loaded with your revision of HP VEE in the directory specified. Scroll down the list to highlight **hp3478a.cid**, then click **OK**.

   Tip: You can also double-click on a highlighted file to select it.

   The *.cid files signify the compiled instrument driver files. Notice that the ID Filename field in the Instrument Driver Configuration box has been filled in for you. Explanations of the other entries follow:

   Sub Address: VXI cards with multiple ports or channels require a **0** entered in this field. Sub addresses are also used by non-VXI cardcage instruments for identifying plug-in modules.

CUTTING YOUR TEST DEVELOPMENT TIME WITH HP VEE

Incremental Mode: Leave the default, unless you'd like to send the entire instrument command string for your instrument state each time you change a setting.

Error Checking: Leave the default, unless you need extra throughput or you're not worried about checking for I/O errors.

6. Click **OK** in both the **Instrument Driver Configuration** and **Device Configuration** boxes.

   Note: *An instrument object named Multimeter in the driver file hp3478a is now in your list of available instruments. It does not have a bus address specified, because it is NOT LIVE at present. (Before B.02.00 you'll see @000, which means you don't have an instrument present.) You can develop your program in this mode, and add an address later, when you're ready to connect the instrument to your computer.*

7. Click **Save Config** to close the **Instrument Select or Configure** box. (Before B.02.00, click Save to close the Configure I/O Devices box.)

You have now added the HP 3478A Multimeter to your device list. You could use this driver while programming, even though the actual instrument was not present. The next exercise will show you how easy it is to add the instrument later.

To Add the Physical Instrument to your Configuration

1. Select **I/O => Instrument...**, and click **Edit Instrument...** with the **Multimeter** highlighted. (Before B.02.00, you select I/O => Configure I/O..., and click Edit with the Multimeter highlighted.)

2. Double-click the **Address** field to highlight the current entry, type **723**, then click **OK**.

   (If the HP-IB select code is not 7, replace 7 with that number.)

Two Easy Ways To Control Instruments

3. Click **Save Config** to save your changes.

To Select an Instrument to Use in your Program

1. Select **I/O => Instrument....**

2. Highlight your selection, in this case the **Multimeter (hp3478a @ 723)**, click **Instrument Panel** in the **Instrument Type** menu, then click **Get Instr**. (Before B.02.00, highlight selection and click State Driver.)

   If you had chosen Direct I/O, you would have gotten a Direct I/O object with the same name talking to an instrument at the address specified.

3. Place the outline of the **Multimeter panel** where you want it and click to place it.

   You may now use the instrument panel in your program like any other HP VEE object.

Try the **On Your Own** example to make sure you understand the configuration process, then we'll do an exercise that configures an instrument for **Direct I/O**.

On Your Own

Configure an HP 54601A Oscilloscope without the instrument present, and call it **Digit_Scope**. Then put it in the work area, as though you were going to use it in a program.

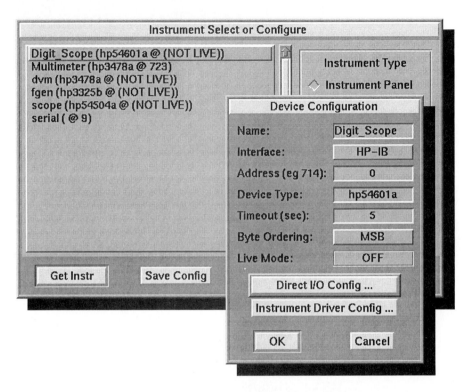

Fig. 3-6. The Device Configuration for Digit_Scope

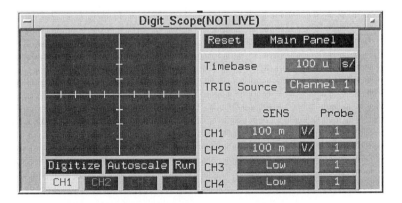

Fig. 3-7. The Digit_Scope Instrument Panel

Lab 3-2: Configuring a Function Generator for Direct I/O

When you don't have a driver for a particular instrument, or you want higher throughput, use the **Direct I/O** object. Let's configure a function generator (HP 3325B) using **Direct I/O**.

1. Select **I/O => Instrument...** to get the **Instrument Select or Configure** dialog box. (Before B.02.00, click I/O => Configure I/O... .)

2. Click **Add Instrument...** to get the **Device Configuration** dialog box. (Before B.02.00, click Add... .) Then edit the **Name** field to **FuncGen** and press the **Tab** key.

    Note: We are using the HP-IB interface here (IEEE488). To configure Serial, GPIO, or VXI instrumentation, see HP VEE documentation.

3. Click **Direct I/O Config...** to get the **Direct I/O Configuration** dialog box, as shown in Figure 3-8.

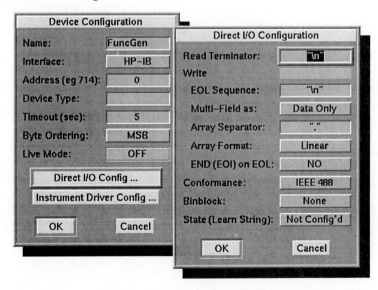

Fig. 3-8. The Direct I/O Configuration Dialog Box

CUTTING YOUR TEST DEVELOPMENT TIME WITH HP VEE

HP VEE selects default values based on your previous selection of an interface. Edit these values, if necessary.

4. Click **OK** to return to the **Device Configuration** box, and notice that the **Device Type** field is not completed, because you're not configuring an instrument panel. Click **OK** to return to the **Instrument Select or Configure** box. (Before B.02.00, you return to Configure I/O Devices.)

5. Notice that **FuncGen ((null) @ (NOT LIVE))** is now highlighted. The (null) means that there was no entry in the Device Type field, since there was no driver file. If you have an instrument, fill in the Address field. Click **Save Config** to preserve your new configuration and return to the work area. (Before B.02.00, you'd see FuncGen(@000) and you'd click Save in the Configure I/O Devices box.)

6. Select **I/O => Instrument....** Highlight **FuncGen** and click **Direct I/O** for **Instrument Type**. Click **Get Instr** and place the **Direct I/O** object where you want it. (Before B.02.00, you'd highlight FuncGen and click Direct I/O.)

Fig. 3-9. The FuncGen Direct I/O Object

Of course, you have to configure I/O transactions, before the object above can do useful work in your program. We'll teach you how to do that in the Using Direct I/O section, but first try this On Your Own exercise to make sure you understand the configuration process.

On Your Own

Configure any HP-IB instrument you have for Direct I/O. You can experiment sending and receiving commands when we get to the Using Direct I/O exercises.

Using an Instrument Driver

We'll use the HP 3325B Function Generator for these exercises. The principles are the same in using any instrument panel. You use an instrument panel instead of programming an instrument directly, because it saves you time in the development and modification of your programs. You change the settings on an instrument through menu selections or editing fields in dialog boxes. If the instrument is connected and Live Mode is on, the changes you make will register on the instrument.

To use an instrument panel in a program you simply add inputs and/or outputs as needed, and connect it to other objects to make a program. You can use several instances of the same driver in a program to set the instrument to different states. HP VEE allows you to iconize a driver to save space or to retain the open view for an easy reminder of instrument settings. You can even change settings while a program is running. We'll practice first, and then you can experiment using your own instruments.

To Change Settings on an Instrument Panel

1. Select **I/O => Instrument....**

2. Double-click **fgen** to select the pre-configured HP 3325B and place it on the left. (This process would be the same regardless of the instrument, as long as the instrument had been configured and added to your list.)

   Make sure the local address on the instrument is set to 7; otherwise, edit your configuration to the proper address.

3. Click **Sine** in the **Function** field to get a pop-up menu, then select **Triangle**. See Figure 3-10.

CUTTING YOUR TEST DEVELOPMENT TIME WITH HP VEE

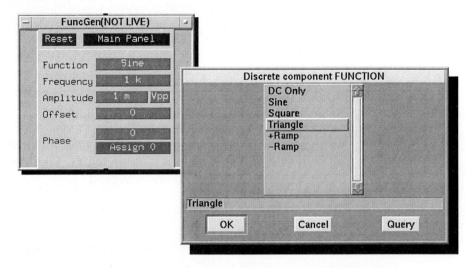

Fig. 3-10. The Function Pop-up Menu on the HP3325B

4. Click the field to the right of **Frequency**.

5. Type 100 in the **Continuous component FREQUENCY** dialog box that appears, and click **OK**.

Note that your **Frequency** setting has now changed.

Employ the same methods to change the instrument settings on any driver.

To Change Instrument Panels

Most drivers have more than one panel to simplify the user interface. To move to a different panel you click Main Panel to get a menu of panels.

1. Click **Main Panel** and select **Sweep Panel** from the menu presented.

    Return to the **Main Panel**.

To Add Inputs and/or Outputs to an Instrument Panel

You can control settings or read data from an instrument by adding data inputs and/or outputs to the driver. The input and output areas are shown in the figure below.

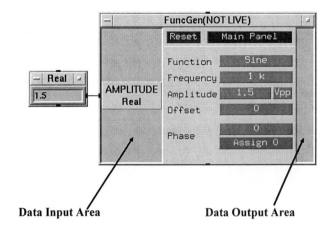

Data Input Area   Data Output Area

Fig. 3-11. The Data Input and Output Areas on a Driver

1. Place the mouse pointer over the data input area of the function generator instrument panel, and press **CTRL-a** to add a data input terminal.

   A list box of the instrument components appears.

2. Select the desired component from the menu presented.

   Note: *You could also open the object menu and select Add Terminals => Select Input Component. Then select the desired component field on the driver.*

Follow the same process to add a data output, except you place the mouse pointer in the data output area instead of the input area.

To Delete Data Input or Output Terminals

1. Place the mouse pointer over the terminal and press **CTRL-d**.

   *Note: You could also open the object menu and select **Terminals** => **Delete Input...** from the object menu and choose the appropriate input from the menu presented.*

On Your Own

Set a state on the HP 3325B Function Generator. Change the Function setting to a Square wave. Add input components for Amplitude and Frequency. Create input dialog boxes for the amplitude and frequency and modify the titles to user prompts. Enter different values for the amplitude and frequency, and run your program to see if the settings are changed after user inputs. (If an instrument is attached, then its settings will change if **Live Mode** is on.)

Using Direct I/O

Let's explore the most fundamental operations: writing text commands, reading data, and uploading/downloading instrument states.

To Write Text Commands to an Instrument

(a) Sending a Single Quoted String

Most HP-IB instruments use alphanumeric strings for commands sent to the instrument. Let's suppose you want to send a command to the HP3325B Function Generator to set the amplitude to 5 volts. The command string is "AM 5 VO". After configuring the instrument for Direct I/O and selecting it from the available devices, you would do the following:

1. Click the transaction bar to get the **I/O Transaction** dialog box, as shown below.

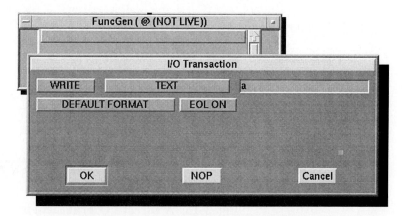

Fig. 3-12. The I/O Transaction Dialog Box

The button labeled WRITE holds a menu including the actions READ, WRITE, EXECUTE, and WAIT. In this context, you want to write data to an instrument, so use the default selection. Open the object menu and consult Help to find out what each action means.

You can also use three of the other default selections: TEXT, DEFAULT FORMAT, and EOL ON. However, the field containing a must be edited to our text command string.

WRITE TEXT transactions are of this form:

WRITE TEXT ExpressionList [Format]

ExpressionList is a single expression or a comma-separated list of expressions. When you edit **a**, you will be creating an ExpressionList in the form of a single quoted string of text. DEFAULT FORMAT means that HP VEE will automatically determine an appropriate text representation based on the data type of the item being written. For example, text strings are sent without conversion, but a variable containing a scalar integer such as 4427 in decimal notation would be converted to four text characters. EOL ON signifies that the end-of-line sequence specified during configuration will be sent.

2. Click the input field labeled **a** and type **"AM 5 VO"**, then click **OK**.

You now see the transaction bar labeled with **WRITE TEXT "AM 5 VO" EOL**, as shown below. The text in quotation marks is the command that will be sent to the HP3325B when your program runs.

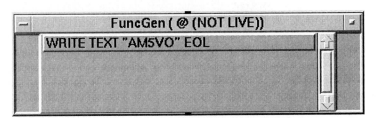

Fig. 3-13. A Direct I/O Transaction

In most cases this process will be the same for sending text commands to instruments. However, there are instruments that specify characters sent at the end of each command or at the end of a group of commands. You need to get this information from the instrument documentation, then include it in the Direct I/O Configuration dialog box.

(b) Sending an Expression List

Another variation of sending text command strings is brought out in the following exercise. Suppose you want to loop through a number of frequencies in the function generator. How would you do that using a single Direct I/O transaction? (Ans: Use a variable for the frequency as a part of an Expression List, and add a data input for that variable to the Direct I/O object.)

1. After putting the **Direct I/O** object for the HP3325B in the work area, click the transaction bar to get the **I/O Transaction** dialog box.

   You can use all of the defaults except for the command string. In this case, you need the format "FR", <frequency number>, "HZ". This is an Expression List, each expression being separated by commas. The frequency number will be signified by the variable A, which you'll add to the Direct I/O object as a data input.

2. Click the field containing **a** and type **"FR",A,"HZ"**.

   This command string sends the frequency A in Hz.

3. To add a data input pin, place the mouse pointer over the **Direct I/O** data input area and press **Ctrl-a**.

   HP VEE adds a data input pin labeled A Any.

4. Select **Flow => Repeat =>For Range** and place it to the left of the **Direct I/O** object.

5. Connect the **For Range** data output pin to the **Direct I/O** data input pin.

6. Edit the fields in **For Range** to: **From 10, Thru 1.8M,** and **Step 50k.**

   This means For Range will send out numbers ranging from 10 to 1.8 million in steps of 50,000. As those numbers are received by the Direct I/O object, the command string will tell the function generator to sweep those same frequencies. Your Direct I/O setup should look like Figure 3-14.

CUTTING YOUR TEST DEVELOPMENT TIME WITH HP VEE

Fig. 3-14. Direct I/O Setup Using an Input Variable

7. (optional) Connect an HP3325B to your computer and edit the configuration of this **Direct I/O** object to include the address of the instrument. Run this program and you will see the instrument sweeping through these frequencies.

To Read Data From an Instrument

Instruments send data to a computer in many different formats. You must know what datatype you want to read, and whether the data is returned as a single value (scalar) or an array. You can find this information in the instrument documentation or you can use the HP VEE Bus I/O Monitor in the I/O menu to examine the data being returned. This information determines how you will configure the HP VEE transaction. Since READ TEXT transactions are the most common, we will discuss them here. Other encodings for READ besides TEXT are BINARY, BINBLOCK, and CONTAINER, which are discussed in detail in the HP VEE documentation.

(a) Reading Measurements from a Multimeter

Let's use the HP3478A Multimeter for an example. It's already configured at address 723 to be run with the HP VEE examples. Suppose the Multimeter is connected to the HP3325B Function Generator you used in the last exercise. When the generator sends out a certain frequency you would like the multimeter to trigger a reading and send the results back to HP VEE. Here's how you would configure the transactions for the multimeter:

Two Easy Ways To Control Instruments

1. Select **I/O => Instrument...**, highlight **dvm (hp3478a @ 723)**, click **Direct I/O**, then click **Get Instr**.

2. Click the blank transaction bar to get the **I/O Transaction** dialog box.

3. Highlight **a** and type **"T5"**, then click **OK**.

   T5 is the command for a single trigger to the multimeter.

4. Open the object menu and click **Add Trans...** to add another transaction bar and open the I/O Transaction dialog box.

   *Shortcut: Double-click the area immediately below the last transaction to add another transaction and display its **I/O Transaction** dialog box.*

5. Click **WRITE** and select **READ** from the pop-up menu.

   You'll notice that there are new buttons appearing in the I/O Transaction box resulting from this selection.

6. Change the ExpressionList input field containing **a** to **X**. Press **Tab** to move to the next field.

   Data returned from an instrument is sent to data output pins. We will add one in a moment, and the default name of the pin is X, so we have labeled our variable by the same name.

7. Leave the **REAL FORMAT** default.

   The multimeter returns single readings as real numbers.

8. Leave **DEFAULT NUM CHARS** as is.

   The default for the number of characters is 20. If you want to change this number, click on **DEFAULT NUM CHARS** to toggle to **MAX NUM CHARS** and change the number **20** to the number of characters you want.

9. Leave **SCALAR** as is and click **OK**.

CUTTING YOUR TEST DEVELOPMENT TIME WITH HP VEE

You will see your transaction displayed on the bar as:

READ TEXT X REAL

Note: *If the instrument is returning an array of values, just click on SCALAR in the I/O Transaction dialog box to get the Select Read Dimension list box, as shown below. Once you've selected the array dimension, you will also have to specify a size for the array.*

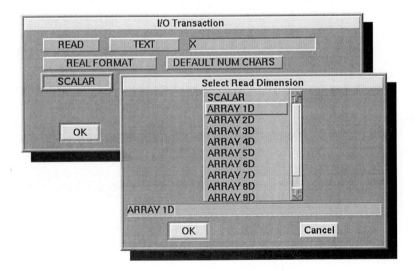

Fig. 3-15. The Select Read Dimension List Box

11. Place the mouse pointer over the data output area and press **Ctrl-a** to add a data output pin labeled **X** for the returned measurement.

Your two Direct I/O transactions should look like Figure 3-16.

Two Easy Ways To Control Instruments

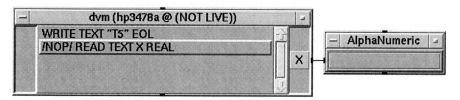

Fig. 3-16. Direct I/O Configured to Read a Measurement

The process we followed in the above exercise would be similar regardless of the data format for the **READ TEXT** transaction. The table on the next page includes a brief description of the other data formats supported. For a more detailed discussion of each item refer to HP VEE documentation.

Table 3-1. Formats for READ TEXT Transactions

Format	Description
CHAR	Reads *any* 8-bit character.
TOKEN	Reads a contiguous list of characters as a unit called a token. Tokens are separated by specified delimiter characters that you specify such as a space or comma.
STRING	Reads a list of 8-bit characters as a unit. Most control characters are read and discarded. The end of the string is reached when the specified number of characters has been read, or when a newline character is encountered.
INTEGER	Reads a list of characters and interprets them as a decimal or non-decimal representation of an integer. The only characters considered to be part of a decimal INTEGER are 0123456789-+. VEE recognizes the prefix 0x (hex) and all Non-Decimal Numeric formats specified by IEEE 488.2: #H (hex), #Q (octal), #B (binary).
OCTAL	Reads a list of characters and interprets them as the octal representation of an integer. These characters include 01234567. VEE recognizes the IEEE 488.2 Non-Decimal Numeric prefix #Q for octal numbers.
HEX	Reads a list of characters and interprets them as the hexadecimal representation of an integer. These characters include 0123456789abcdefABCDEF. The character 0x is the default prefix; it is not part of the number and is read and ignored. VEE also recognizes the IEEE 488.2 Non-Decimal Numeric prefix #H for hexadecimal numbers.

Format	Description
REAL	Reads a list of characters and interprets them as the decimal representation of a Real (floating-point) number. All common notations are recognized including leading signs, signed exponents, and decimal points. The characters recognized to be part of a REAL are 0123456789-+.Ee. VEE also recognizes certain characters as suffix multipliers: P for 10^{15}, T for 10^{12}, G for 10^9, M for 10^6, k or K for 10^3, m for 10^{-3}, u for 10^{-6}, n for 10^{-9}, p for 10^{-12}, f for 10^{-15}.
COMPLEX	Reads the equivalent of two REALs and interprets them as a complex number. The first number read is the real part, and the second number is the imaginary part.
PCOMPLEX	Reads the equivalent of two REALs and interprets them as a complex number in polar form (phasor notation). The first number is the magnitude and the second is the angle. You may specify units of measure for phase in the transaction.
COORD	Reads the equivalent of two or more REALs and interprets them as rectangular coordinates.
TIME STAMP	Reads one of the specified HP VEE time stamp formats which represent the calendar data and/or time of day.

To Upload and Download Instrument States

Some instruments offer a learn string capability. The learn string embodies all the function settings that compose an instrument state. Direct I/O will upload this learn string, save it with that particular Direct I/O object, and later download it to the instrument in your program. The procedure to follow is a simple one.

1. Set your instrument to the desired state manually.

2. Open the **Direct I/O** object menu and click **Upload State**.

    Now this state is associated with this particular instance of the **Direct I/O** object.

3. Open an **I/O Transaction** dialog box by clicking a blank transaction bar.

4. Click **TEXT**, highlight **STATE (LEARN STRING)** from the **Select Write Encoding** list box, and click **OK**. Then click **OK** to close the **I/O Transaction** box.

Uploading and downloading are controlled by your settings in the Direct I/O Configuration dialog box. If Conformance is IEEE 488.2, then HP VEE will automatically handle learn strings using the 488.2 *LRN? definition. If Conformance is IEEE 488, then Upload String specifies the command used to query the state, and Download String specifies the command that precedes the state string when downloaded. Look at the example in Figure 3-17.

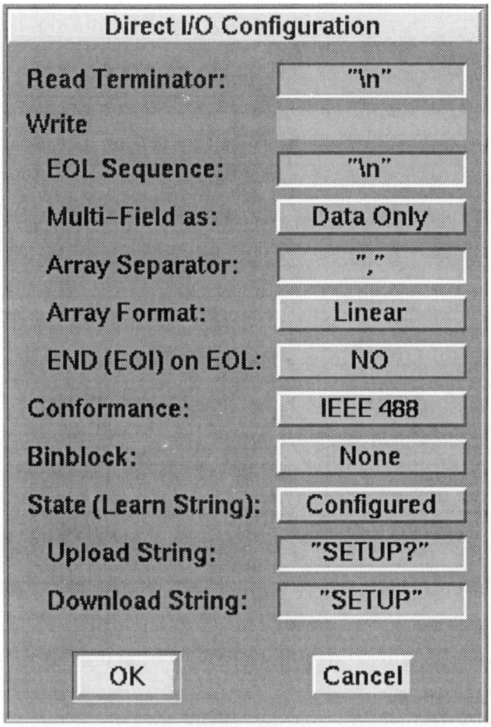

Two Easy Ways To Control Instruments

Direct I/O Configuration	
Read Terminator:	"\n"
Write	
EOL Sequence:	"\n"
Multi-Field as:	Data Only
Array Separator:	","
Array Format:	Linear
END (EOI) on EOL:	NO
Conformance:	IEEE 488
Binblock:	None
State (Learn String):	Configured
Upload String:	"SETUP?"
Download String:	"SETUP"
OK	Cancel

Fig. 3-17. Configuring for Learn Strings

Conformance can only hold IEEE 488 or IEEE 488.2. Here we're using the HP 54100A Digitizing Oscilloscope, which conforms to IEEE 488 and requires a "SETUP?" to query the learn string and "SETUP " to precede the learn string when downloading. When you select Configured for State (Learn String) two more fields appear, Upload String and Download String. The proper strings have been entered in their input fields.

Chapter 3 Checklist

You should now be able to perform the following tasks. Review the appropriate topics, if necessary, before moving on to the next chapter.

- Explain the benefits of using instrument drivers and Direct I/O.

- Explain the process for controlling instruments.

- Configure an instrument for a state driver.

- Configure an instrument for Direct I/O.

- Change settings on an instrument driver.

- Add and delete component inputs and outputs.

- Move to different panels on an instrument driver.

- Use Direct I/O to write commands to an instrument.

- Use Direct I/O to read data from an instrument.

- Upload and download instrument states using learn strings.

Analyzing and Displaying Test Data

4

Average Time to Complete: 1.5 hr.

Overview

This chapter gives you the basics on HP VEE analytical and display capabilities. You'll find out where to locate the right math objects for your applications, and how to display your test results, so that you can turn data into useful information easily and quickly.

In this chapter you'll learn about:

- HP VEE data types
- HP VEE analysis capabilities
- Using math objects
- Using the Formula object
- HP VEE display capabilities
- Customizing your displays

HP VEE Data Types

The following are brief descriptions of HP VEE data types. Just read through them quickly. More important issues involving the usage of these data types will be explained in the coming chapters. A container carries data between objects in HP VEE. Each container has data of a specific type and shape. The types are explained in the table below. Shape is expressed as a Scalar or an Array. (A Scalar is a single number including numbers expressed as two or more components such as Complex numbers.) The dimension may be specified for an Array, such as Array 1D for a one-dimensional array, Array 2D for a two-dimensional array, and so on.

In general, you won't be concerned with data types or shapes, because most objects operate on any HP VEE data type and will automatically convert data to the type required for that object. For example, if a Magnitude Spectrum display receives a Waveform data type, HP VEE automatically performs a Fast Fourier Transform to convert it from the time domain into the frequency domain. Occasionally, however, an object will only take a particular data type, so it's good to be aware of them.

Data Type	Description
Int32	A 32-bit two's complement integer (-2147483648 to 2147483647).
Real (or REAL64)	A 64-bit real that conforms to the IEEE 754 standard (+/- 1.797693138623157 E308).
PComplex	A magnitude and phase component in the form (mag, @phase). Phase is set by default to degrees, but can be set to radians or gradians with the **File => Preferences => Trig Mode** setting.

Analyzing and Displaying Test Data

Data Type	Description
Complex	A rectangular or Cartesian complex number having a real and imaginary component in the form (real, imag). Each component is Real. For example, the complex number 1 + 2i is represented as (1,2).
Waveform	A composite data type of time domain values that contains the Real values of evenly-spaced, linear points and the total time span of the waveform. The data shape of a Waveform must be a one-dimensional array (Array 1D).
Spectrum	A composite data type of frequency domain values that contains the PComplex values of points and the minimum and maximum frequency values. The domain data can be mapped as log or linear. The data shape of a Spectrum must be a one-dimensional array (Array 1D).
Coord	A composite data type that contains at least two components in the form (x,y,...). Each component is Real. The data shape of a coord must be a Scalar or an Array 1D.
Enum	A text string that has an associated integer value. You can access the integer value with the ordinal(x) function.
Text	A string of alphanumeric characters.
Record	A composite data type with a field for each data type. Each field has a name and a container, which can be of any type and shape (including Record).

In addition to the ten data types above, HP VEE has three more data types used *only* for instrument I/O. All integer values are stored and manipulated internally by HP VEE as Int32 data types, and all real numbers are stored and manipulated by HP VEE as Real64 data types. However, instruments generally support 16-bit integers or 8-bit bytes, and some instruments support 32-bit reals. To accomodate these situations, HP VEE also supports the following data types for instrument I/O:

Instrument I/O Data Type	Description
Byte	An 8-bit two's complement byte (-128 to 127). (Byte is used in **READ BINARY**, **WRITE BINARY**, and **WRITE BYTE** instrument I/O transactions.)
Int16	A 16-bit two's complement integer (-32768 to 32767).
Real32	A 32-bit real that conforms to the IEEE 754 standard (+/-3.40282347E+/-38.

HP VEE will automatically convert these data types into the appropriate internal data type. For rules on those converstions, consult HP VEE documentation.

HP VEE Analysis Capabilities

The following list of mathematical functions comes from the cascading menus in the Math and AdvMath menus. We've also listed functions that are not explicity included in the menus. This list will give you an overview of the analysis capabilities available. If HP VEE does not have a math function you need, you still have several options available. You can create the function with the Formula object, which we'll discuss later in this chapter; you can write the function in a compiled language such as C and link it to HP VEE; or you can communicate with another software application from HP VEE.

You will immediately understand what many of the objects in the following list do; however, some of them will look confusing at first. To get an explanation for a particular object, just select the object and consult Help in its object menu.

Math Menu

<u>+ - * /</u>

+, -, *, /, ^, mod, div

<u>Relational</u>

==, ~=, !=, <, >, <=, >=

<u>Logical</u>

AND, OR, XOR, NOT

<u>Bitwise</u>

bit(x,n), bits(str), setBit(x,n), clearBit(x,n), bitAnd(x,y), bitOr(x,y), bitXor(x,y), bitCmpl(x), bitShift(x,y)

Real Parts

abs(x), signof(x), ordinal(x), round(x), floor(x), ceil(x), intPart(x), fracPart(x)

Complex Parts

j(x), re(x), im(x), mag(x), phase(x), conj(x)

String

strUp(str), strDown(str), strRev(str), strTrim(str), strLen(str), strFromThru(str,from,thru), strFromLen(str,from,len), strPosChar(str,char), strPosStr(str1,str2)

Generate

ramp(numElem,from,thru), logRamp(numElem,from,thru), xramp(numElem,from,thru), xlogRamp(numElem,from,thru)

Power

sq(x), sqrt(x), cubert(x), recip(x), log(x), log10(x), exp(x), exp10(x)

Polynomial

1: poly(x, [a0 a1]), 2: poly(x, [a0 a1 a2]), 3: poly(x, [a0 a1 a2 a3]), N: poly(x, [a0 a1 ... aN])

Trig

sin(x), cos(x), tan(x), cot(x), asin(x), acos(x), atan(x), acot(x), atan2(y,x)

Hyper Trig

sinh(x), cosh(x), tanh(x), coth(x), asinh(x), acosh(x), atanh(x), acoth(x)

Analyzing and Displaying Test Data

Time & Date

now(), wday(aDate), mday(aDate), month(aDate), year(aDate), dmyToDate(d,m,y), hmsToSec(h,m,s), hmsToHour(h,m,s)

AdvMath Menu

Array

init(x, value), totSize(x), rotate(x, numElem), concat(x,y), sum(x), prod(x), sort(x)

Matrix

det(x), inverse(x), transpose(x), identity(x), minor(x, row, col), cofactor(x, row, col), matMultiply(A,B), matDivide(number, denom)

Probability

random(low, high), randomize(x, low, high), randomSeed(seed), perm(n, r), comb(n, r), gamma(x), beta(x, y), factorial(n), binomial(a, b), erf(x), erfc(x)

Statistics

min(x), max(x), median(x), mode(x), mean(x), sdev(x), vari(x), rms(x)

Frequency Distribution

magDist(x, from, thru, step), logMagDist(x, from, thru, logStep)

Calculus

integral(x), deriv(x, 1), deriv(x, 2), deriv(x, order), defIntegral(x, a, b), derivAt(x, 1, pt), derivAt(x, 2, pt), derivAt(x, order, pt)

Regression

linear, logarithmic, exponential, power curve, polynomial

Data Filtering

polySmooth(x), meanSmooth(x, numPts), movingAvg(x, numPts), clipUpper(x, a), clipLower(x, a), minIndex(x), maxIndex(x), minX(x), maxX(x)

Bessel

j0(x), j1(x), jn(x, n), y0(x), y1(x), yn(x, n), Ai(x), Bi(x)

Hyper Bessel

i0(x), i1(x), k0(x), k1(x)

Signal Processing

fft(x), ifft(x), convolve(a, b), xcorrelate(a, b), bartlet(x), hamming(x), hanning(x), blackman(x), rect(x)

Other Functions Not Explicitly in the Math Menus

- WhichOS( ) and whichPlatform( ) functions

- The triadic operator: *(condition ? expression1 : expression2)*. If the *condition* is true, the result of *expression1* is returned; otherwise, the result of *expression2* is returned.

- Subarray syntax: A[2:4], for example, returns the third through fifth elements of the array A. (All HP VEE arrays have zero-based indexing.)

- Build array syntax: [1 3 6], for example, builds a 3 element array with the values 1,3, and 6.

Analyzing and Displaying Test Data

- Global variables: You can use any global variable's name in an expression instead of the Get Global object.

    Note: All functions can be nested.

- Record Syntax: Records use a dot syntax to identify fields. For example, *rec.b* indicates the *b* field in the Record called *rec*.

Using Math Objects

Let's work through an example. The principles will be the same using any object from the math menus.

Lab 4-1: Calculating Standard Deviation

Generate a cosine waveform of at a frequency of 1 kHz, amplitude of 1 V, a time span of 20 ms, represented by 256 points. Calculate its standard deviation and display it.

1. Select **Device => Virtual Source => Function Generator**.

2. Select **AdvMath => Statistics => sdev(x)**.

3. Double-click **sdev(x)** to get to the open view and open the object menu to consult **Help**.

    Note: The sdev(x) object is defined as the square root of the variance of x, and x may be of the type Int32, Real, Coord, or Waveform. Since the Function Generator outputs a Waveform data type, this program will run without error.

4. Connect the **Function Generator** to **sdev(x)**.

4 - 9

CUTTING YOUR TEST DEVELOPMENT TIME WITH HP VEE

5. Select **Display** => **AlphaNumeric** and connect it to the **sdev(x)** data output pin.

6. Run your program. It should look like Figure 4-1.

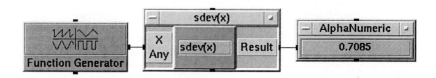

Fig. 4-1. Calculating Standard Deviation

On Your Own

Generate a cosine wave. Calculate its variance and the root mean square. Display your results.

===

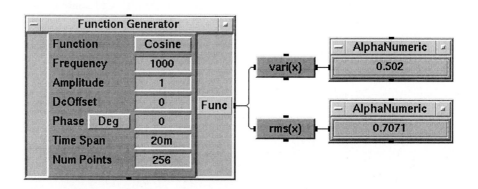

Fig. 4-2. On Your Own Solution: Variance and RMS

4 - 10

Using the Formula Object

The Formula object can be used to write mathematical expressions in HP VEE. The variables in the expression are the data input pin names. The result of the evaluation of the expression will be put on the data output pin. Examine the figure below. The input field for the expression is in the center of the object. A default expression (2*A+3) simply indicates where your formula should go. Just double-click this field and input your own expression.

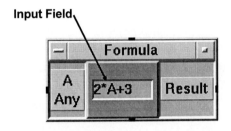

Fig. 4-3. The Formula Object

To Evaluate a Simple Expression with the Formula Object

Let's evaluate the expression, 2*A^4-B, where A=2 and B=1. (Notice the ^ sign for exponentiation.)

Note: The variable names are not case-sensitive.

1. Select **Math => Formula**. Click the **Formula** input field and type **2*A^4-B**.

CUTTING YOUR TEST DEVELOPMENT TIME WITH HP VEE

2. Place the mouse pointer over the data input area and press **Ctrl-a** to add an input pin.

   It will be labeled B Any by default, but you could rename it to suit your expression.

3. Select **Data => Constant=>Integer**, clone it by selecting **Clone** from the object menu, and connect the two **Integer** objects to the **Formula** inputs **A Any** and **B Any**.

4. Enter **2** in the **A** input box and **1** in the **B** input box.

5. Select **Display => AlphaNumeric** and connect it to the output of Formula, and run your program.

   You should get **31** for an answer, as shown in the figure below.

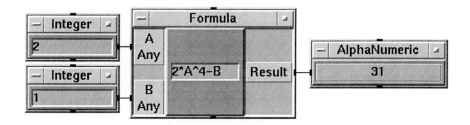

Fig. 4-4. Evaluating an Expression

To Use an HP VEE Function in the Formula Object

Let's generate a cosine wave and calculate the standard deviation and root mean square using the Formula object.

1. Select the **Function Generator, Formula,** and **AlphaNumeric** objects and connect them together using their data pins.

Analyzing and Displaying Test Data

2. Clone the **Formula** object by opening the object menu and selecting **Clone**, and place it just below the first one. Connect the **Function Generator** data output pin to the second **Formula** object.

3. Clone another **AlphaNumeric** display and connect it to the second **Formula** object.

4. Enter **sdev(A)** in the first **Formula** object, and **rms(A)** in the second one.

You'll recall that these are the two math functions we used from the Statistics submenu in the AdvMath menu. Notice that they can be called as functions or independent objects.

5. Run your program.

You'll see the same answers putting these functions into the Formula object as you did when you used them as independent objects, as shown below.

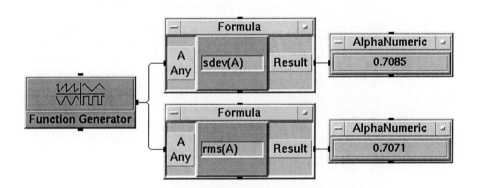

Fig. 4-5. Formula Examples Using HP VEE Functions

4 - 13

CUTTING YOUR TEST DEVELOPMENT TIME WITH HP VEE

On Your Own

1. Use the **ramp** object in the **Math => Generate** submenu to create an array of numbers from **1** to **4096**. Calculate the standard deviation of this array and display it.

2. Do the same thing described in number one, but do it using the **ramp( )** function.

3. Do the same tasks as described in number two, but nest functions and use only two objects.

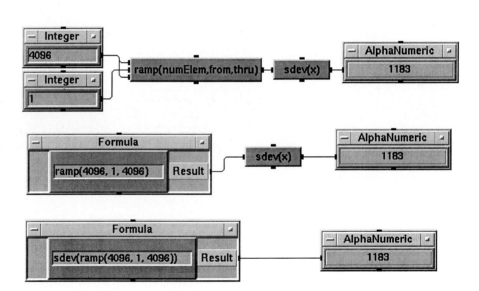

Fig. 4-6. On Your Own Solution: Ramp and SDEV

You have to delete the input terminal on the Formula object to avoid an error message, because all data input pins must be connected and have data before an object can operate. However, connecting the sequence input/output pins or the data output pin is optional.

4 - 14

Display Capabilities

The following table gives brief descriptions of the display objects you have at your disposal. Skim through it quickly. We'll cover the displays in more detail as we use them in examples.

Display	Description
AlphaNumeric	Display values as text or numbers. Requires SCALAR, ARRAY 1D, or ARRAY 2D.
Logging AlphaNumeric	Displays values as text or numbers when repeatedly logged. Requires SCALAR or ARRAY 1D.
Meter	Displays numbers in the format of an analog meter along with the decimal number. Ranges of the meter may be color-coded. Requires Scalar data.
XY Trace	Graphically displays mapped arrays or a set of values when y data is generated with evenly-spaced x values. The x value that is automatically generated depends on the data type of the trace data. For example, a Real trace would generate evenly-spaced Real x values; whereas, a Waveform trace would generate x values for time.
Strip Chart	Graphically displays the recent history of data that is continuously generated while the program runs. For each y input value, the x value is incremented by a specified Step size. When new data runs off the right side of the display, the display automatically scrolls to show you the latest data.

CUTTING YOUR TEST DEVELOPMENT TIME WITH HP VEE

Display	Description
Complex Plane	Displays Complex, Polar Complex (PComplex), or Coord data values on a Real vs. Imaginary axis.
X vs Y Plot	Graphically displays values when separate data information is available for X and Y data.
Polar Plot	Graphically displays data on a polar scale when separate information is available for radius and angle data.
Waveform (Time)	Graphically displays Waveforms or Spectrums in the real time domain. Spectrums are automatically converted to the time domain using an Inverse Fast Fourier Transform (ifft). The x axis is the sampling units of the input waveform.
Spectrum (Freq)	A menu that contains frequency domain displays: Magnitude Spectrum, Phase Spectrum, Magnitude vs Phase (Polar), and Magnitude vs Phase (Smith). Inputs must be Waveform, Spectrum, or an array of Coords. Waveform inputs are automatically changed to the frequency domain with a Fast Fourier Transform (fft).

Note: The Beep object, used to give an audible signal to the test operator, and the Note Pad object, used for documentation, are also in the Display menu, but are not used for presenting test data.

Analyzing and Displaying Test Data

Customizing Displays

Displays may be customized in a variety of ways. Not only can you label, move and size them like all HP VEE objects, but you can also change the x/y scales, modify the traces, add markers, or zoom in on parts of the graphical display. Let's work through an example to illustrate some of these features. You'll use the Noise Generator to generate a waveform, and then display it with the Waveform (Time) display. You'll change the X scale, zoom in on a wave segment, and use the markers to measure the distances between points on the waveform. The same principles may be applied to all the graphical displays.

To Display a Waveform

1. Select **Device => Virtual Source => Noise Generator**.

2. Select **Display => Waveform (Time)**.

3. Connect the data output of the **Noise Generator** to the data input of **Waveform (Time)** and run your program.

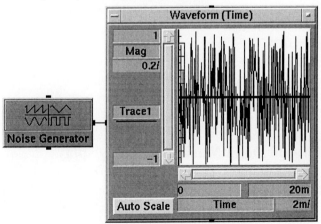

Fig. 4-7. Displaying a Waveform

4 - 17

To Change the X and Y Scales

1. Click the right input field below the **x** axis where it says **20m** and enter **1m**.

   This alters the time span of the display from 20 milliseconds to 1 millisecond.

2. Click the lower input field on the **y** axis where it says **-1**, and enter **- .5**.

   You'll see the display immediately adjust to the new y scale of -0.5 to 1 for Mag. You could also alter any of the other scales in the same way

To Zoom In on Part of the Waveform

1. Open the **Waveform (Time)** object menu and click **Zoom => In**.

   The cursor becomes a small right angle. By pressing and holding the left mouse button you can draw a square on the graph outlining the area you want to enlarge.

2. Outline an area of the waveform including several peaks, and release the mouse button.

   The display zooms in to this selected area of the waveform. Notice the x and y scales change automatically.

To Add Delta Markers to the Display

1. Open the Waveform (Time) object menu and select **Markers => Delta On**.

You will see two white arrows pointing up and down at one of the data points on the waveform. Also, notice that the display records the x and y coordinates of these markers at the bottom of the display. To measure the x or y distance between two peaks, just click one of the other peaks. You'll see one of the markers jump to that new peak with the new coordinates recorded at the bottom of the display, as shown in the figure below.

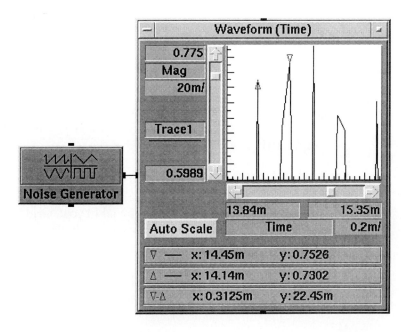

Fig. 4-8. Delta Markers on a Waveform Display

HP VEE will automatically interpolate between waveform data points, if you open the object menu and select Markers => Interpolate Center.

To Change the Color of the Trace

1. Open the object menu and click **Traces & Scales...**.

   A Traces and Scales dialog box appears that allows you to change the name(s) of the trace(s), the color, the type of line, and how points are displayed. You can also change the scale names, ranges, log or linear mappings, and colors.

   Note: With version B.02.00 you can also change these values at run time by using the Traces and Scales control inputs. See HP VEE documentation for more information.

2. Click the button next to **Color** near the top of the dialog box, select the color you want, then click **OK**. Click **OK** to exit the **Traces and Scales** dialog box.

   The trace will now be displayed in the new color.

Other display characteristics such as Panel Layout, Grid Type, Clear Control, and Add Right Scale may be customized in a similar fashion as the features in the exercise above.

Note: HP VEE also includes Plot in the display object menus, which allows you to plot test results on the display without printing out the rest of the program.

For Additional Practice

To learn about other HP VEE objects and gain more practice do some of the exercises in *Appendix B: Additional Lab Exercises* in the *General Programming Techniques* section. Solutions are provided with a discussion of key points.

Chapter 4 Checklist

Use the following checklist to determine whether there are topics you need to review before going to Chapter 5.

- Describe the main data types in HP VEE, and the three data types that are used for instrument I/O only.

- Describe some of the main areas of analytical capabilities in HP VEE.

- Find an online Help explanation for any object in the Math or AdvMath menus.

- Describe the relationship between input pins and variables in an HP VEE math object.

- Evaluate a mathematical expression using the Formula object.

- Use an HP VEE function in a mathematical expression in the Formula object.

- Describe major display capabilities in HP VEE.

- Customize a graphical display in terms of the scales used, the part of the waveform seen, the markers used, and the color of the trace.

5

Storing and Retrieving Test Results

Average Time to Complete: 2 hrs.

Overview

This chapter will teach you the fundamentals of storing and retrieving test data. You'll learn how easy it is to create arrays of the right data type and size to hold your test results, and then how to access any part of that data for analysis or display. Getting data to and from files was introduced in a Chapter 2 exercise. Now we'll go into greater detail on the flexibility and power of the To/From File objects. For more elaborate tests, developers usually need to store several types of data in a single structure. HP VEE satisfies this need with the Record data type. One or more Records may be stored in a file called a Dataset. You can easily perform sort or search operations on datasets. In effect, this provides you with a simple, customized test database that is easy to create and maintain.

In this chapter you'll learn about:

- Putting test data into arrays

- Using the Collector object

- Using the To/From File objects

- Creating mixed data types using Records

- Performing search and sort operations using DataSets

- Creating simple test databases using the Dataset objects

Using Arrays to Store Test Results

In Chapter 4 you had an overview of the HP VEE data types, which can be stored as scalar values (that is, a single number such as 9 or (32, @10)) or as arrays from 1 to 10 dimensions.

Indexing for arrays is zero-based in HP VEE, and brackets are used to indicate the position of the array element. For example, if the array A holds the elements [4 5 6], then A[0] = 4, A[1] = 5, and A[2] = 6. The colon is used to indicate a range of elements. For instance, A[0:2] = [4 5 6] in the array above. The asterisk, *, is a wildcard to specify all elements from a particular array dimension. A[*] returns all elements of array A. Commas are used to separate array dimensions. If B is a two-dimensional array with three elements in each dimension, B[1,0] returns the first element in the second row of B.

To Create an Array for Your Test Results

The easiest way to create an array is to use the Collector object. Let's use the For Count object to simulate 4 readings from an instrument, which you will put into an array and then print the results. The principles will be the same regardless of the data type or the size of the array, since the Collector will take any data type and create the array size automatically depending on the number of elements sent.

1. Select **Flow => Repeat => For Count**, **Data => Collector**, and **Display => AlphaNumeric**.

    Double-click the **Collector** to get the open view, and read through **Help** in the object menu to understand the object.

    For Count outputs increasing integer values starting at 0 depending on the number of iterations you specify in the input field. Highlight the default number **10** by double-clicking, then type **4**. **For Count** will output 0, 1, 2, and 3.

Storing and Retrieving Test Results

The Collector receives data values through its Data Any terminal. When you're finished collecting data, you "ping" the XEQ Any terminal to tell the Collector to construct the array. You can use the For Count sequence output pin to ping the Collector XEQ pin. The Collector displays a button that toggles between a 1 Dim Array and n+1 Dim Array.

2. Click **n+1 Dim** in the **Collector** to change the selection to **1 Dim Array**.

3. Connect the **For Count** data output pin to the **Data Any** input pin on the **Collector**.

4. Connect the **For Count** sequence output pin to the **XEQ Any** input pin on the Collector.

   The XEQ Any pin is a control pin that exists on several different objects, that tells HP VEE when you want that object to execute. In this case, you want the object to fire after all of the data for the array has been collected.

5. Connect the **Collector** data output pin to the **AlphaNumeric** data input pin.

   You should enlarge **AlphaNumeric** to accomodate the array, so place the mouse pointer over the object and press the right mouse button to get the pop-up object menu. Then select **Size**, move the mouse pointer to the size you want, and click to get the enlarged object. (Recall that you could also enlarge AlphaNumeric when you first selected it by using "click and drag" on the object outline.)

6. Run your program. It should look like the one below.

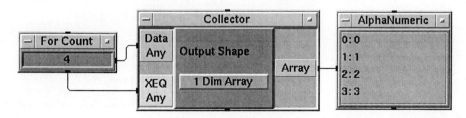

Fig. 5-1. The Collector Creating an Array

To Extract Values from an Array

You could do this in one of two ways: use the bracket notation in an expression, or use the Access Array => Get Values object. We'll use expressions in the Formula object for the following example. You'll add several objects to the program in the first exercise.

1. Delete the data line between the **Collector** and **AlphaNumeric** by placing the mouse pointer over the line, pressing **Shift-Ctrl**, and then clicking the left mouse button. Then iconize the **Collector**.

2. Select **Math => Formula** and clone it. Move **AlphaNumeric** to the right, and put both **Formula** objects to the right of the **Collector**.

3. Connect the **Collector** data output to the data inputs of the **Formula** objects. Enter **A[2]** in the upper **Formula** input field, and **A[1:3]** in the lower **Formula** input field.

   A[2] will extract the third element of the array as a Scalar; A[1:3] will return a sub-array of three elements holding the second, third, and fourth elements of A (meaning the array on the A Any terminal).

4. Clone **AlphaNumeric** and connect a display to each **Formula** object.

5. Run your program. It should look like the one below.

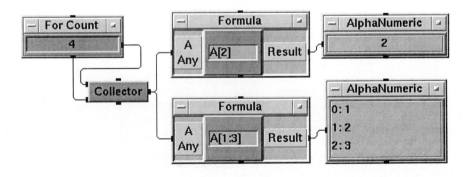

Fig. 5-2. Extracting Array Elements with Expressions

Using the To/From File Objects

We've used the To File and From File objects in Chapter 2. Now we'll discuss them in more detail. Before working on an exercise, there are some basic concepts you should understand about these objects:

- A data file is opened on the first READ or WRITE transaction after the program begins. When the program ends, HP VEE closes any open files automatically.

- HP VEE maintains one read pointer and one write pointer per file regardless of how many objects are accessing the file. The read pointer identifies the next data item to be read, and the write pointer indicates where the next data item should be written.

- You can append data to existing files or overwrite them. If the Clear File at PreRun & Open setting is checked in the open view of the To File object, then the write pointer starts at the beginning of the file; if not, the pointer is positioned at the end of the existing file. Each WRITE transaction appends information to the file at the location of the write pointer. If an EXECUTE CLEAR transaction is performed, the write pointer moves to the beginning of the file and erases its contents.

- A read pointer starts at the beginning of a file, and advances through the data depending on the READ transactions. You may perform an EXECUTE REWIND in the From File object to move the pointer back to the beginning of the file without affecting any data.

Understanding I/O Transactions

Before we do the lab exercise on the To/From File objects, let's look at "I/O transactions" in more detail. I/O transactions are used by HP VEE to communicate with instruments, files, strings, the operating system, interfaces, other programs, HP BASIC/UX, and printers. For example, look at the To File object in Figure 5-3.

CUTTING YOUR TEST DEVELOPMENT TIME WITH HP VEE

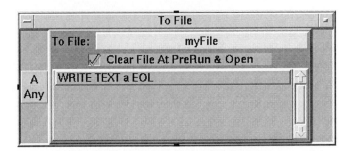

Fig. 5-3. The To File Object

You are sending data to the specified file, myFile. You can add inputs to accept data from your program. The bar is called a transaction bar. It contains the default transaction statement: WRITE TEXT a EOL . When you click it, an I/O Transaction dialog box appears, which configures your specific transaction statement..

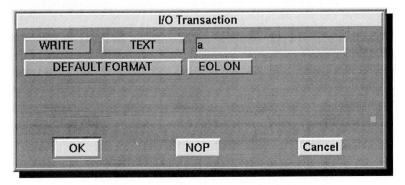

Fig. 5-4. An I/O Transaction Dialog Box

There are different forms of this dialog box depending on which object you're using, but there are certain common elements we want to stress: the "actions", the "encodings", the "expression list", the "format", and the "end-of-line" (EOL) sequence. An I/O transaction to write data is usually in the following format:

        <action> <encoding> <expression list><format><EOL>.

Storing and Retrieving Test Results

The tables and comments that follow will give you a basic understanding of these elements.

The most common actions available are **READ, WRITE, EXECUTE**, and **WAIT**.

Action	Explanation
READ	Reads data from the specified source using the specified encoding and format.
WRITE	Writes data to the specified target using the specified encoding and format.
EXECUTE	Executes a specific command. For example, EXECUTE REWIND repositions a file's read or write pointer to the beginning of the file without erasing the contents. EXECUTE CLOSE closes an open file.
WAIT	Waits the specified number of seconds before the next transaction.

Note: There are also a number of actions for I/O => Advanced I/O Operations that you can examine by exploring the objects in that menu.

Encodings and formats refer to the way data is packaged and sent. For instance, a TEXT encoding sends data as ASCII characters. The TEXT encoding could be formatted in a number of ways. For example, let's say you want to send a string of letters and numbers to a file. A WRITE TEXT STRING transaction would send the entire string represented by ASCII characters. A WRITE TEXT REAL transaction would only extract the Real numbers from the same string and send them using ASCII characters for the

5 - 7

individual digits. The following table provides brief explanations of encodings:

Encodings	Explanations
TEXT	Reads or writes all data types in a human-readable form (ASCII) that can easily be edited or ported to other software applications. HP VEE numeric data is automatically converted to text.
BYTE	Converts numeric data to binary integer and sends or receives the least significant byte.
CASE	Maps an enumerated value or an integer to a string and reads/writes that string. For example, you could use CASE to accept error numbers and write error messages.
BINARY	Handles all data types in a machine-specific binary format.
BINBLOCK	Uses IEEE488.2 definite length block headers with all HP VEE data types in binary files.
CONTAINER	Uses HP VEE specific text format with all data types.

An "expression list" is simply a comma-separated list of expressions that need to be evaluated to yield the data sent or received. The expression may be composed of a mathematical expression, a pin name, a string constant, an HP VEE function, a user function, or a global variable.

Data formats were presented in Chapter 3 in conjunction with reading data from instruments. Most of these formats apply to all I/O transactions. Consult Chapter 3 or HP VEE documentation for further discussion of formats.

Storing and Retrieving Test Results

EOL (end-of-line sequence of characters) may be turned on or off, and you can specify the EOL sequence by opening the object menu of most of the I/O => To objects and selecting Config....

Let's do the lab, so these abstractions are rooted in something more concrete.

Lab 5-1: Using the To/From File Objects

The purpose of this lab exercise is to teach the process of getting test data to and from files. Let's store and retrieve three common test result items: a test name, a time stamp, and a one-dimensional array of Real values. The same process will apply to all HP VEE data types.

To Send a Text String to a File

1. Select **I/O => To => File**.

   The default file is **myFile**, which can easily be changed by clicking the **To File** input field to get a list box of files in your home directory. You can leave this default. Click the box next to **Clear File At PreRun & Open**. By default HP VEE appends new data to the end of an existing file. You need to check this box to be certain the file is cleared before you write new data. **WRITE TEXT a EOL** is the default transaction. It means that you will write the data on pin **a** using **TEXT** encoding and a specified end-of-line sequence. HP VEE is *not* case-sensitive; you can use lower-case or upper-case strings for pin names.

2. Click the transaction bar to get the **I/O Transaction** dialog box. (Refer to Figures 5-3 and 5-4, if necessary.)

3. Double-click the expression list field to highlight the **a**, and type **"Test1"**, then click **OK**. (You need the quotation marks to indicate a Text string.)

If you typed **Test1** without the quotation marks, HP VEE would interpret this as a pin name or global variable name. You can leave the other defaults, since you want to want the action **WRITE**. The encoding **TEXT** will send the data using ASCII characters. The **DEFAULT FORMAT** will choose an appropriate HP VEE format such as **STRING**. And finally, the default **EOL** sequence is the escape character for a new line **\n**.

You should now have **WRITE TEST "Test1" EOL** in the transaction bar. This transaction means you will send the string **Test1** to the specified file. If this were the only transaction, you would delete the input terminal **A Any**, but we will use it in a moment, so leave it there for now.

To Send a Time Stamp to a File

The object now( ) in the Math => Time & Date menu gives the current time expressed as a Real Scalar. The value of the Real is the number of seconds since 00:00 hours on Jan. 1, 0001 AD. Therefore, now( ) returns a value about 62.89G. HP VEE provides this format, because it's easier to manipulate mathematically and conserves storage space. If you want to store the time stamp in a more readable format, use the TIME STAMP FORMAT in the To File object.

1. Double-click just below the first transaction bar in the **To File** object to get a new **I/O Transaction** box.

2. Double-click the expression list input field to highlight the **a** and type **now( )**.

   The now( ) function will send the current time from the computer clock in a Real format, but let's change that to the Time Stamp Format.

3. Click **DEFAULT FORMAT** to get the **Select Text Format** box, select **TIME STAMP FORMAT**, then click **OK**. HP VEE now adds some additional buttons to I/O Transaction dialog box.

Storing and Retrieving Test Results

Click **Date & Time**, select **Time** (displays time without the date), then click **OK**.

Click **HH:MM:SS** (hour, minute, and second format) to toggle to **HH:MM** (hour and minute format).

Click **24 HOUR** (military time format) to toggle to **12 HOUR** (am or pm format).

Your box should look like Figure 5-5.

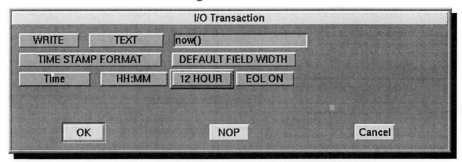

Fig. 5-5. The TIME STAMP I/O Transaction Box

Click **OK**.

Your second transaction bar should now have the statement:
   WRITE TEXT now( ) TIME:HM:H12 EOL.

To Send a Real Array to a File

Let's create a one-dimensional array of four elements using the For Count and Collector objects. Then we'll append this to myFile.

1. Select **Flow => Repeat => For Count** and **Data => Collector**. Change the default value in **For Count** to 4. Connect the data output of **For Count** to the data input of the **Collector**. Connect the **For Count** sequence output pin to the **XEQ** pin on the **Collector**. Iconize the **Collector**.

CUTTING YOUR TEST DEVELOPMENT TIME WITH HP VEE

The Collector will now create the array [0 1 2 3], which you can send to your data file.

2. Connect the **Collector** data output to the **A Any** terminal.

3. Double-click below the second transaction bar in the **To File** object.

4. Click **DEFAULT FORMAT**, select **REAL FORMAT**, then click **OK** to return to the **I/O Transaction** box.

You now have new buttons in the box regarding your **REAL FORMAT** selection. You can leave all of the default choices, but you might want to investigate the menus for future reference. Click **OK** to close the **I/O Transaction** box. You'll now see **WRITE TEXT a REAL STD EOL** on the third transaction bar, as shown below. (The configured **I/O Transaction** box is also displayed.)

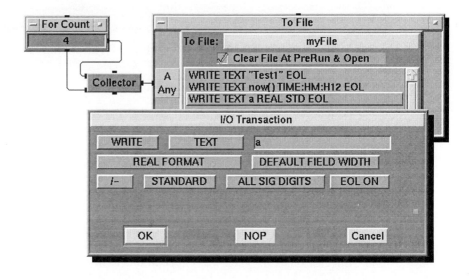

Fig. 5-6. Storing Data Using the To File Object

Storing and Retrieving Test Results

To Retrieve Data Using the From File Object

When you're using From File, you need to know how the data was stored. You will see later in this chapter that you can store and retrieve data using To DataSet or From DataSet, in which case you don't have to know what kind of data is in the file. In this example, you know that you stored the name of a test in a String Format, followed by a time stamp in Time Stamp Format, and finally an array of Real numbers. You will now create three transactions in From File to read that data back into HP VEE.

1. Select **I/O => From => File** and place it below the **To File** object.

2. Connect the sequence output pin of the **To File** object to the sequence input pin of the **From File** object.

   This sequence connection assures you that To File has completed sending data to myFile, before From File begins to extract data.

3. Leave the default data file, **myFile**, since you sent data to this file. Then click the transaction bar to get the **I/O Transaction** dialog box. Click **REAL FORMAT** and change it to **STRING FORMAT**. See Fig. 5-7.

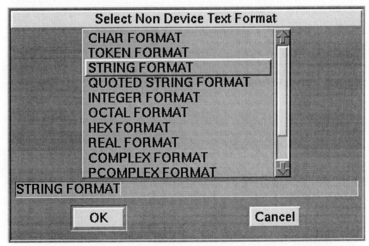

Fig. 5-7. The Select Non Device Text Format Box

5 - 13

CUTTING YOUR TEST DEVELOPMENT TIME WITH HP VEE

All of the other defaults are correct, so click **OK** to close the **I/O Transaction** box.

You should now see the transaction statement: **READ TEXT x STR**.

You now need to add two more transactions to read back the time stamp and the real array.

4. Add a data output by moving the mouse pointer over the data output area and pressing **Ctrl-a**. A dialog box appears labeled **Select output to add**. Select **Y** and click **OK**. HP VEE adds the data output terminal **Y**. To add a third terminal, repeat the same procedure. Since the label **Y** is being used, HP VEE will offer you a data output terminal labeled **Z**. Select **Z** and click **OK**. You now have three outputs labeled **X**, **Y**, and **Z**.

5. Double-click below the first transaction bar. The **I/O Transaction** dialog box appears. Double-click on the expression list input field to highlight **x** and type **y**. This means that you want the second transaction to read data back to pin **y**. Change **REAL FORMAT** to **STRING FORMAT**, then click **OK**.

   Note: If you want to read the time stamp back as a text string, then use the STRING FORMAT. The TIME STAMP FORMAT converts the time stamp data back to a Real number.

6. Double-click below the second transaction bar to go directly to the **I/O Transaction** dialog box. Edit **x** to **z**, so that the Real array is read back to the **Z Any** output terminal. **REAL FORMAT** is correct in this case, but you need to change **SCALAR** to **ARRAY 1D**.

   Now the **I/O Transaction** box adds a **SIZE** button. In this case, we know the array has four elements, so edit **10** to **4** and click **OK**.

   Note: If you don't know or remember the size of an array, you may toggle SIZE: to TO END:. This will read data to the end of the array without HP VEE knowing its exact size. You could use this feature to read the entire contents of a file as a string array to examine the file contents.

Storing and Retrieving Test Results

You will now see **READ TEXT y STR** on the second transaction bar and **READ TEXT z REAL ARRAY:4** on the third. Iconize **From File**.

7. Select **Display => AlphaNumeric** and clone it twice to get three displays. Connect them to the three data output pins on **From File**. Size the second display to be wider to hold the time stamp, and the third one to be higher for the array.

   Note: *Recall that you can size the AlphaNumeric displays as you clone them, just as you could with any object by clicking and dragging the object outline when you first select it from the menu.*

8. Run your program. It should look like the one below.

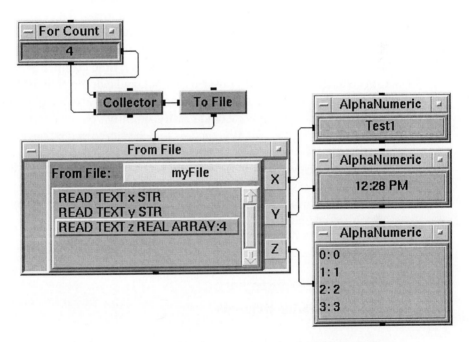

Fig. 5-8. Retrieving Data Using the From File Object

Using Records to Store Mixed Data Types

The Record data type can store different data types in a single data container. Any HP VEE data type including Record could be used. The data can be be in the shape of a Scalar or an Array. So you could store the test name, the time stamp, and the real array in the preceding example in a single data structure. The individual elements in a Record are stored as fields and are accessed using a dot notation. For example, Rec.Name would access the field, Name, within a Record called Rec. If you created an array of records then Rec[2].Name would signify the Name field in the third record in the array. (Recall that all arrays start their indexing at 0.)

There are several benefits to structuring your test data using the Record data type. First, you can create logical groupings of mixed data types in a single container, which makes a program easier to develop and maintain. For example, you might use the following fields for a record storing test data: test name, value returned, pass or fail indicator, time stamp, nominal value expected, upper pass limit, lower pass limit, and a description of the test. Secondly, manipulating a single data container rather than eight separate ones in the example above would greatly simplify your program and make it much more readable. Finally, records may be stored and retrieved from DataSets in HP VEE. A DataSet is a special file created to store records. When you retrieve records from a DataSet, you don't have to know what data types are inside. HP VEE provides you objects to retrieve, sort, and search the information stored in DataSets. So, in effect, you have a simple, customized database for your test results.

Lab 5-2: Using Records

This section teaches you the fundamentals of using the Record datatype. You'll learn how to build a record, retrieve a particular field in that record, set a chosen field, and unbuild the entire record in one step. Along the way you'll use the time stamp function, now(), in a different way. The last two

Storing and Retrieving Test Results

sections in the chapter will show you how to use DataSets to simplify common test development tasks.

To Build a Record

You'll build a Record with three fields: the name of a test stored as a String, a time stamp stored as a Real Scalar, and simulated test results stored as a four element Array of Reals. When you retrieve these fields in the next exercise, you'll see that you can convert the time stamp into a number of different formats for display.

1. Create your test name by selecting **Data => Constant => Text** and entering **Test1** in the input field. Iconize **Text**.

2. Select **Math => Time & Date => now( )** and place it below **Text**.

3. Select **Data => Constant => Real** and place it below **now( )**.

    You can turn this Scalar Real into an Array 1D by clicking config... in the Real object menu and specifying the number of array elements you want.

4. Open the object menu for **Real** and click **config....** Enter **4** in the **Array Elements** input field and click **OK**. Enter four values into this array by double-clicking next to element **0000** to highlight the first entry, then input the values **2.2, 3.3, 4.4, 5.5** using the **Tab** key between each entry and the **Enter** key when you're done. Iconize **Real**.

5. Select **Data => Build Data => Record** and place it to the right of the three other objects. Add a third data input terminal, so you can input three fields. Open each terminal by double-clicking over the terminal and rename the three input terminals to **testname, time,** and **data**.

    The Output Shape on the Build Record object toggles between Scalar and Array. The Scalar default will be the correct choice for the majority of situations. For a discussion of the Array selection, see HP VEE documentation.

6. Connect the **Text** object to the **testname** terminal, **now()** to the **time** terminal, and **Real** to the **data** terminal on the **Build Record** object.

7. Run your program in this stage of development. Double-click on the **Result** data output terminal to examine your record. It should look like the figure below.

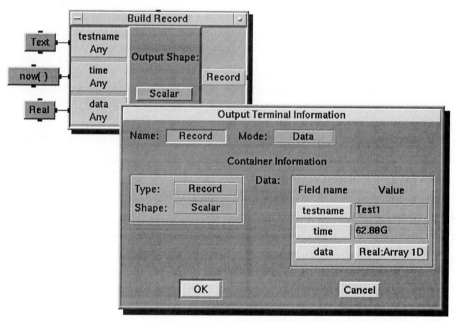

Fig. 5-9. Output Terminal Information on a Record

You can clearly see the three fields and their values. If you click on the **Real: Array 1D** button, a list box will show you the actual values. Notice that the time stamp has been stored as a Real Scalar. We'll show you how to convert that to a more readable form in the following exercise. Click **OK** to close the **Output Terminal Information** dialog box.

Storing and Retrieving Test Results

To Get a Field From a Record

Let's add to the program you already have. You'll use the Get Field object to extract each of the three fields from the record, then display the values for each.

1. Select **Data => Access Record => Get Field**.

   The data input labeled Rec Any will take any record regardless of the number and type of fields. Rec.A is the default selection in the input field, but this can edited to retrieve any field. Rec refers to the record at the data input terminal by the same name.

2. Clone **Get Field** twice and place the objects to the right of **Build Record**.

3. Connect **Build Record** data output to all three **Get Field** objects.

Since the three fields were stored as testname, time, and data, you'll have to edit the Get Field objects to get the appropriate field.

4. Edit the three **Get Field** object input fields to **Rec.testname**, **Rec.time**, and **Rec.data**.

5. Select **Display => AlphaNumeric** and clone it twice. Connect the three displays to the three **Get Field** objects. Size the third display to be about three times higher than the other displays to accomodate the real array.

Now you'll reconfigure the second display to present the time stamp using hours, minutes, and seconds in a 24 hour time format.

6. Open the second AlphaNumeric display object menu and select **Number Formats....** Click to the left of **Global Format** to remove the check mark.

   You can now set your own display format for this particular display. Click the button labeled **Standard** next to **Real**. Highlight **Time Stamp** in the **Select Real Format** list box and click **OK**. You will now see the dialog box, **Set Number Formats**, as shown in Figure 5-10.

CUTTING YOUR TEST DEVELOPMENT TIME WITH HP VEE

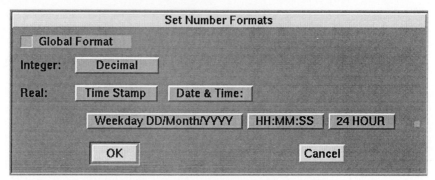

Fig. 5-10. The Set Number Formats Box

7. Click **HH:MM:SS** to toggle to **HH:MM**. Click **24 HOUR** to toggle to **12 HOUR**.

8. Run your program and save it as **getfield.vee**. See Fig. 5-11 below.

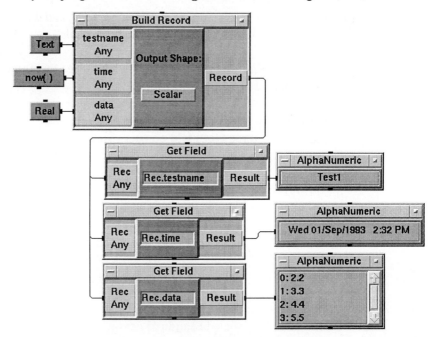

Fig. 5-11. Using the Get Field Object

Notice that the second display will now give you the weekday, the date, and the time expressed in hours, minutes, and an am or pm designation.

Now that you know the basics of building a record and getting a particular field from that record, we'll show you how to change the value in a field using the Set Field object.

To Set A Field in a Record

You might want to use the same Record several times with different tests, so this exercise teaches you how to alter data in specific fields. We'll modify getfield.vee. Delete all objects after Build Record. Recall that pressing Ctrl-d with the mouse pointer over the desired object will delete it.

1. Select **Data => Access Record => Set Field** and place it to the right of **Build Record**. Connect their data pins together.

    Set Field works by setting the field specified in the box labeled Rec.Field to the value specified in the box labeled 2*A+3. You simply edit those labels to the names appropriate to your program. You connect the incoming record to Rec Any and the incoming new value to A Any. The modified record will be put on the data output terminal labeled Rec.

2. Edit **Rec.Field** to **Rec.data**, since you will change the value of the four element array in the **data** field. Also, edit **2*A+3** to **A**, since you will put the new values for the array on the input terminal, **A Any**.

3. Select **Data => Constant => Real**. Open the object menu and select **config....** Enter **4** to the right of **Array Elements:**.

    If the new values for the record field are contained in an array, it must have the same size as the current array.

    Enter the values **1, 2, 3, 4** into **Real** and connect it to the **Set Field** input labeled **A Any**. (Remember to highlight the first entry and use the **Tab** key when creating the new array.)

CUTTING YOUR TEST DEVELOPMENT TIME WITH HP VEE

Now let's use Get Field to extract the field Rec.data from the record and display the results.

4. Select **Data** => **Access Record** => **Get Field** and edit the field specified from **Rec.A** to **Rec.data**. Connect the data output of **Set Field** to the data input of **Get Field**.

   Note: You could also have used a Formula object with A.data in the expression field.

5. Select an **AlphaNumeric** display, size it to accomodate an array, and connect it to the **Get Field** output pin.

6. Run your program and save it as **setfield.vee**. See the figure below.

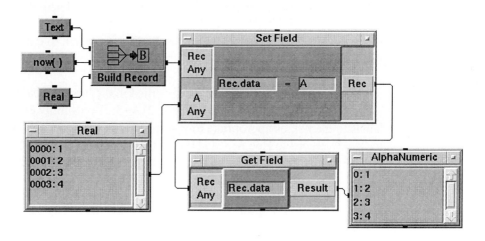

Fig. 5-12. Using the Set Field Object

Storing and Retrieving Test Results

To Unbuild a Record in a Single Step

If you would like to extract all record fields and get a list of the field names and their types, then use the UnBuild Record object. Let's modify setfield.vee. Delete all objects after Build Record.

1. Select **Data => UnBuild Data => Record** and connect it to **Build Record**. Add another data output pin to **UnBuild Record** and rename the **A**, **B**, and **C** outputs to the field names: **testname**, **time**, and **data**.

2. Select an **AlphaNumeric** display and clone it four times. Connect the five displays to the five output terminals on **UnBuild Record**. You will have to enlarge the displays for **Name List**, **Type List**, and **data** to accomodate arrays. Also, reconfigure the **time** display to present time in hours, minutes, and seconds using a 24 hour format.

3. Run your program and save it as **unbuild.vee**. It should look like the one below.

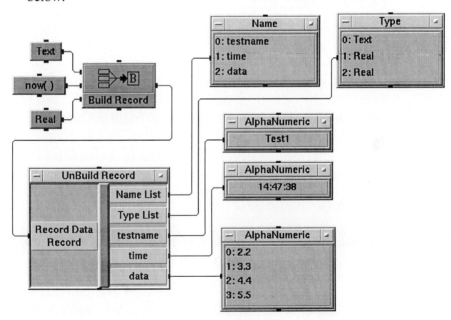

Fig. 5-13. Using the UnBuild Record Object

5 - 23

Notice that the Name List pin gives the names testname, time, and data of the three fields in your record, just as the Type List identifies testname as Text, time and data as Real types.

Using DataSets to Store and Retrieve Records

The advantage of storing records to DataSets instead of files is that you do not have to remember the specific types of the data you saved. With a DataSet you retrieve one or more records, and then HP VEE has objects that will unpack those records. You can also perform sort and search operations on that data creating your own customized test database.

Lab 5-3: Using DataSets

A DataSet is simply an array of Records stored in a file. The purpose of this exercise is to teach you how to get data into and out of a DataSet.

To Store and Retrieve a Record from a DataSet:

First, we'll create an array of ten Records, each containing three fields with a test name, a Real Scalar that could be a time stamp, and an array of Reals. We'll store this array of Records in a DataSet. Then we'll retrieve all ten records and display them.

1. Select **Flow => Start, Flow => Repeat => For Count**, and **Math => Formula**. Connect **Start** to the sequence input pin on **For Count**; connect the **For Count** data output pin to **Formula's** data input pin.

   Double-click the **Formula** expression field to highlight the default expression, and then type **"test" + a**.

Storing and Retrieving Test Results

When you click Start, For Count will output integers zero through nine sequentially to the A pin of Formula. Formula will add these integers to the word "test" and output the result, so you'll get the Text Scalars: test0, test1, test2,...,test9. These values will fill the first fields in the ten Records.

2. Select **Data => Build Data => Record**. Add a data input pin. Connect the data output of **Formula** to the **A** input of **Build Record**.

3. Select **Device => Random Number** and connect its data output to the **B** terminal of **Build Record**. Also, connect the **Formula** sequence output pin to the sequence input pin of **Random Number**.

   Connecting the sequence pins will assure you that on each of the ten iterations of this program a new random number will be put into the B field of that particular record.

4. Select **Data => Constant => Real**. Open its object menu, click **Config...**, type **3** in the **Array Elements** input field, then click **OK**. Highlight each entry in the array (by double-clicking), and type in the numbers **1,2**, and **3**. Open the object menu, click **Change Title...**, type **Real Array**, and click **OK**.. Connect the **Real Array** data output to the **C** terminal on **Build Record**.

5. Select **I/O => To => DataSet** and connect the data output of **Build Record** to its data input. Leave the default file, and click to the left of **Clear File At PreRun**.

   Your program should now put an array of ten records into the DataSet called myFile. See Figure 5-14.

5 - 25

CUTTING YOUR TEST DEVELOPMENT TIME WITH HP VEE

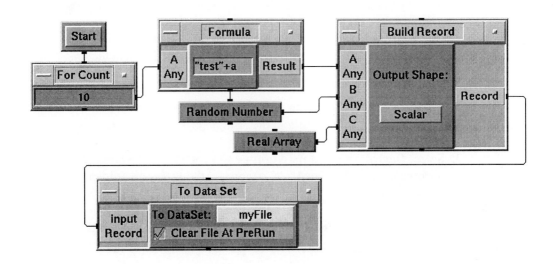

Fig. 5-14. Storing an Array of Records in a DataSet

Now you'll retrieve the array of records and display using the From DataSet and Record Constant objects.

6. Select **I/O => From => DataSet**. Leave the default file name, **myFile**. Click the **Get Records** field to toggle from **One** to **All**. Finally, leave the default of **1** in the expression field at the bottom.

Your configuration means that HP VEE will look at the DataSet in myFile, find "All" the records that fit the criterion in the expression field. If you set Get Records to One, HP VEE would output the first record that met the criterion in the expression field. The 1 signifies a TRUE condition meaning that all of the records fit the criterion, so the entire array of records in that file will be put on the output pin labeled Rec. We will explain other uses of the expression field in later exercises. Consult Help in the object menu for more information.

Connect the **For Count** sequence output pin to the sequence input on the **From Data Set** object. This assures you that the part of the program that

Storing and Retrieving Test Results

sends data to **myFile** is done executing *before* you try to read data from the file.

7. Select **Data => Constant => Record**. Open the object menu, select **Config...**, enter any number *greater than* **0** for **Array Elements**, then click **OK**. Open the object menu and select **Terminals => Add Control Input**. Click **Default Value** from the list box presented, then click **OK**.

You've configured this object for an array instead of a scalar. The record received will become the default value. In this case, Record Constant will receive an array of records from the From Data Set object, and it will format itself to display that array of records.

Connect the **From Data Set** output pin, **Rec**, to the **Default Value** pin on **Record Constant**. If you would like to see this terminal, open the object menu and select **Terminals => Show Terminals**. A dotted line between the two objects indicates a control line. See the figure below.

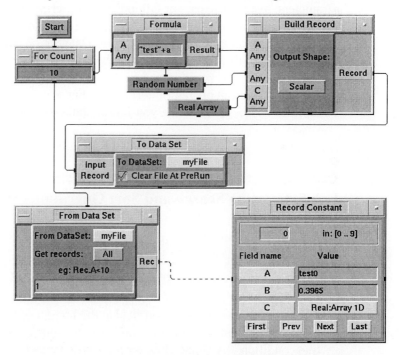

Fig. 5-15. Storing and Retrieving Data Using DataSets

5 - 27

CUTTING YOUR TEST DEVELOPMENT TIME WITH HP VEE

8. Run your program and save it as **dataset1.vee**.

   Note: When using the From Data Set object, if HP VEE doesn't find a record that meets your criterion, you get an error message. A more elegant way to handle this situation is to add an EOF (end-of-file) output pin to the object, which will fire if no records meet your criterion. You can then take whatever action you want programmatically.

Customizing a Simple Test Database

You could store a number of records in a DataSet. Each record could contain different data types describing a particular test: the name, time stamp, test parameters, test values, pass or fail indicator, description of the test, and so on. You could create your own test database, if you could search and sort that data. The expression field in the From Data Set object is used for search operations. And the function sort( ) can be used to sort records using a specified field. First, you'll learn how to search a DataSet for information. Next, you'll create an operator interface for that search operation giving you a simple database. And finally, you'll program a sort operation.

Lab 5-4: Using Search and Sort Operations With DataSets

Let's modify the dataset1.vee program.

To Perform a Search Operation With DataSets

1. Double-click on the expression field at the bottom of the **From Data Set** object to highlight the default expression, the number **1** that evaluates to a true condition. (A single click for the UNIX versions.) Enter **Rec.B>=0.5**.

Storing and Retrieving Test Results

The object will now output all records, whose second field is greater than or equal to 0.5. Let's also add an EOF pin. We won't connect it to anything to avoid making the program too complex. This pin will fire if no records match our criterion in the expression field.

2. Place your mouse pointer over the data output area of the **From Data Set** object, and press **Ctrl-a**. An **EOF** pin will appear. See Figure 5-16.

   Note: *You could also open the object menu, and click Terminals => Add Data Output.*

3. Run your program and save it as **dataset2.vee**.

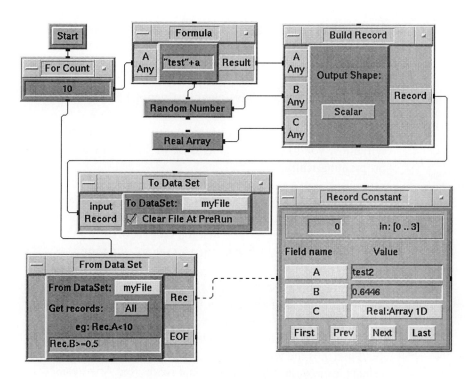

Fig. 5-16. A Search Operation With DataSets

5 - 29

To Create an Operator Interface for your Search Operation

Let's modify dataset2.vee. In this exercise you'll create a menu for extracting data from your test results database. You'll also create a very simple operator interface that can be secured to avoid unwanted modifications to your program.

The specifications of the program are:

- Provide a test menu that will allow the user to select a particular test from test0 through test9, from which they want all related test data.

- Once they have selected the test, the user will click a start button to begin the database search.

- The specified test results will be displayed with the fields and values labeled. The user should be able to interact with the display to gain more detailed information.

- The program should give clear instructions for operation.

With dataset2.vee in your work area, you first need to add a control input that will allow you to input the expression in the From Data Set object programmatically.

1. Open the **From Data Set** object menu and select **Terminals... => Add Control Input...**. Select **Formula** from the menu presented. A **Formula** input terminal appears. Click the **Get records** field to toggle from **All** to **One**, since you only want one test record at a time.

You want the user to select a particular test name. The test names are located in field A of all records. So you need the expression:
        Rec.A==<test name in quotation marks>.
This statement means that the object should output the record whose first field matches the test name the user has selected. For example, if the user selects test3, your expression should read: Rec.A=="test3". The object would then extract the test record for that test, which you could display.

Storing and Retrieving Test Results

Let's create a menu next. The Data => Enum object is used for this purpose. We'll discuss this in more detail in a later chapter. For now, we'll create a menu that allows the user to make selections by clicking a button next to the desired selection.

2. Select **Data => Enum**. Open the object menu and select **Edit Enum Values...**. Click next to **0000:** on the dialog box presented to get a cursor, then type the values **test0, test1, test2,...,test9** using the **Tab** key between each one. Click **OK** and you will see your first entry, **test0**, on a button.

   This is the default menu style for the **Enum** object. To change the format to radio buttons, just open the object menu and click **Format => Buttons**.

   Now **Enum** should display a menu using buttons for the ten menu choices.

   Open the object menu, select **Change Title...** and rename **Enum** to **Test Menu**. Refer to Figure 5-17 on the next page.

As you can see in the figure, the output of your Test Menu goes into a Formula object, which then sends the correct formula to the From Data Set object. Let's create that formula now.

3. Select **Math => Formula**, and enter the following expression: "Rec.A==" + "\"" + A + "\"". Connect the data input pin on the **Formula** object to the **Test Menu** data output pin. Connect the **Formula** data output pin to the control input pin on the **From Data Set** object (labeled Formula Text). Iconize the **Formula** object.

   This probably seems very confusing, so let's break down what you're doing. First of all, you need a Text data type to send to the From Data Set object, which means you want your formula in quotation marks. So, you start with "Rec.A==" in the Formula object. This tells HP VEE to look at the first field (labeled A) of all the records in your DataSet file, and to select the first one (Get records: One) that equals (note the double-equal sign, ==) the <selected test name>. The test name comes from the Test Menu as an Enum data type without quotes, so you need to put quotes around it. A quotation mark is indicated by the escape character \", so you need to add one before and after the input on terminal A of the Formula object. Thus, the final expression in the Formula object is:

5 - 31

CUTTING YOUR TEST DEVELOPMENT TIME WITH HP VEE

"Rec.A==" + "\"" + A + "\"".

This will put the right formula into the From Data Set object. For example, if test2 is selected, then your final formula will read:
   Rec.A=="test2".
The From Data Set object then outputs the first record it finds, whose first field is equal to "test2".

Now you need to create a box displaying instructions for the user. We'll use the Note Pad object for this. Refer to the figure below, then go to step 4.

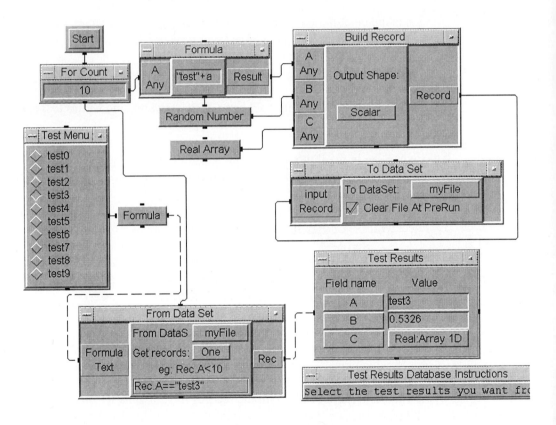

Fig. 5-17. Adding a Menu to the Search Operation

Storing and Retrieving Test Results

4. Select **Display => Note Pad**. Open the object menu, click **Change Title...**, type **Test Results Database Instructions**, then click **OK**.

   The Note Pad should expand in size to accomodate the new size. Click on the Note Pad input area below the title to get a cursor. Type:
   > **Select the test results you want from the**
   > **Test Menu, then click Start.**

   (You might want to use the Size command in the object menu to reduce the size of the object.)

   Note: If you have a version of HP VEE prior to B.02.00, you need to configure the Record Constant for a Scalar for this program to work. (1) Open the Test Results (Record Constant) object menu, select Terminals => Delete Input..., highlight Default Value, then click OK. (2) Open the object menu, select Config..., enter a 0 for Array Elements, then click OK. (3) Open the object menu, select Terminals => Add Control Input, highlight Default Value, then click OK. (4) Connect the From Data Set data output, Rec, to the Test Results control input pin.

   You now have the detail view, as shown in Figure 5-17. Run the program a few times to verify that it works. Remember that you need to select a test on the **Test Menu**, and then you click **Start**.

   Now, you'll create an operator interface in a couple of minutes. When you understand the process, which you'll go over more thoroughly in a later chapter, it will take a few seconds.

5. Select the **Enum** (labeled **Test Menu**), **Start**, **Note Pad** (instructions), and **Record Constant** (labeled **Test Results**) objects by pressing **Ctrl** and clicking these objects.

   All objects selected show a shadow.

   Then select **Edit => Add to Panel**, and your operator interface appears as a panel view. You can then move and size the objects to your taste. One layout is shown in Figure 5-18 on the next page.

5 - 33

CUTTING YOUR TEST DEVELOPMENT TIME WITH HP VEE

Note: If the Add to Panel selection were grayed out, it would mean that you do not have any objects selected in the work area.

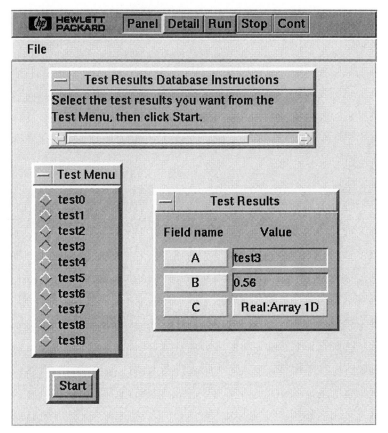

Fig. 5-18. The Operator Interface for Your Database

6. Run your program a few times to be sure it runs properly. Save it as **database.vee**.

Notice that you can get more detailed information on any given record simply by clicking the field names or the values in the Record Constant object (named Test Results).

Storing and Retrieving Test Results

To Perform a Sort Operation on a Record Field

Open your **dataset2.vee** program, and let's modify the end of it. Scroll your work area up for more room. This is the program that sets some condition in the From Data Set object such as Rec.B>=0.5, then HP VEE will extract all of the records that meet that requirement. The array of records that meet the criterion are displayed in the Record Constant object. Now suppose you wanted to sort the resulting records by the second field in ascending order, so that you could tell which tests were failing by the greatest margin. This exercise shows you how to do that.

1. Select **Math => Formula** and connect the **From Data Set** data output pin to the **Formula** object data input pin. Double-click the **Formula** expression field to highlight the default formula, then enter **sort(a, 1, "B")**.

   The Sort object is found in the AdvMath => Array menu, and you can read detailed information on its capabilities in the object menu Help entry. Here, we are calling the sort( ) function from the Formula object. Briefly, the first parameter tells HP VEE to sort the data on Formula's A pin -- an array of records in this case. The second parameter indicates the direction of the sort: any non-zero number indicates an ascending direction, a zero indicates descending. The default direction is ascending. The third parameter, in the case of a Record data type, indicates the name of the field to sort. Therefore, we are performing an ascending sort on the B field in our array of records.

2. Select **Display => AlphaNumeric** and connect it to the data output pin of the **Formula** object.

3. Run your program a few times, and notice how the program sorts all of the records returned from the DataSet file in ascending order by field **B**.

   In Figure 5-19 we have just shown the modified part of the program.

CUTTING YOUR TEST DEVELOPMENT TIME WITH HP VEE

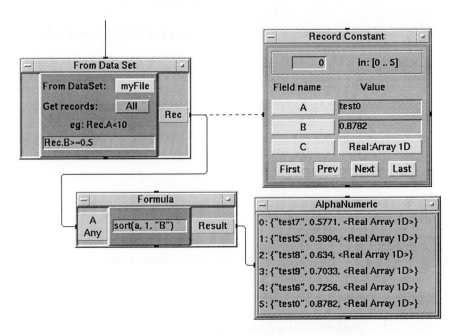

Fig. 5-19. A Sort Operation on a Record Field

Chapter 5 Checklist

You should now be able to perform the following tasks. Review topics, if necessary, before proceeding to the next chapter.

- Explain the basic notation for using arrays.

- Create an array using the Collector object.

- Extract elements from an array using the Formula object.

- Send a string, time stamp, and real array to a file.

- Retrieve a string, time stamp, and real array from a file.

- Use the function now( ) for a time stamp.

- Format time stamps in a variety of ways for display.

- Build and unbuild a record.

- Get and set fields in a record.

- Store a record to a DataSet.

- Retrieve a record from a DataSet.

- Perform a search operation on a DataSet.

- Perform a sort operation on a Record field.

- Combine HP VEE tools to create a simple test database.

Part II: Common Tasks Using HP VEE

6

Generating Reports Easily

Average time to complete: 2 hrs.

Overview

In this chapter the first lab exercise will teach you the basics of generating reports easily. The program you create will use a variety of HP VEE objects, so it will also serve as a review of Part I. You can put test data and comments into a file, edit that file, and then combine it with screen graphics to create a report that will satisfy most application needs.

HP VEE is good at generating straightforward, practical reports. If you want to generate a more elaborate report -- putting your test data into a spreadsheet, for example -- then you need to integrate HP VEE with other software applications. The second lab exercise shows you how to move HP VEE data into an MS Excel spreadsheet.

In this chapter you'll learn about:

- Creating a report header

- Putting test results into a report

- Adding a report summary outside of HP VEE

- Printing screen displays for your report

- Displaying your report from HP VEE

- Moving HP VEE test data into a spreadsheet

Lab 6-1: Generating a Simple Report

This program simulates a test, where a measurement is taken and compared to a limit. If the test value is below or equal to the limit, it passes; otherwise, it fails. The report generated shows the test name, time stamp, and a table of the test results. Each row of this table gives the value measured, the limit, and whether the test passed. A paragraph summarizing the test and the conclusions reached follows the table. The report is accompanied by a detailed screen dump of the program.

The program itself gives a pop-up panel of the report, so the operator can easily check the results. The program is divided into four modules: Build Record Array, Write Report Header, Write Test Results, and Display Report. You create the overall structure of the program first. Then you program the details of each module. The purpose of each module will be explained as you create the program.

To Create an Overall Program Structure

You use four UserObjects to make your test modular. The first builds an array of three records. Each record holds a measured value, the test limit, and a pass/fail indicator. After the test data has been simulated and put into the array, the second module generates a report header in a file. The third module takes the array of test results, formats them, and adds them to the report file. The final module produces a pop-up panel displaying the report file.

After the main report has been generated, you add a summary with the text editor of your choice, and print a screen dump of the program. Let's begin by creating the four UserObjects that will be used for the modules.

1. Change the title to **Generating a Report**.

2. Select **Device => UserObject** and edit the name to **Build Record Array**.

Generating Reports Easily

Since this module will need to send its array of records to the module labeled Write Test Results, you need to add a data output pin. For now let's create a "stub", which will send some data out this terminal until you program the actual Build Record Array subprogram.

3. Add a data output pin to the **Build Record Array UserObject**. Select **Data => Constant => Real**, put it inside **Build Record Array**, and connect it to the data output terminal labeled **X**.

   You can leave the default value of **0** for the **Real** constant. This object will act as the "stub", until the **UserObject** is programmed according to specifications.

   Iconize **Build Record Array** and move it to the left work area.

4. Select **Device => UserObject**, rename it **Write Report Header**, then iconize it. Place it in the upper-center work area.

   This module needs no inputs or outputs, because it just sends a report header to a file; however, you do need to make sure the header is written to a file before the test results, so you need to connect its sequence output pin to the sequence input pin of the next module, Write Test Results.

5. Select **Device => UserObject**, label it **Write Test Results**, add a data input pin, and iconize it. Move it to the right of **Build Record Array**.

   The data input pin accepts a record array from the **Build Record Array UserObject**, which holds all the simulated test results.

   Connect the **Build Record Array** data output pin to the **Write Test Results** data input pin.

   Also, connect the **Write Report Header** sequence output pin to the **Write Test Results** sequence input pin.

6. Select **Device => UserObject**, label it **Display Report**, iconize it, and place it below **Write Test Results**. Connect the sequence output pin of **Write Test Results** to the sequence input pin of **Display Report**.

CUTTING YOUR TEST DEVELOPMENT TIME WITH HP VEE

You need to connect the sequence pin to assure that the entire report has been written to a file, before you read the file into a display.

7. Run your program to assure yourself that the main program structure works properly. Save it as **repstruc.vee**. See the figure below.

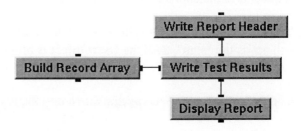

Fig. 6-1. The Overall Program Structure

Why are there separate modules for writing the header and body of the report? Because you send the header to the file once. The body of the report includes a table with the test results. Here you use another To File object in a loop that sends the data to the file one row at a time. You could put these procedures in the same module, but separating them emphasizes the differences in programming methods.

To Create an Array of Records to Store Test Data

Once again, to overcome the need to have particular instruments, you simulate test data, so that you can focus on the process of generating a report. Each record needs three fields to store a test value, a test limit, and a pass/fail indicator. You create an array with three elements, each one holding a test record. The principles are the same regardless of the number or type of fields and the size of the array.

Generating Reports Easily

1. Editing **repstruc.vee**, expand the **Build Record Array** object to the open view. Then click the maximize button (a small square at the upper right-hand corner of the **UserObject** title bar) to expand the object to full screen view.

2. Delete the **Real** number object you were using for a stub.

First, you'll need a Build Record object with three input pins.

3. Select **Data => Build Data => Record** and place it to the right-center of the work area within the UserObject. Add a third data input terminal to **Build Record**.

4. Double-click the **A Any** terminal and change the name to **Value**. Then change the name of **B Any** to **Limit** and **C Any** to **PassFail**.

   You use the Collector object to create your array. The Random Number object is used to generate values between 4.8 and 5.2, a constant Real object holds the limit 5, and two constant Text objects hold PASS and FAIL text strings.

5. Select **Device => Random Number** and place it on the left side of the work area. Double-click **Random Number** to get its open view. Double-click the input field labeled **Range from** and change the **0** to **4.8**. Press Tab to move to the **Range to** field and change the **1** to **5.2**. Iconize **Random Number** and connect it to the **Value** terminal of **Build Record**.

6. Select **Data => Constant => Real** and place it to the left of the **Limit** terminal on **Build Record**. Change the **0** to a **5**. Also, change the name from **Real** to **5**. Iconize it and connect it to the **Limit** terminal.

For the PassFail terminal you need to test the Random Number output to see if it's less than 5, which would indicate a PASS; otherwise, you want to generate a FAIL. Use the If/Then/Else object for the test, constant Text objects for PASS and FAIL, and a Junction object to gate the proper text string into the PassFail terminal.

7. Select **Flow => If/Then/Else** and place it to the right of **Random Number**. Double-click the input field of the **If/Then/Else** object and

CUTTING YOUR TEST DEVELOPMENT TIME WITH HP VEE

enter **A<=5**. Also, change the name to **A<=5**. Connect the **Random Number** data output pin to the **A Any** terminal on **If/Then/Else**. Iconize the object.

If the expression you just entered is evaluated as true, when data is received at A Any, then the object fires the Then pin; otherwise, the Else pin is fired. (Any expression that evaluates to a non-zero number will be true; any expression that evaluates to zero is false.) In this case, if the random number generated is less than or equal to five then you want to make a PASS text string go into terminal PassFail of the Build Record object.

8. Select **Data => Constant => Text** and place it to the left of the **PassFail** input terminal. Clone it and place the clone just below. Enter **PASS** in one object and change the name to **PASS**. Then enter **FAIL** in the other one and change the name to **FAIL**. Iconize both of them.

    *Note: You'll attach both of these to a **Junction** object in a moment. **Junction** acts as an OR gate with multiple inputs. It is often used when you want two or more inputs to connect to an input pin. When data is received at one of the **Junction** inputs, it outputs the same data. The data is passed through in the order that it's received at the input pins.*

9. Select **Flow => Junction** and place it to the right of the **Text** objects. Expand it to open view and consult **Help** in the object menu, if you want to read a more detailed discussion. Then iconize it and attach **PASS** to the **A Any** terminal and **FAIL** to the **B Any** terminal. Connect the **Junction** data output to **PassFail** on **Build Record**.

    You now want to trigger the text objects to execute at the right time, so you'll connect their sequence in pins to the If/Then/Else object to accomplish this.

10. Connect the **Then** pin on **If/Then/Else** (labeled A<=5) to the sequence input pin on the **PASS** object. Connect the **Else** output pin to the **FAIL** object sequence input pin.

You have now created one record, but you need three, so you'll attach a For Count object set to 3 to Random Number and use the Collector to build the array of records.

11. Select **Flow => Repeat => For Count** and place it over **Random Number**. Change **For Count** from **10** to **3**, change its name to **For 3**, connect its data output to the sequence in pin on **Random Number**, and iconize **For 3**.

12. Select **Data => Collector** and place it to the right of **Build Record**. Double-click the **Collector** to get an open view. Connect the **Build Record** data output to the **Data Any** input pin on **Collector**. Connect the **For 3** sequence out pin to the **XEQ** pin on **Collector**, and iconize it. Finally, connect the **Array** output pin on the **Collector** to the **X** output terminal on the **Build Record Array UserObject**.

13. Run your program at this stage and save it as **repgen.vee**. See the figure below.

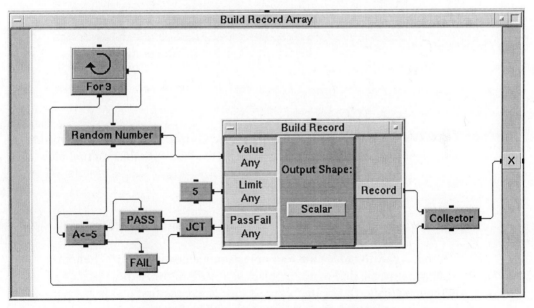

Fig. 6-2. The Build Record Array Module

If you've done everything correctly, you can double-click on the X terminal of Build Record Array to see that you've created an array of three elements, each one containing three fields named Value, Limit and PassFail. See the figure below. Notice that you can click on the Next button to examine the values in each record.

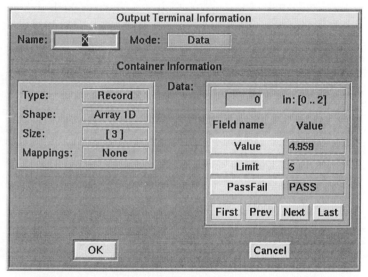

Fig. 6-3. The Output Terminal Information Box

Click **OK** when you're done examining the **Output Terminal Information** box. Iconize the **UserObject** after you've read the optimization tip below.

Optimization Tip: Alternative Way to Program If/Then/Else

There is a way to reduce the four objects implementing the **If/Then/Else** statement to a single **Formula** object. HP VEE allows a three-part expression (called a "triadic" expression), where the first part is an expression to be evaluated as true or false. The first part is followed by a question mark. Two values follow the question mark separated by a colon.

Generating Reports Easily

The first value is put on the output pin, if the evaluation is true, and the second value is output if the evaluation is false. The format is:

(<expression> ? <output value if TRUE> : <output if FALSE>).

So, for the UserObject you just programmed labeled Build Record Array, you could use the following expression in a Formula object:

(A<=5 ? "PASS" : "FAIL").

See the figure below.

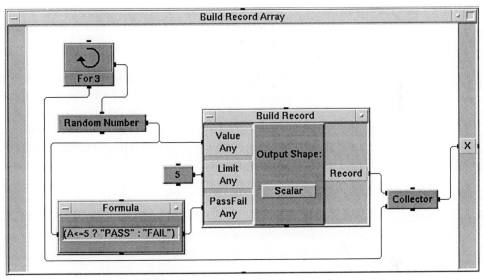

Fig. 6-4. Alternative Way to Program If/Then/Else

To Create a Report Header

Basically you create a report header by using a transaction per line with the To File object. You have to pay close attention to how many spaces you're using with text strings for column headers, but the process is straightforward.

1. Double-click the **Write Report Header** icon to get the open view, then click on the maximize button to get the full screen view.

   There will be no inputs or outputs, because you'll just be sending the header information to a file.

   Tip: *In the future you may want to have an input for the filename. This is an optional control pin on To/From File objects.*

2. Select **I/O => To => File** and place it in the right-center of your work area. Make sure **Clear File at PreRun and Open** is checked. Click on **myFile**, delete the name using the **Backspace** key, type **report1.txt** and click **OK**. Delete the input terminal **A**. You won't need it for this exercise. (MyDataFile replaces myFile on UNIX systems.)

   Note: *Recall that when editing a filename, you could also delete the present entry by pressing Ctrl-a to move the cursor to the extreme left of the input field. Then press Ctrl-k to delete the name. This is the faster way when you have a long path in front of the filename.*

3. Click the first transaction bar to get the **I/O Transaction** dialog box. Double-click the input field to highlight the **a**, then type "LIMIT TEST" and click **OK**.

   The quotation marks indicate a TEXT constant.

4. Double-click just below the transaction above to get another **I/O Transaction** dialog box. Highlight the **a** again, and type 18 equal signs followed by a newline character (\n) enclosed by quotation marks to use as a divider bar ("==================\n"). Click **OK**.

Generating Reports Easily

Next, you'll put in a time stamp using a date and time format.

Until now, each transaction had just one value to send to a file, but you can send a list of values to a file with a single transaction. In the following step you'll configure a transaction with two values to send to a file. The input field in the I/O Transaction dialog box can take a list of expressions separated by commas. You are going to send the function now( ), followed by the escape character "\n". Now( ) tells HP VEE to send a time stamp. The "\n" is an escape character that means a new line, so HP VEE will skip a line in the report1.txt file. You can combine these escape characters with quoted text to format your report. You'll do just that in the next few steps. The following table shows you the escape characters available to you.

Escape Character	ASCII Code (decimal)	Meaning
\n	10	Newline
\t	9	Horizontal Tab
\v	11	Vertical Tab
\b	8	Backspace
\r	13	Carriage Return
\f	12	Form Feed
\"	34	Double Quote

6 - 11

CUTTING YOUR TEST DEVELOPMENT TIME WITH HP VEE

Escape Character	ASCII Code (decimal)	Meaning
\'	39	Single Quote
\\	92	Backslash
\ddd		The ASCII character corresponding to the three-digit octal value *ddd*.

6. Double-click just below the last transaction in **To File**. Edit the input field in the **I/O Transaction** dialog box to **now( )**, **"\n"**. Then click **DEFAULT FORMAT** to get the **Select Text Format** list box. Double-click **TIME STAMP FORMAT**. Click on **24 HOUR** to toggle to **12 HOUR** format (which will give you an A.M. or a P.M. with the time), on **Weekday DD/Month/YYYY** to toggle to **DD/Month/YYYY**, and on **HH:MM:SS** to toggle to **HH:MM**. Click **OK**.

You will now see **WRITE TEXT now( ),"\n" DATE:DMY TIME:HM:H12 EOL** on the transaction bar. (You may have to enlarge **To File** to see the whole line.)

7. Configure a transaction to send **"Value   Limit   Result\n"**.

   Note: *The escape character "\n", immediately following Result tells HP VEE to skip the next line. (The EOL ON in this dialog box already tells HP VEE to go to a new line). Any escape character can be embedded within a text string in this way.*

The column headers have five spaces between the words. The number of spaces depends on how many letters are in the headers and how wide you want your columns to be. See the figure below.

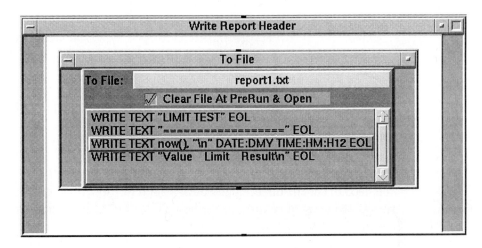

Fig. 6-5. The UserObject Labeled Write Report Header

You have now completed your header. You'll test this part of the program when you program the Display Report module. Iconize Write Report Header.

To Write Test Results to a File

This module receives a three element array of records with the fields: Value, Limit, and PassFail. You want to cycle through the records, extracting each of the three fields, and placing them in a row in your report table. To do that you use three Formula objects using the expression, A[B].fieldname, where A signifies the array at terminal A, and B is the array index depending on the value at the terminal B, and fieldname is one of the three fields mentioned above.

You can turn EOL (end-of-line) off, which allows you to use different transactions that will add data to the same line in your file. This will become clear as you work through this exercise.

The principles involved in cycling through an array of records to extract data and spacing the data items on a row in your report are applicable to most reports. Once you understand the general process, you will be able to choose among the many options HP VEE provides very easily.

1. Expand the **Write Test Results** icon to open view, and then maximize it to full screen.

2. Select **Math => Formula** and place it in the upper-center of your work area. Add a data input terminal. Now clone it twice and place the three objects in a vertical line. Enter the formulas **A[B].Value**, **A[B].Limit**, and **A[B].PassFail** in the three objects from top to bottom. Also, edit the names to **Value**, **Limit**, and **PassFail**. Iconize all three.

You need to change the B input values from 0 to 1 to 2 in order to cycle through the array of records, so the best choice for the job is the For Count object. When set to 3, it will output 0, 1, and 2.

3. Select **Flow => Repeat => For Count** and place it to the left of the **Formula** objects. Edit its default value to **3**, change the name to **For 3**, and connect its output to all three **B Any** terminals on the **Formula** objects. (That's the lower data input pin on each object.) Iconize **For 3**.

4. Now connect the **A Any** input on **Write Test Results**, which will hold the incoming array, to the three **A Any** input pins on the **Formula** objects.

5. After moving all of these objects to the left of your work area, select **I/O => To => File** and place it to the right of the **Formula** objects. Add two data input pins. Click on **myFile** to get the **Write data into what file?** dialog box. Delete **myFile**, type in **report1.txt**, and click **OK**.

Since all **To File** objects use the same file pointer they will all show the same selection for **Clear File At PreRun & Open**. In this case, since you checked it on the other **To File** object in the **Write Report Header** module, it will be checked.

Connect the three **Formula** objects to the three data input pins on the **To File** object.

Generating Reports Easily

You are now going to send the first two record fields to report1.txt with one transaction. You'll use a field width of 6 characters, a fixed number notation that freezes the number of fractional digits on a Real number, and a vertical bar to separate the columns. Here's how you do it.

6. Click on the first transaction bar and edit the **I/O Transaction** input field to **A," | ",B," | "**. (There is a space before and after each vertical bar.)

   This means that the value at terminal **A** is sent, followed by a vertical bar with a space on either side, followed by the value at terminal **B**, followed by another vertical bar. Since you want to add one more value to the line, click **EOL ON** to toggle to **EOL OFF**.

   Click **DEFAULT FORMAT** and select **REAL FORMAT** instead. Click **DEFAULT FIELD WIDTH** and type **6** in the **FIELD WIDTH** input field. Click **STANDARD** to get the **Select Real Notation** dialog box, and select **FIXED**. Type **4** for **NUM FRACT DIGITS**. This means the value 5.1234567 would be shown as 5.1234. Click **OK**.

   The transaction bar should now read **WRITE TEXT A," | ",B," | " REAL FIX:4 FW:6 RJ**. You may have to enlarge **To File** to see the whole line. Don't forget you can move your workspace to the side, if you need more room; anything that goes off the screen is still preserved as part of your program.

Now you need to complete the line in your report file with a Text entry.

7. Double-click just below the first transaction bar to get the I/O Transaction box, and edit the input field to **C**, since that's the terminal that will hold the **PassFail** data. Change **DEFAULT FORMAT** to **STRING FORMAT**. Change **DEFAULT FIELD WIDTH** to **FIELD WIDTH: 5**. Click **OK**.

8. Run your program and double-click on the **A**, **B**, and **C** terminals of the **To File** object to see the data going to the file. The formatting can be checked by viewing the contents of **report1.txt** with your favorite editor. The module should resemble Figure 6-6 on the next page.

CUTTING YOUR TEST DEVELOPMENT TIME WITH HP VEE

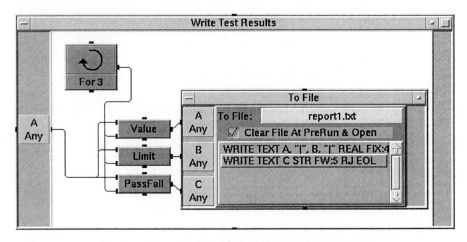

Fig. 6-6. The UserObject Labeled Write Test Results

Iconize this module.

Optimization Tip: Putting the Formulas into the To File Object

Instead of using Formula objects and data input pins, you could optimize this UserObject by entering the three formulas in the input fields of the I/O Transaction boxes. For example, instead of typing in A,"|",B,"|", you could enter A[B].Value,"|",A[B].Limit,"|", where A is the To File input holding an array of records and B is the index number of a particular record. Similarly, the second transaction would use A[B].PassFail instead of the terminal C and a Formula Object.

Examine Figure 6-7 to understand the optimization.

6 - 16

Generating Reports Easily

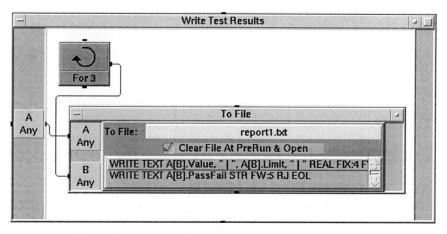

Fig. 6-7. Optimized Version of Write Test Results

To Display a Report

In this UserObject the From File object reads the entire report1.txt file as an array of strings. Then it feeds it to the Logging AlphaNumeric display. An operator interface will only show the display and an OK button for the user to indicate when he or she is done.

1. Enlarge the **Display Report UserObject** to get the open view, then click on the maximize button to open it to full screen size.

2. Select **I/O => From => File** and place it in the left work area.

   Change the **From File:** selection to **report1.txt**. Click the transaction bar and change **REAL FORMAT** to **STRING FORMAT** in the **I/O Transaction** box. Click **SCALAR** and select **ARRAY 1D** in the list box that appears. Click **SIZE:** to toggle to **TO END: (*)**. (This means you will read to the end of an array, even though you don't know its size.) Click **OK**. Use **Size** from the object menu to make the **From File** box smaller.

6 - 17

CUTTING YOUR TEST DEVELOPMENT TIME WITH HP VEE

3. Select **Display => Logging AlphaNumeric** and place it to the right of **From File**. Connect the **X** terminal on **From File** to the data input on the display. Open the **Logging AlphaNumeric** object menu and deselect **Show Title** by clicking on its checkmark.

   This will create a more readable panel.

4. Select **Flow => Confirm (OK)** and place it below **Logging AlphaNumeric**. Double-click on it to get the open view and change its title from **OK** to **DONE**. Then iconize it again.

   You don't have to connect it to anything, since the UserObject will not finish execution until all objects inside have executed. The OK object will not execute until the user clicks it.

Now, we will create a clear operator interface.

5. Select **Logging AlphaNumeric** and **DONE** (the **OK** object).

   Reminder: *Multiple objects can be selected by pressing Ctrl and clicking on the desired objects.*

6. Open the **Edit** menu in the **Display Report UserObject** by placing the mouse pointer over the background and clicking the right mouse button. Select **Edit => Add to Panel**.

   You'll now see the panel view of **Display Report** with your display and **DONE** (the **OK** object) button. Arrange them and size the panel.

7. Open the **Display Report** object menu and click **Show Panel on Exec**. Iconize **Display Report**. Save the program as **repgen.vee**.

   See the next two figures for the detail view of **Display Report** and the program while running.

   Run your program. (You must click **DONE** to stop it completely.)

Generating Reports Easily

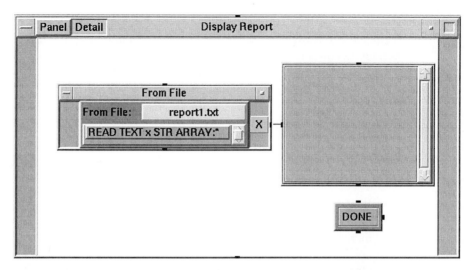

Fig. 6-8. The Display Report UserObject (Detail View)

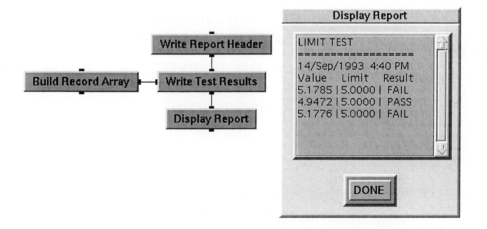

Fig. 6-9. The Repgen.vee Program

You'll notice that the display doesn't indicate the blank lines, but you'll find them in the *report1.txt* file you created. (Examine the file with any text editor.) The From File object automatically strips out any blank lines from a file when using a String Format.

6 - 19

Now, you still need to add a summary to your report. All you need to do is open the text file you created and edit in the summary paragraph (with your favorite editor). Any part of your report that's greater than two lines should be done in this way. You could also make titles boldface in this way or use different fonts to make your report more elaborate.

Printing Options

- If you would like to print a detailed view of your entire program, even though it may not all be visible, use the Print All... command in the File menu. This will also give you the option of printing detailed views of your UserObjects in your report as well. Printer configuration menus will allow you to print directly to a printer or to a file. Recall that this option will also print identification numbers on the objects, if you've run the veedoc utility on your program.

- If you would like your program to print a screen automatically at some point in your program, use the Print Screen option in the I/O menu.

- If you would like to print your display programatically, then open the display's object menu and select Terminals => Add Control Input ... and select Print (or Plot on some displays).

Using Spreadsheets With HP VEE

A very practical way to generate a report is to get your test data into a spreadsheet. You can then manipulate or format the data any way you want. For many, the ability to print their data in a spreadsheet along with screen graphics and textual comments would be a very good solution to their need to communicate test results. This lab exercise will give you a way to do that with MS Excel, vers. 4.0. This example uses HP VEE for Windows, but you could create the text file on UNIX, and then send it to a PC over the LAN.

Lab 6-2: Generating a Report With MS Excel

In this lab exercise you'll first create simulated test data stored in a DataSet as an array of records. Your goal will be to unpack the array of records and put that data into a file in a format that can be read into MS Excel. Then you will have your program automatically run MS Excel and load the test data into a spreadsheet. The field names of the records will become the column titles in the spreadsheet: TestName, Data1, Data2, Data3, Data4, and Data5. The first field of each record will hold the particular test name; these names will be used for the row names in the spreadsheet (test0 through test9). The rest of the spreadsheet will hold simulated test data. Finally, you'll use MS Word to import the spreadsheet as a key part of your report.

Does it sound complicated? It's not. You'll be surprised at how simple this is. Create the program in the figure below. (Refer to Lab 5-3 for help.)

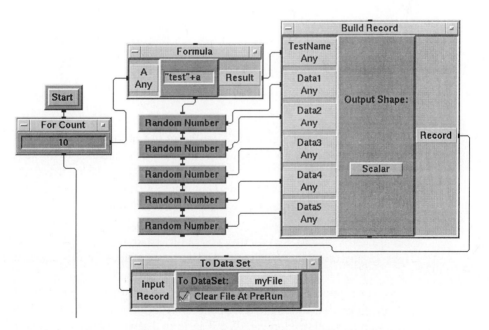

Fig. 6-10. Simulating Test Data in a File

Notice that you have to add data input terminals to the **Build Record** object. You also need to rename these terminals using the following: **TestName**, **Data1**, **Data2**, **Data3**, **Data4**, and **Data5**. The sequence out line on the For Count object triggers a From Data Set object that will check that you have stored the right data in myFile. See the figure below.

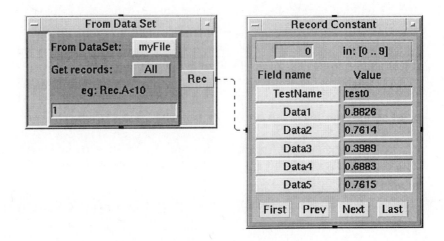

Fig. 6-11. Checking the Simulated Test Data

Figure 6-11 is the final part of the program in Figure 6-10. The sequence output pin from the **For Count** object should be connected to the sequence input pin of the **From Data Set** object. Now that you know this data is in this file, you need to extract it and put it into a file that can be read by MS Excel. MS Excel can read a Text file of strings using each string as a row in your spreadsheet. Data that goes into the individual columns will be separated by spaces. (Actually, you could separate the data with commas, tabs, or any other special character. We'll use spaces for this example.)

You can create the following as a separate program, as long as you have run the program that stores the test data into myFile, or you can extend the first program in this lab exercise. We'll assume that you have already stored the simulated data in **myFile**. Save the first program as **excel1.vee**.

Generating Reports Easily

1. Select **I/O => From => DataSet**. Click the **Get records** field to toggle from **One** to **All**. This will pull all of the records from **myFile**.

2. Select **Data => Constant => Record**. (Before B.02.00 you need to use Config... in the object menu to configure this object for an array. You can specify the number of array elements to be any value greater than zero.) Open the object menu and select **Terminals => Add Control Input...** . Select **Default Value** from the list box presented. (The Default Value control pin will automatically format the Record Constant object to hold whatever Record data it receives.)

The Record Constant will verify the data in *myFile*. Next, we need to get the Record field names and put them in the first string of the file that will be imported by Excel. Let's call that file *excelvee.txt*.

3. Select **Data => Unbuild Data => Record**. Expand it to open view and delete the terminals named **Type List**, **A**, and **B**. You'll only need the **Name List** terminal. Then iconize it again. Connect its data input terminal to the data output of the **From Data Set** object.

   The field names of your Record will now be output in an array. Now, you want to send each element of that array separated by spaces to the excelvee.txt file.

4. Select **I/O => To => File**. Change the **To File:** field to **excelvee.txt**. Check **Clear File at PreFun & Open**. Connect the input labeled **A** to the output of the **Unbuild Record** object.

   Now click on the transaction bar to get the **I/O Transaction** dialog box. Get a cursor in the expression list field and type:
         a[0]," ",a[1]," ",a[2]," ",a[3]," ",a[4]," ",a[5]," ".
   Change **DEFAULT FORMAT** to **STRING FORMAT**. Change **DEFAULT FIELD WIDTH** to **FIELD WIDTH: 1**. You do this, because you want a *single* space delimiting columns for the spreadsheet. You know that each name has at least one character. HP VEE will automatically expand the field width to accomodate a word that is greater than one character. Change **ALL CHARS** to **MAX NUM CHARS: 6** to limit the number of characters in each Real number sent to the spreadsheet. Click **OK** to close the dialog box.

Double-click just below the first transaction bar to get another **I/O Transaction** dialog box. Double-click the **a** to highlight it and type " " (a space between quotation marks). Click **OK**. This will give you a blank line in the spreadsheet below the column titles.

Now, you need to send the ten records with simulated data to the excelvee.txt file. You can do this using the formula box to extract one record at a time from the DataSet. That record will be parsed in a To File object, so that each field will be separated by a single space. The resulting string will be appended to the excelvee.txt file.

5. Select **Flow** => **Repeat** => **For Count** and connect its sequence input pin to the sequence output pin of the **From Data Set** object. Leave the default number, since you'll want to cycle through 10 records.

6. Select **Math** => **Formula**, add a data input pin, and change the formula to **A[B]**. Connect the **A** input to the **Rec** output on the **From Data Set** object. Connect the **B** input to the **For Count** data output.

These connections will take the array of 10 records from myFile, and extract a record at a time, and put that scalar record on the Formula data output pin.

7. Open the **To File** object menu, select **Clone**, and place it below the first **To File** object. Connect the data input pin to the Formula data output pin. Click the first transaction bar to get the **I/O Transaction** box. Delete the entries in the expression list field and type:
a.TestName," ",a.Data1," ",a.Data2," ",a.Data3," ",a.Data4, " ",a.Data5.
This will separate the fields in your record with spaces.

Change **ALL CHARS** to **MAX NUM CHARS: 6**. Then click **OK**.

Click the second transaction bar and press **Ctrl-k** to delete it.

8. Run your program. Then save it as **excel2.vee**.

See the following two figures to check your program.

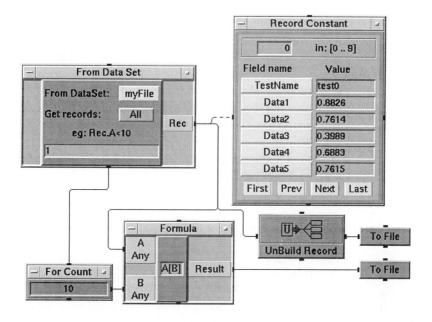

Fig. 6-12. The Excel2.vee Program

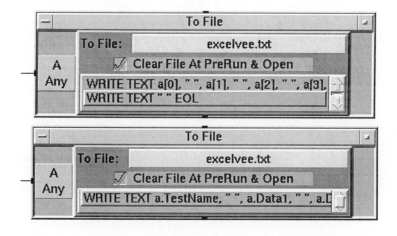

Fig. 6-13. The To File Object Configurations

6 - 25

CUTTING YOUR TEST DEVELOPMENT TIME WITH HP VEE

At this stage you could now manually load your file, excelvee.txt, into MS Excel. You simply select **File => Open** in **MS Excel**. Change to the drive and directory where your file is located. Then select **excelvee.txt** in the **File Name** field. Click the button labeled **Text...** . Select **Space** in the **Column Delimiter** menu. Make sure **File Origin** is **Windows (ANSI)**, then click **OK** to close the **Text File Options** window. Click **OK** to close the **Open** window and your file should appear in a spreadsheet.

You can make this process automatic by using the To/From DDE object.

To Put HP VEE Data into a Spreadsheet Automatically

*Note: This will only work on HP VEE for Windows. On the Unix versions you would have to move your **excelvee.txt** file to a PC over the LAN, and then load it manually into MS Excel.*

1. Open your **excel2.vee** program.

2. Select **I/O => To File**. Change the **To File** field to **excelvee.txt**. Make sure that **Clear File At PreRun & Open** is checked. Delete the input terminal. Configure the transaction statement to read: **EXECUTE CLOSE**. Iconize **To File**. Connect its sequence input pin to the sequence output pin of the **For Count** object.

3. Select **I/O => To/From DDE** and place it below the **To File** object in step 2.

   Notice that Excel and Sheet1 are the default entries for Application and Topic. Now, you only need to configure an I/O transaction.

4. Click the transaction bar to get an **I/O Transaction** dialog box. Change **READ (REQUEST)** to **EXECUTE COMMAND:**. You get the command from the **MS Excel Function Reference**, which looks like the following: "[OPEN(\"c:\\vee_user\\excelvee.txt\",3,,3)]".

Generating Reports Easily

Notice the backslashes before the quotation marks and backslashes in the path name. These are escape characters; see pages 6-11 and 6-12 for their meaning. Click **OK** to close the box.

Connect the **To File** sequence output pin (the **To File** object with the **EXECUTE CLOSE** transaction) to the sequence input pin on the **To/From DDE** object.

This object will launch the Excel application and put your HP VEE data into a spreadsheet. See the next two figures.

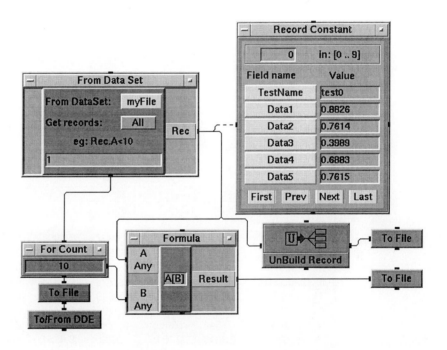

Fig. 6-14. Adding the To/From DDE Object

6 - 27

CUTTING YOUR TEST DEVELOPMENT TIME WITH HP VEE

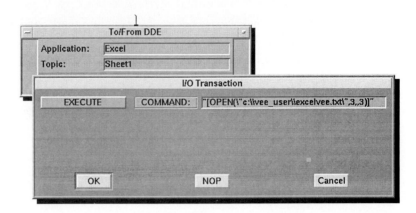

Fig. 6-15. I/O Transaction for the To/From DDE Object

Figure 6-16 an the next page shows the resulting spreadsheet of HP VEE test data. You could then select the spreadsheet, select **Edit => Copy**, which would put the spreadsheet on the clipboard. Start MS Word, position the cursor where you want the spreadsheet, and select **Edit => Paste Special** from MS Word. Choose **Formatted Text (RTF)** in the **Paste Special** dialog box, then click **Paste Link**.

	A	B	C	D	E	F	G
1	TestName	Data1	Data2	Data3	Data4	Data5	
2							
3	test0	0.7796	0.8436	0.9967	0.9996	0.6114	
4	test1	0.3924	0.2662	0.2972	0.8401	0.0237	
5	test2	0.3758	0.0926	0.6771	0.0562	0.0087	
6	test3	0.9187	0.2758	0.2728	0.5878	0.6911	
7	test4	0.8375	0.7264	0.4849	0.2053	0.7437	
8	test5	0.4684	0.4579	0.9491	0.7444	0.1082	
9	test6	0.599	0.3852	0.7349	0.6089	0.5723	
10	test7	0.3613	0.1515	0.225	0.4251	0.8028	
11	test8	0.517	0.9899	0.7515	0.3455	0.1689	
12	test9	0.6572	0.4918	0.0635	0.6997	0.5047	
13							
14							

Fig. 6-16. The Spreadsheet of Test Data in MS Excel

Not only will your spreadsheet appear in the MS Word document, but every time the spreadsheet is updated in MS Excel, your changes will appear in the spreadsheet in your MS Word document. In MS Word you could add any items necessary or take advantage of the many formatting options to complete your report.

Optimization Tip Using the To File Object

Whenever you're sending an array of data to a file, you can use Config... in the object menu to specify an EOL (end-of-line) sequence and an array separator. For example, in Figure 6-13 you could program the first To File object in a single transaction that would read *WRITE TEXT a, "\n" EOL*. The lower-case *a* refers to the array received at pin *a*. In this case, you would configure the To File object to use a space separator (enter " " in the Array Separator field after selecting Config...). The newline character ("\n") would skip an extra line in the file.

If you're storing arrays in files to send to Excel, you might want to use a tab ("\t") for an array separator, since this is the default column delimiter in Excel.

Notes on Sending Data to Lotus 1-2-3, Release 4

You can also send data to Lotus 1-2-3 quite easily. 1-2-3 uses the newline character to indicate rows. A period, space, colon, or semicolon separates columns. So you would save your file of data in the same way you did for Excel making sure to use one of the acceptable column delimiters. From 1-2-3 you would then perform the following actions: (1) select *File => Open*, (2) type the file name, (3) click *Combine*, (4) select *Formatted Text* and click *OK*, (5) and finally click *OK* to import your file.

Chapter 6 Checklist

You should now be able to perform the following tasks. Review topics, if necessary, before proceeding to the next chapter.

- Create an overall structure for a program.

- Create an array of records to store test results.

- Create a report header.

- Use escape characters to aid formatting.

- Use the To File object to generate a report.

- Format a table of test results.

- Display a report using the panel view of a UserObject.

- Explain three different print options you might use to illustrate your report with screen displays.

- Create a program that automatically puts HP VEE data into a spreadsheet.

7

Integrating Programs In Other Languages

Average time to complete: 1 hr.

Overview

One of the great advantages of HP VEE is that it integrates well with other applications and programs. In this chapter you'll learn the easiest way to integrate compiled programs and operating system commands with HP VEE.

First, there is a conceptual discussion about the Execute Program object: how it specifies programs and parameters, how it uses the operating system commands, and the distinctions between the UNIX and MS Windows versions of the object. Then you'll do three lab exercises -- one for PC users and two for UNIX users.

In this chapter you'll learn about:

- The Execute Program object

- Using operating system commands from HP VEE

- Calling compiled programs from HP VEE

Understanding the Execute Program Object

There are three major ways to run programs in other languages from HP VEE. The first method uses the Execute Program object to escape HP VEE and run another program, application, or operating system command. This method is the most versatile and easy to use. The second method links compiled functions in other languages to HP VEE, either through Shared Libraries in UNIX operating systems or Dynamic Link Libraries in MS Windows. Although this way is slightly more difficult to execute, it will give you significant performance gains. Refer to Chapter 11 for exercises using Shared Libraries and Chapter 13 for a discussion of Dynamic Link Libraries. The third method is specifically designed for HP BASIC/UX programs and will be discussed in Chapter 14.

The Execute Program object is located in the I/O menu and looks like the next two figures. Notice that in the PC version the Execute Program object does not use transaction I/O to communicate with programs, and so you don't add data input and output pins to pass data to your compiled program. The UNIX version does use transaction I/O, and so we've added input and output pins and created a ficticious program to better illustrate how the object would be used.

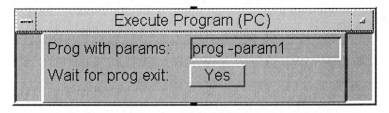

Fig. 7-1. The Execute Program Object (PC)

Integrating Programs In Other Languages

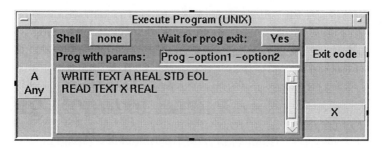

Fig. 7-2. The Execute Program Object (UNIX)

Using the Execute Program Object (PC)

You use this object to run the following from HP VEE:

- Compiled programs written in other languages

- **.BAT** or **.COM** files

- MS DOS system commands, such as **dir**

The *Prog with params* (program with parameters) field will hold the same words you would type at a DOS prompt. If you were running a program in C, you would enter the executable file name -- myprog.exe, for example. (You can omit the .exe extension.) If the program has parameters, they would follow the executable file name preceded by a hyphen: myprog -param1 -param2, for instance. If you want to run a DOS system command, you first need to run the DOS command interpreter with the /c option (i.e., command.com /c <system command>). This option tells the command interpreter to read the string following the /c as a system command. The first lab exercise has an example of this.

The *Wait for prog exit* field, when set to Yes, will not fire the sequence out pin until the program is done executing. When set to No, the sequence out pin fires before the specified program is done executing.

7 - 3

Using the Execute Program Object (UNIX)

UNIX is designed to run a number of programs called processes concurrently. If HP VEE initiates another program, HP VEE is called the parent process and the program initiated is called the child process. The Execute Program object spawns a child process, either directly or through a command shell. The Shell field opens a menu with the following choices: none, sh, csh, and ksh. If the Shell field is set to none, the first token in the Pgm with params field is interpreted as the name of an executable program, and the following tokens are assumed to be parameters. If you have shell-dependent features in the Pgm with params field, such as standard input and output redirection (< and >), wildcards (*, ?, [a-z]), or pipes (|), you need to specify a shell; otherwise, select none because it yields a faster execution speed.

The *Wait for prog* exit field toggles between Yes and No. Regardless of the setting, HP VEE spawns a child process, if one is not already active. And all transactions specified in the Execute Program object execute.

When set to Yes:

> The child process must terminate before the data output pins are fired.

When set to No:

> The child process fires the data output pins and remains active. The performance of your program is greater with this setting.

Pgm with params accepts:

- The name of an executable program file and command line parameters

- A command that will be sent to a shell for interpretation

You may add input or output terminals to the Execute Program object. Data is received from an HP VEE program on an input pin, and then you perform a WRITE TEXT transaction to send the data to the child process. A READ

Integrating Programs In Other Languages

TEXT transaction reads data from the child process, and places it on a data output pin for use by your HP VEE program.

You may also send the name of your program or shell command to the Execute Program object by adding the data input terminal labeled Command Text, which is available by adding data inputs.

Now that you understand the fundamentals of this object, let's try some lab exercises.

Lab 7-1: Using a System Command (PC)

Calling a compiled program in another language is straightforward. You just type the executable file and any parameters into the Execute Program (PC) object. On the other hand, executing an MS DOS system command is a little tricky, so this exercise clarifies this process. For example, if you want your HP VEE program to execute a *dir* command, you first need to run the DOS command interpreter, as this example will show.

1. First, run the MS DOS application in windows. Go to the root directory and create a directory called **ch7** using the **mkdir** command. Change to that directory and use **edlin tmp** to create a new file called **tmp**. When **edlin** opens this file for you, enter **e** at the asterisk to save it and go back to DOS. Return to HP VEE.

2. Select **I/O => Execute Program (PC)**. Click the **Prog with params** field to get a cursor, then type:

   command.com /c dir > c:\ch7\tmp

   This will run the DOS command interpreter, which will run the system command to display the current directory, and redirect the output (>)to the tmp file instead of the computer screen. Leave **Yes** for the **Wait for prog exit** selection.

CUTTING YOUR TEST DEVELOPMENT TIME WITH HP VEE

3. Select **I/O => From => File** and place it below **Execute Program**. Connect the sequence out pin of **Execute Program** to the sequence in pin of the **From File** object.

   Click the **From File:** input field labeled **myFile** to get a list box, double-click the input field to highlight **myFile**, type **\ch7\tmp**, then click **OK**.

   Click the transaction bar to get the **I/O Transaction** box, change **REAL FORMAT** to **STRING FORMAT**, change **SCALAR** to **ARRAY 1D**, change **SIZE: (10)** to **TO END: (*)**, then click **OK**.

   The transaction bar should now read: **READ TEXT x STR ARRAY:*** .

   This transaction will read the contents of the tmp file.

4. Select **Display => Logging AlphaNumeric** and connect its data input pin to the **From File** data output.

5. Run your program. It should look like the figure below.

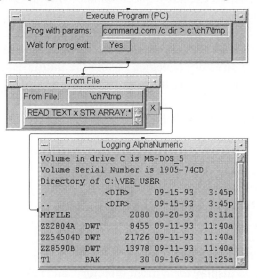

Fig. 7-3. Using Execute Program (PC)

Lab 7-2: Using a System Command (UNIX)

In this exercise you'll use the operating system command ls, which lists the filenames in a directory. Since this is not a shell-dependent command, you can set Shell to *none*. Then you'll program a variation of this exercise using a shell-dependent feature, the pipe (|).

To List the Files in a Directory

You'll use the UNIX operating system command *ls*, to list the files. In this case, you want *ls* to terminate before HP VEE continues with your program, so you set the *Wait for child exit* field to Yes. To read the output of *ls*, you use a READ TEXT transaction with a STRING FORMAT in the shape of a one-dimensional array. Since you don't know how many files are in the directory, you choose the TO END: (*) option when configuring the I/O transaction.

1. Select **I/O => Execute Program (UNIX)** and place it in the upper-left work area.

2. Make sure the **Shell** field is set to **none** and the **Wait for child exit** field is set to **Yes**.

3. Click the **Pgm with params** field and enter: **ls /tmp**.

   You could specify any directory. We're using /tmp as an example.

4. Add a data output terminal. The default will be named **X**.

   Since you are not using an exit code from the child process, you may disregard the terminal labeled **Exit code**.

5. Click the transaction bar to get the **I/O Transaction** box. Edit the default variable **a** to an **X**, since data from the child process will be read into that output terminal.

CUTTING YOUR TEST DEVELOPMENT TIME WITH HP VEE

Change **WRITE** to **READ**. Change **REAL FORMAT** to **STRING FORMAT**. Change the shape of the data from **SCALAR** to **ARRAY 1D**. And finally, toggle the **SIZE:** button to **TO END: (*)**. Click **OK**.

Your transaction bar should now read: **READ TEXT X STR ARRAY:*** .

6. Select **Display => Logging AlphaNumeric** and connect its data input pin to the **X** terminal on the **Execute Program** object.

7. Run your program. It should look like the one below.

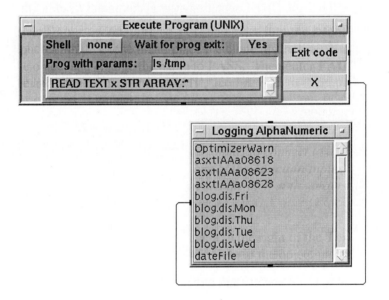

Fig. 7-4. Listing the Files in a Directory (UNIX)

Integrating Programs In Other Languages

To List the Files in a Directory Using a Shell

This variation of the last exercise is for instructional purposes. You'll use a shell-dependent feature, a pipe (|), which sends the output of one operating system command to another. The second command will be *wc*, which stands for word count. The *wc* command counts lines, words, and characters in the named files. The command *wc -l filename* counts the number of lines in the specified file. You'll count the number of lines in a directory, then display the number and the files.

1. Select **I/O => Execute Program (UNIX)**. Set the **Shell** field to **sh**, which is needed to use the shell features, "|" and ";". Enter the command, **ls /tmp|wc -l;ls /tmp**, in the **Pgm with params** field. Add two data output terminals, one labeled **X** and the other labeled **Lines**.

   Configure your first transaction to: **READ TEXT Lines INT**. **Lines** replaces the default variable **a**.

   Configure a second transaction to: **READ TEXT X STR ARRAY:Lines**. **Lines** should be entered in the **SIZE** field, when specifying the length of the array.

2. Select **Display => AlphaNumeric** and **Display => Logging AlphaNumeric**. Connect **AlphaNumeric** to the **Lines** output and **Logging AlphaNumeric** to the **X** output pin.

3. Run your program. It should look like the Figure 7-5.

CUTTING YOUR TEST DEVELOPMENT TIME WITH HP VEE

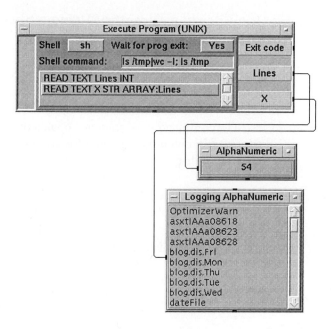

Fig. 7-5. Using a Shell Command with a Pipe

Now that you understand the basic process for using operating system commands, let's call a program written in C using input and output pins on the Execute Program object.

Lab 7-3: Using Compiled Programs

Although you'll use a program written in C for this exercise, the same principles apply to any compiled programs in other languages. First, use your favorite editor to write the following program and save it in AddOne.c. Then compile it using the following command: *cc AddOne.c -o AddOne*.

Integrating Programs In Other Languages

```
#include <stdio.h>

main ( )

{

  int c;

  double val;

  setbuf(stdout,NULL);        /* turn stdout buffering off */


  while (((c=scanf("%lf",&val)) != EOF) && c > 0) {

    fprintf(stdout,"%g\n",val + 1);

    fflush(stdout);           /* force output back to VEE */

  }

  exit(0);
```

Fig. 7-6. The C Program Listing for AddOne.c

Note: *You might want to just read through this exercise, if you're not familiar with programming in C.*

HP VEE uses *stdin* and *stdout* of the C program to transfer data. The program simply reads a Real number from standard input, which will be your HP VEE program, in this case. Then AddOne adds one to the value and sends the result back to HP VEE. The program in the figure below uses two standard C routines, *setbuf* and *fflush* to force data through *stdout* of the C program. In practice, either *setbuf* or *fflush* is sufficient. Using *setbuf(file,NULL)* turns off buffering for all output to file, which will be stdout in this case. Using *fflush(file)* flushes any already buffered data to file.

For those of you who don't know C, here's a simple explanation of the program. The #include attaches a standard library of I/O routines to your program. The main body of the program first declares an integer variable c, and a real (double) variable *val*. The buffering is turned off in the *stdout* file.

The *while* loop reads one value at a time. If the value is not the EOF character and it is greater than 0, the value is incremented by one and printed to the *stdout* file. The *fflush* routine forces the output back to HP VEE.

The *exit(0)* sends no exit code back to HP VEE. You could send a number back using *exit( )* and it would appear at the Exit code terminal. You could use this routine to flag a particular condition in your C program.

After you have compiled this program, put the executable file AddOne, in any directory you want. Here we'll assume it's in the root directory. Now you can create your HP VEE program.

1. Select **Data => Real Slider** and place it to the left side of the work area. Rename it **Number**.

    You use the Real Slider by placing the mouse pointer over the slider bar, pressing the left mouse button, and dragging it up or down. You can select a range of real values using the input fields on the slider. The value selected is displayed at the top of the slider.

    Change the upper range from **1** to **100**.

2. Select **I/O => Execute Program (UNIX)** and place it to the right of the **Real Slider**. Add an input terminal and connect it to the **Real Slider** object. Make sure **Shell** is set to **none** and **Wait for child exit** is set to **Yes**. Add a data output terminal. Enter the executable file *(pathname)***AddOne**, in the **Pgm with params** field. (I will enter my entire pathname here. You enter yours.)

    Configure two transactions: **WRITE TEXT a EOL** and **READ TEXT X REAL**.

    This will write the value at terminal **A ANY** to your **AddOne** program, the program will increment the value, and return it to terminal **X**.

Integrating Programs In Other Languages

3. Select **Display => AlphaNumeric**, rename it **Result**, and connect it to the **X** terminal on the **Execute Program** object.

4. Select an input value with the **Real Slider** and run your program. It should look like the figure below.

   Tip: *If you would like your program to run automatically after selecting a number on the slider, open the Real Slider object menu and click the Auto Execute box.*

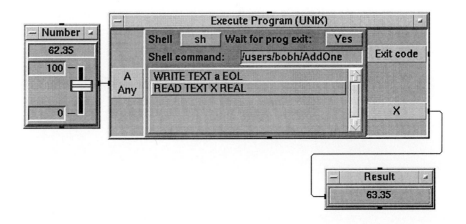

Fig. 7-7. Running a C Program Using Execute Program

You now understand the fundamentals of running a compiled program in another language. When you use a different compiled language, you will still need to turn buffering off to standard output or flush already buffered data. Refer to Chapters 11 and 14 for other methods of integrating other programs with HP VEE.

Chapter 7 Checklist

You should now be able to perform the following tasks. Review topics, if necessary, before moving on to the next chapter.

- Explain the purpose of the Execute Program object.

- Give an overview of the configuration settings on the Execute Program object.

- Explain the general process of how the Execute Program object sends data to/from a program on a UNIX platform. Explain how the PC platform differs.

- Run operating system commands from HP VEE.

- Run programs in other languages from HP VEE using the Execute Program object.

Leveraging Your HP VEE Test Programs

8

Average Time to Complete: 1 hr.

Overview

In the last chapter, you learned how to combine programs written in other languages with your HP VEE programs. This is especially important for test development today because of the strong pressures to reduce time to market. Test developers need to leverage their past work and to program in such a way that their tests will be easy to modify in the future.

Part of the solution is creating well-documented, modular programs, which we discussed in Chapter 2. Another part is learning how to incorporate past HP VEE programs into your current tests, the subject of this chapter.

In this chapter you'll learn about:

- Merging existing HP VEE programs with your tests

- Defining a user function

- Creating, calling, and editing functions

- Creating, merging, importing, and deleting function libraries

CUTTING YOUR TEST DEVELOPMENT TIME WITH HP VEE

Merging HP VEE Programs

The easiest way to leverage your programming is to merge a past program with your current test. This is done using the Merge... command in the File menu. You are presented with a list box displaying the *lib* subdirectory from the HP VEE home directory. This directory contains many useful programs, which expand your power. For example, you could merge a program that gives you a bar chart display or one that provides a data entry keypad for accepting numeric user input such as ID numbers. You could also switch to another directory and merge a program that you've written. Once the program has been merged, it can be edited to suit your current needs.

Lab 8-1: Merging a Bar Chart Display Program

This is a very simple exercise to show you how to merge an existing program with your present one. Although you'll use a program from the HP VEE *lib* directory, you could do the same thing with one of your own programs. You'll create an array with five values from 1 to 5 using the ramp( ) function. Instead of displaying the array with one of the internal HP VEE displays, you'll merge the BarChart program with the program you're creating.

1. Select **Math => Formula** and place it in your left work area.

2. Delete the data input terminal.

3. Change the default formula to **ramp(5,1,5)**.

   The first parameter is the number of elements desired in the ramp array. The second parameter is the starting number, and the third is the last number. For more information on this function selecdt Math => Generate => ramp(numElem,from,thru), and examine Help in its object menu.

4. Click on **File => Merge...** to get the **Merge File** list box. Select **BarChart** and place it to the right of the **Formula** object. Connect the two objects.

5. Run your program. It should look like the figure below.

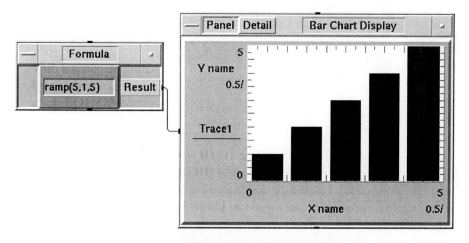

Fig. 8-1. Merging the BarChart Program

Notice that the Bar Chart Display takes a one-dimensional array and displays the values as vertical bars. It uses the number of bars necessary to display the values in the array. If you want to examine how it's programmed, open the detail view of the display. By searching through this library directory you can get some ideas on programs you might like to create to make your job easier.

Using Functions

Most programming languages use functions to create subprograms that perform specific tasks. First, we'll define an HP VEE function. Then you'll have some lab exercises to show you how to create, call, and edit HP VEE user-defined functions. Once you understand the basics, you'll learn how to create libraries of functions, which can be merged into your programs in the development phase or imported at runtime.

Defining an HP VEE User Function

There are three types of user-defined functions in HP VEE:

(1) **User Function**

- Created by selecting Make UserFunction in the object menu of a UserObject.

- You can call the User Function from different places in your program by using the Call Function (Device => Function => Call) or an expression (from the Formula object, for example).

- You edit the User Function by clicking on Edit => Edit UserFunction ... and selecting the appropriate User Function from the list box presented.

- All changes made to one User Function will be inherited by other User Functions of the same name in your program.

- You can easily transfer User Functions from one program to another either by merging them in during program development or by importing them at runtime (Device => Function => Import Library).

(2) **Compiled Functions**

- Created outside of HP VEE using a compiled language. These functions are then put in a library, which is linked to HP VEE at runtime (refer to Chapters 11 and 13 for a more detailed discussion).

- To call these functions, you first have use the Import Library object to link them to your program. Then you may call them using the Call Function object or an expression.

(3) **Remote Functions**

- Similar to a User Function except that it runs on a remote host computer connected by your Local Area Network (refer to Chapter 14 for detailed information).

Lab 8-2: User Function Operations

In this Lab exercise you'll convert a UserObject to a User Function, call it from a program, and edit it. In the next exercise we'll discuss moving User Functions between programs.

To Create a User Function

In this exercise you'll create a UserObject named ArrayStats, which will accept an array, calculate its maximum value, minimum value, mean, and standard deviation, and put the results on its output pins.

1. Select **Math => Formula**, change its title to **ramp(10,1,10)**, delete its default input pin, then change its defualt expression to **ramp(10,1,10)**.

    This will create a 10 element array from 1 to 10.

2. Select **Device => UserObject** and place it to the right of the **Formula** object. Rename it **ArrayStats**, add one data input terminal for the array,

add four data ouput terminals for the results. Rename the output terminals: **Max**, **Min**, **Mean**, and **Sdev**. Select **max(x)**, **min(x)**, **mean(x)**, and **sdev(x)** from the **AdvMath** => **Statistics** menu, place them in the **UserObject**, and connect their data inputs to A and their data outputs to the appropriate output terminals. Also, connect the **Formula** object to the **UserObject**.

3. Select **Display** => **AlphaNumeric**, clone it three times, and connect the displays to the **UserObject** output pins.

4. Run your program. It should look like the one below.

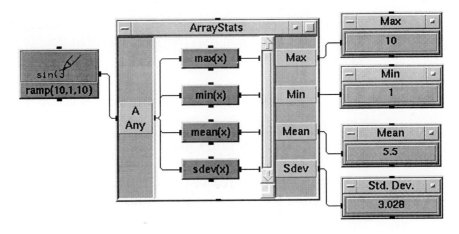

Fig. 8-2. ArrayStats Before Creating a User Function

5. Open the **ArrayStats UserObject** menu and click **Make UserFunction**. See Figure 8-3.

You see the UserObject named ArrayStats replaced by a Call Function object calling a User Function named ArrayStats. It will produce the same functionality as the UserObject ArrayStats. In addition, you can call it from different places in the program and all changes to the User Function are inherited by all others of the same name.

If you wanted to use ArrayStats elsewhere in your program, you would click on Device => Function => Call, change the default expression name to ArrayStats, and the necessary input and output terminals will be added for you.

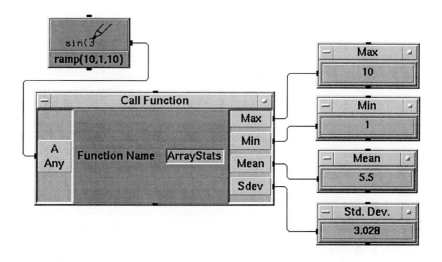

Fig. 8-3. Calling the User Function ArrayStats

To Edit a User Function

Let's suppose you wanted to edit ArrayStats to deliver a record with four fields giving the array statistics. Notice how quickly you can do that in the following exercise.

1. Delete the four **AlphaNumeric** displays.

2. Select **Edit => Edit UserFunction...** and select **ArrayStats** from the **Edit UserFunction** list box.

   All of the User Functions in your program will be displayed here.

3. Open the **UserFunction: ArrayStats** menu, click on size, and enlarge the editing window.

4. Delete the four lines going to the output terminals. (Press **Ctrl-Shift** and click on the line you want to delete.)

5. Select **Data => Build Data => Record** and place it to the right side of the **UserFunction: ArrayStats** editing window. Add two data input terminals. Label the four terminals after the statistical functions: **max**, **min**, **mean**, and **sdev**. Connect the four inputs with the appropriate objects. Rename the **Max** output terminal **X** (Double-click **Max**, type the new name, click **OK**). Delete the other **UserFunction** data output terminals. Connect the **Build Record** output to the **X** output terminal on the **User Function** editing window. Click **Done**.

Before you click **Done**, your editing should look like the figure below.

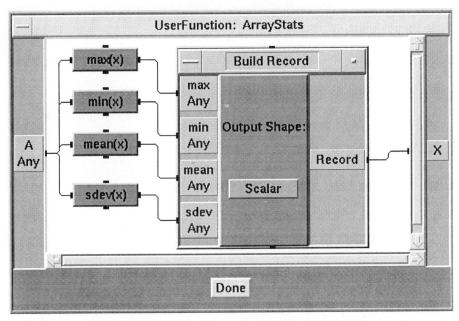

Fig. 8-4. Editing the UserFunction ArrayStats

6. Open the **Call Function** object menu and click **Configure Pinout**.

Note: *This will adjust the number of pins to match your recent edits. You must do this any time you change the number of inputs or outputs in a User Function.*

An excellent way to display a record is by using the Record Constant object. You use the Default Value control input to accept a record from ArrayStats. HP VEE will automatically configure the Record Constant to hold the incoming record. It sounds confusing, so let's do it to clarify what we mean.

7. Select **Data => Constant => Record** and place it to the right of the **Call Function** object. Open the **Record Constant** object menu and click **Terminals => Add Control Input....** Select **Default Value** from the list box presented. Now connect the **Call Function** data output to the control input pin on the **Record Constant** object.

   Notice that control lines are indicated by dotted lines to differentiate them from data lines.

8. Run your program. It should look like the figure below.

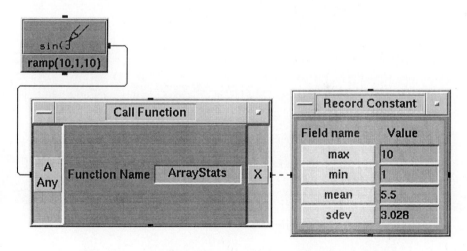

Fig. 8-5. After Editing ArrayStats Output to a Record

To Call a User Function from an Expression

Now you'll learn how to call ArrayStats from an expression in the Formula object.

1. Delete the **Call Function** object from the previous exercise.

2. Select **Math => Formula** and replace the default formula with **ArrayStats(A)**.

   Now the Formula object will take the input at terminal A Any, feed it to the User Function ArrayStats, which will deliver the record of statistics to terminal X.

   Connect the **ArrayStats Formula** object to the **ramp(10,1,10) Formula** object and the **Record Constant**.

3. Run your program. It should look like the figure below.

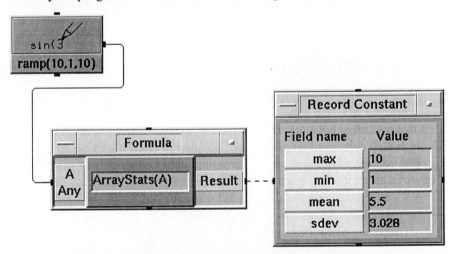

Fig. 8-6. Calling the ArrayStats User Function

Notice that the functionality of ArrayStats in the Formula object is exactly the same as it was in the Call Function object. We have used a Formula object in this example, but you could call ArrayStats from any input field that accepts expressions.

Note: When you are calling a User Function from an expression, the User Function will only deliver a single output (the uppermost data output pin). If you need all of the outputs, or they cannot be put into a Record, then you will have to use the Call Function object.

Reminder: When calling a User Function from an expression, input terminals are used as function parameters to pass to your function. If no data is passed to your function, you must still include empty parentheses after the function name; otherwise, HP VEE will think you're referring to a Global variable or input terminal. For example, if the User Function called MyFunction has no input parameters, you must write MyFunction( ) in an expression. The Call Function object does not require the parentheses, because HP VEE knows you are referring to a function.

Using Libraries With HP VEE User Functions

When you save a program, the User Functions you created are automatically saved as well. You have already learned how to merge a past program into your current program with the Merge... command. You can also use the Merge Library... command in the File menu to import User Functions from a particular file. That file might hold an HP VEE program, or you might have created a group of logically related User Functions to use as a library. The merged User Functions can be edited and used exactly like the ones you created locally. This is an effective way to leverage your HP VEE test programs.

There is another way to bring outside User Functions into your active program using the Import Library and Delete Library objects in the Device => Function menu. With the Merge... command the User Functions are copied into your active program; whereas, the Import Library object accesses the original functions in another file without making a copy. The functions are imported at runtime at the point in the program when they're needed.

You can then delete them programmatically. This spreads out the load times and conserves disk space. If you use this technique, you may not edit the functions imported. Instead you can modify them in their original files, or use the Merge... command.

Lab 8 - 3: Creating and Merging a Library of User Functions

When you save any program you automatically save the User Functions associated with it. The Merge Library... command in the File menu will merge the User Functions from the specified file into your active program. You can think of this group of functions as a library. In this exercise you'll use the report generation program from Chapter 6, change the four UserObjects to User Functions, creating a library within that program. You'll resave the report program, then create a new program that merges your newly created library of User Functions. It may sound like a lot of work, but it's easy to do.

1. Use the **File => Open...** command to recall the report generation program from Chapter 6, *repgen.vee*. It should look like the figure below.

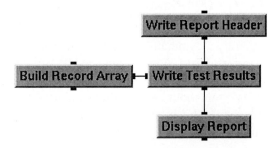

Fig. 8-7. Report Generation With UserObjects

2. Open the **UserObjects** and change their names to **BuildRecAry**, **ReportHeader**, **ReportBody**, and **ReportDisplay**.

   You are creating names that will have no spaces, because this is a requirement of a User Function.

3. Open the four **UserObject** menus and click on **Make UserFunction**.

   Each UserObject is replaced by a Call Function object that calls that particular User Function. Notice that the Call Function object does not require parentheses when referring to a User Function. If you were calling the function from a Formula object, you would need to include parentheses whether or not the function used parameters.

   Run your program and note the functionality is exactly the same as before. Use the **File => Save As...** command and name it **Report1.vee**.

   Your program should look like the figure below.

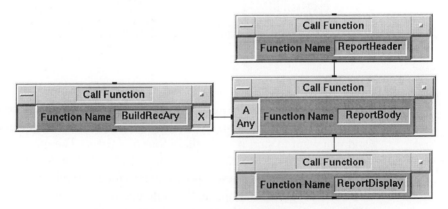

Fig. 8-8. Report Generation With User Functions

4. You have now created a library of four functions. You can see them listed by clicking **Edit => Edit UserFunction...**, as shown in the figure below. Click **Cancel** to close the list box.

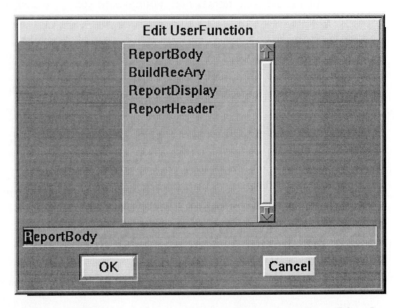

Fig. 8-9. Your Library of User Functions Listed

You're now going to create a new program and merge this library into it. Let's suppose you want to build a library of functions for generating reports, and you want to start it using these four functions. The new program will simply contain a Note Pad object explaining each function in the library. You could then create new report generation User Functions, merge them with this program, and update the Note Pad object to keep track of them. Whenever you had to create a new report, you could simply use the Merge Library... command to leverage all the functions from this program, which you'll call RepGen.

5. Select **File => New**. Since you've already saved your program, you can select **No, clear** from the **Save changes first?** prompt that appears.

6. Select **File => Merge Library...** . Select **Report1.vee** from the **Merge Library** list box.

Select **Edit => Edit UserFunction** to make sure your library from **Report1.vee** transferred to your new program. When you use the Merge Library... command, you can edit the merged functions just like functions you created locally.

7. Select **Display => Note Pad** and type the **User Function** descriptions similar to the ones shown in the figure below. Then save your new program as **libmerge**.

   Note: *You can save a "program" of User Functions for the purpose of creating a library, even though there is no actual HP VEE program calling these functions.*

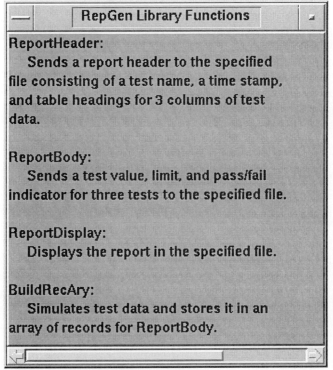

Fig. 8-10. The RepGen Library of UserFunctions

Lab 8 - 4: Importing and Deleting Libraries

There are times when you just want to import a function at runtime, but you don't need to edit it. Then you might want to delete it to conserve memory and disk space. The Import Library and Delete Library objects were designed for this situation. In the following exercise, you'll import functions from your libmerge program. Then you'll call the BuildRecAry function to simulate some test data, display it, and finally delete the library to free up memory and disk space.

1. Select **Device** => **Function** => **Import Library** and place it in the upper-left work area.

    The menu in the Library Type field allows you to select a User Function, a Compiled Function, or a Remote Function. In this case you want a User Function library so leave the default. The Library Name shows myLibrary as a default. This name is used as a "handle" by your HP VEE program to distinguish between different libraries being imported. The Delete Library object uses this name to identify the library to be deleted. You can use the default name.

    The File Name field will show you a dialog box of the VEE_USER directory by default on a PC. (UNIX systems access your home directory.) You simply need to specify the file that holds the library of functions. You can type the complete path, if you want to access another directory.

    Click the default name **myFile** to get the list box. Select **libmerge.vee** (from Lab 8-3). This file will usually be in C:\VEE_USER in B.02.00. HP VEE automatically displays the complete path in the File Name field.

    Open the object menu and select **Load Lib** to import the library immediately instead of waiting until runtime. This command is very useful in the development stage. Notice that the Edit => Edit UserFunction... command is grayed out, because you cannot edit imported functions.

2. Select **Device => Function => Call** and place it below the **Import Library** object. Connect their sequence pins to make sure **Import Library** executes first.

3. Open the **Call Function** object menu and click **Select Function** to show you a list of the functions you imported with your **Load Lib** command. Select **myLibrary.BuildRecAry**. (Prior to B.02.00 you did not need to specify the library, just the function name, as shown in Figure 8-12.)

   HP VEE automatically inserts this function in the Function Name field and adds the required output terminal. You could also have entered myLibrary.BuildRecAry in the Function Name field to accomplish the same results. Use Select Function when you can't remember the names of the functions in the library.

4. Select an **AlphaNumeric** display, enlarge it, and connect it to the **Call Function** data output.

5. Select **Device => Function => Delete Library** and place it below the **Call Function** object. Connect the sequence pins, so the library is deleted after the BuildRecAry function has been called. You can leave the default **Library Name**, since this is the same one you used with the **Import Library** object.

6. Run your program. It should look like the one below.

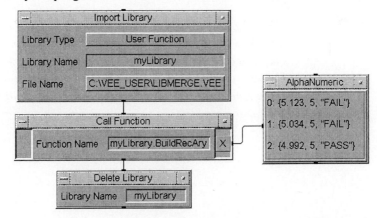

Fig. 8-11. **Importing and Deleting a Library (B.02.00)**

CUTTING YOUR TEST DEVELOPMENT TIME WITH HP VEE

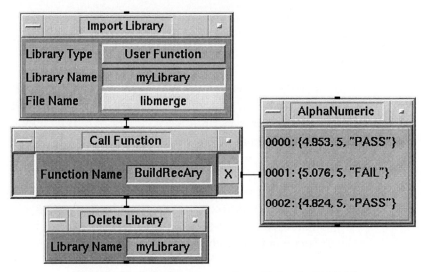

Fig. 8-12. Library Operations Prior to B.02.00

The figure above shows the lab exercise using HP VEE prior to the B.02.00 release (versions B.00.01 and B.01.00). Notice that you did not have to use the <library name>.<function name> format; you only needed to specify the function name.

> *Note:* What happens if merged or imported functions have the same names as local functions? With merged functions HP VEE will give you an error. With imported functions HP VEE will allow it, but will use the local functions. If two imported libraries have the same function names, the results will be indeterminate.

Chapter 8 Checklist

You should now be able to perform the following tasks. Review topics, if necessary, before moving on to the next chapter.

- Merge an entire HP VEE program with your current program.

- Define a User Function and compare it to a Compiled Function and a Remote Function.

- Create, call, and edit a User Function.

- Create, merge, import, and delete User Function libraries.

9

Test Sequencing

Average time to complete: 2 hr.

Overview

This chapter teaches the fundamentals of using the Sequencer object, one of the most significant features of HP VEE. Some of the benefits of the Sequencer include:

- Easy development of a test plan

- Wide array of branching capabilities between tests

- Major component for building a customized test executive

- Ability to call tests in HP VEE and other languages

- Automatic logging of test results

In this chapter you'll learn about:

- The Sequencer object

- Configuring a test for the Sequencer

- Creating a test execution order based on runtime results

- Accessing data logged by the Sequencer

- Ways to pass data to/from Sequencer tests

- Performing analysis on logged data from the Sequencer

- Storing Sequencer test data

In this chapter you'll work through two lab exercises. The first one shows you how to configure a test for the Sequencer object, to add or insert or delete a test in your test execution flow, and to access the test data that's been logged by the Sequencer. To keep things simple, you'll simulate test results with the random( ) function. This way you can focus all your attention on the characteristics of the Sequencer.

The second lab will be more challenging. You'll learn how to structure data passed to tests using global variables, to call User Functions from the Sequencer, and to log Sequencer data to files. Performing analysis on parts of that data will complete your basic skills, and you'll begin to see the power at your disposal when developing test plans.

Using the Sequencer Object

The Sequencer object implements a specified test order based on runtime results. Each test may be an HP VEE User Function, a Compiled Function, or a Remote Function, which returns a single result. That result is compared to a test specification to determine whether or not it passes. The Sequencer then uses a pass or fail indicator to determine the next test it should perform. You have six different options for branching to the next test. These options include executing the next test, repeating the same test, or jumping back to an earlier test. We'll discuss these in detail in the following lab exercise. The Sequencer can even ask for user input to decide what course of action to take. After the specified tests have been executed, the Sequencer automatically logs the test data to an output terminal. From this point the data can be analyzed and displayed, or stored to a file for future investigation.

The Sequencer object is simple and powerful. Let's get started with an easy example, so that you can visualize what we're talking about.

Test Sequencing

Lab 9 - 1: Creating a Test Execution Order

In this lab you'll simulate test results using the random( ) function, establish a test execution order, learn how to modify that order, and retrieve specific data from the logged results. Fields in the Sequencer will be discussed as they arise in the exercise.

To Configure a Test

The steps will apply to the specific example of implementing the random( ) function with a certain range of test results expected, but the principles may be employed when configuring any test.

1. Select **Device => Sequencer** and place it in your upper-left work area.

2. Select **Display => AlphaNumeric** display, place it below the **Sequencer**, increase its width, and connect its data input to the **Log** output terminal on the **Sequencer** object.

3. Click the **Sequencer** transaction bar to get the **Sequence Transaction** dialog box.

   The TEST field has a default name of test1, which you can leave. This is just the label for the test in the Sequencer; it is not the test function itself. The FUNCTION field (testFunc(a) is the default) holds the actual function that performs the test. In this case, you'll replace the default with the random( ) function. The random(low,high) object is located in the AdvMath => Probability menu. Recall that you can call this math function from an expression field without actually using the object in the menu. If you don't provide the parameters low and high, which is what we're going to do in this example, the function will use the default parameters 0 and 1.

4. Click the **FUNCTION** input field, which currently holds **testFunc(a)**, and type **random( )**.

9 - 3

CUTTING YOUR TEST DEVELOPMENT TIME WITH HP VEE

Note: Be sure not to press Enter after you type something, since that tells HP VEE that you're done editing the dialog box. Either click on new fields you want to modify or press Tab to move forward to different fields. Shift-Tab will move the cursor backward.

Random( ) will return a Real value between 0 and 1 simulating a test result. This result will be compared to the test specification. **SPEC NOMINAL** represents the expected test value; the default is **.5**. Change this to **.25**, and then alter the upper **RANGE** field (on the far right) from **1** to **.5**. You can leave the other defaults as they are. This configuration will lead to a PASS result in approximately half of the runs. Your dialog box should look like the figure below.

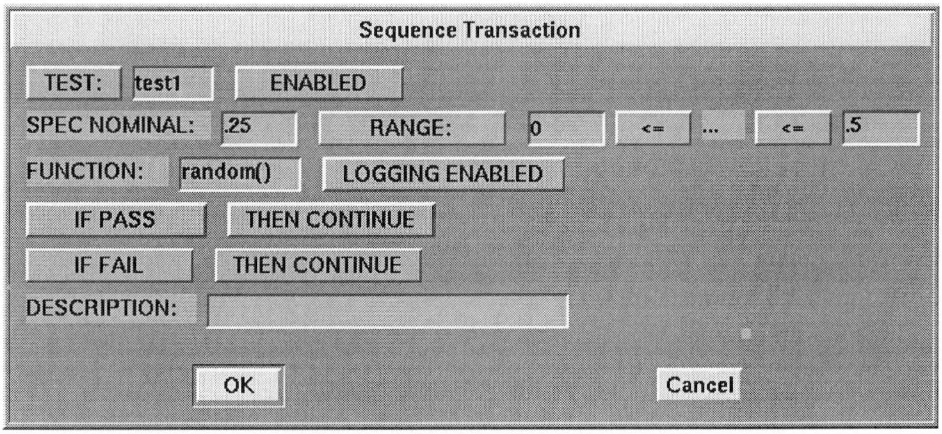

Fig. 9-1. The Sequence Transaction Dialog Box

Click **OK** to close the dialog box. You will now see the transaction **test1 0 <= (.25) <= .5** on the first transaction bar. This means that test1 will pass if the returned value is in the range from 0 to .5 with the end points included. The expected result is about .25.

5. Run your program, and you will see the name of the test, the test result, and the pass-fail indicator (**1** for **PASS**, **0** for **FAIL**) in the display.

Before proceeding study the following table to understand the various choices in the Sequence Transaction dialog box. Open the dialog box again

Test Sequencing

by clicking on the transaction bar. Open the various menus and make sure you understand the different options available to you when configuring a test.

Sequence Transaction Field	Explanation
TEST:	The TEST: button toggles to EXEC:. The TEST: field holds the unique name used to reference this test in the Sequencer. The default names start with test1 and increment with each test. Choosing TEST: means that a test result will be compared to specifications and branching will occur to the next test based on your configuration. You may toggle TEST: to EXEC:, which means that the test will be executed without a comparison between a test result and specifications. For example, you might choose EXEC: when your User Function is setting up global variables. Selecting EXEC: will also disable logging for this test.
ENABLED	This button gives you four menu choices. ENABLED executes the test under all conditions. ENABLED IF: executes the test, if the stated expression evaluates to TRUE. For example, the test might be enabled if the input pin A holds the value 1 (A == 1). ENABLED IF: may be used for audit test control. You might want a particular test to execute every ten runs, for instance. DISABLED and DISABLED IF: are just the opposite of the first two menu choices.
SPEC NOMINAL:	The expected value from the test.

CUTTING YOUR TEST DEVELOPMENT TIME WITH HP VEE

Sequence Transaction Field	Explanation
RANGE:	This menu includes RANGE:, LIMIT:, TOLERANCE:, and %TOLERANCE:. RANGE: fields signify the range of test values that signify a PASS condition. You may also choose from the usual comparisons: >, >=, <, <=, ==, !=. LIMIT: uses just one value for a comparison of test data. The TOLERANCE: selection states the passing range of values by adding or subtracting the specified tolerance to the SPEC NOMINAL: value. %TOLERANCE: states the passing range of values by adding and subtracting a percent tolerance of the SPEC NOMINAL: value to the nominal specification.
FUNCTION:	The FUNCTION: field specifies which test to run. You can call User Functions, Compiled Functions, Remote Functions, or you can write in an expression to be evaluated. The result of the function you call is tested against your specifications. If a User Function returns more than one value, HP VEE assumes the top output pin holds the result to be tested.
LOGGING ENABLED	This button toggles to LOGGING DISABLED. If logging is enabled, each test logs a record. By selecting Logging Config... in the object menu you can choose which fields you want from a list that includes: Name, Result, Nominal, High Limit, Low Limit, Pass, Time Stamp, and Description. Name, Result, and Pass are the default selections.
IF PASS	This button toggles to IF PASS CALL:. If your test passes, HP VEE goes to this line for branching instructions. IF PASS tells HP VEE to branch according to your selection in the following menu. See THEN CONTINUE. IF PASS CALL: tells HP VEE to call the stated function, then go to the branching menu selection.

Test Sequencing

Sequence Transaction Field	Explanation
THEN CONTINUE	This button holds a menu with six branching options. THEN CONTINUE simply executes the next test configured in the Sequencer. THEN RETURN: tells HP VEE to stop executing tests and put the specified expression on the Return output pin of the Sequencer. THEN GOTO: jumps to the test named in its field. THEN REPEAT repeats the current test up to the number of times specified in the MAX TIMES: field. If the PASS/FAIL condition still exists after the maximum number of repeats, then HP VEE continues with the next test. THEN ERROR: stops execution by generating an error condition with the given error number. An error can be trapped with the Error output pin on the Sequencer. No other output pins will send data. THEN EVALUATE: calls the specified User Function, which must return a string that states a branching menu option. Valid strings results from the User Function are: "Continue", "Return <expr>", "Goto <name>", "Repeat <expr>", "Error <expr>", where <expr> is any valid HP VEE expression and <name> is the name of a test in the sequence. This option allows you to ask the user what to do next.
IF FAIL	IF FAIL toggles to IF FAIL CALL:. If your test fails, HP VEE goes to this line for branching instructions. Options are the same as for IF PASS.
DESCRIPTION:	This field holds Text comments on your test. They will show on the Sequencer transaction bar and can be stored with your test record by using the Logging Config... choice in the object menu.

To Add or Insert or Delete a Test

In this section you'll add another test transaction to the Sequencer object. You can use the same random( ) function to simulate a test result, but this time you'll compare the result to a limit instead of a range of values.

1. Double-click below the first **Sequencer** transaction bar to get the **Sequence Transaction** dialog box.

   Notice that HP VEE gives you the default name **test2**. You can use that. Change **SPEC NOMINAL** from .5 to .25. Click **RANGE:** to get the **Select Spec Type** dialog box. Select **LIMIT:**. Choose < for your operator. Change **1** to **.5** for your limit.

   Change the **FUNCTION** field from **testFunc(a)** to **random( )**. Leave the other default selections and click **OK** to return to the **Sequencer**.

   *Note: You could also add a transaction after the highlighted one by selecting **Add Trans...** from the object menu.*

You have just added a second transaction to your Sequencer test plan. The transaction bar should read: **test2 (.25) < .5**. Now let's suppose you want to insert a transaction between these two tests.

2. Make sure the second transaction bar is highlighted. Then open the object menu and select **Insert Trans...** .

   Change the **TEST** name field to **Insert**. Change the **FUNCTION** field to **random( )**. Then click **OK**. You will now see **Insert 0 <= (.5) <= 1** on the second transaction bar. Run your program to see the three records from your three tests. You may have to enlarge your display to see all the entries.

Now you'll delete **Insert**.

3. Click the **Insert** transaction bar, place the mouse cursor over the **Insert** transaction bar, and press **Ctrl-k** to delete **Insert**.

Test Sequencing

Note: You could also click the target transaction bar and select *Cut Trans* from the object menu. You can also paste a transaction that has been cut by choosing *Paste Trans* from the object menu (Ctrl-y is the shortcut). And in a similar fashion you can copy a transaction with the *Copy Trans* selection.

4. Run your program and note the two records of data from the two tests. Save the program as **seq1.vee**.

   Note: The braces indicate a Record data type. The Sequencer outputs a Record of Records, as you can see in the AlphaNumeric display. This means you could put the sequencer in a loop and run the same sequence of tests several times yielding an array of Records of Records.

   Your program should look like the figure below.

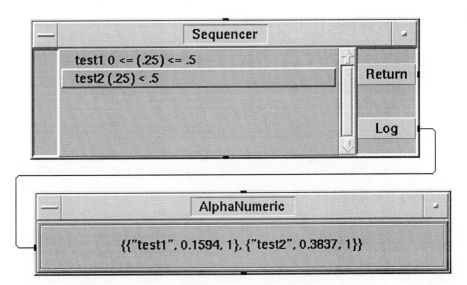

Fig. 9-2. A Simple Sequencer Example

To Access Logged Test Data

The Sequencer outputs a Record of Records. Each test uses the test name as its field name in the Sequencer record. The fields within each test are named according to your logging configuration. Using the default configuration with the fields Name, Result, and Pass you could access the result in test1 with the notation Log.Test1.Result, as shown below.

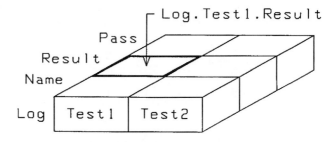

Fig. 9-3. A Logged Record of Records

Let's build on the last exercise to try this out. Open **seq1.vee**.

1. Select **Math => Formula** and place it below your display. Change the input terminal name from **A** to **Log** and connect it to the **Sequencer Log** terminal.

   Change the default formula to **Log.Test1.Result**. (Remember that HP VEE is not case sensitive and the capitals in the names are for clarity in documentation.)

   We have renamed the input pin; however, you could leave the default name A. Your formula would then read A.Test1.Result.

   Select an **AlphaNumeric** display and connect it to the **Formula** output.

Test Sequencing

2. Run your program and you will see that you have accessed the **Result** field in **Test1**. Save the program as **seq2.vee**.

Your program should look like the figure below.

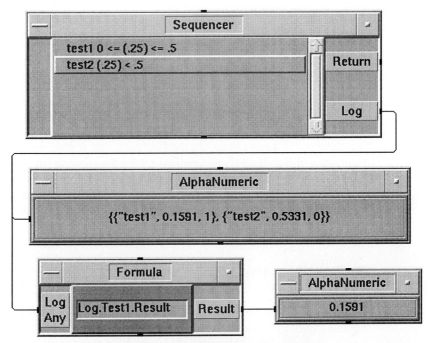

Fig. 9-4. Accessing Logged Data

Note: Each test creates a record as it executes within the Sequencer, which can be used in subsequent tests. For example, you could enable test2 if test1 passed (ENABLED IF: test1.pass == 1). If you need to access test data in an expression field while the test is still running, test data is stored in the temporary record **thistest**.

3. Change the formula to read **Log.test1** and run your program again.

You can now see that you have retrieved the entire record for test1 indicated by the braces around the three values in the display.

9 - 11

4. By changing the formula, try accessing the **result** and **pass** fields in both **test1** and **test2**. Select **Logging Config...** in the object menu and add the **Nominal** and **Time Stamp** fields to your logged records. Access these new fields with the **Formula** object.

Lab 9 - 2: Passing Data in the Sequencer

In the first lab exercise you learned how to alter the test execution order and access the logged test data. In this lab you'll create a User Function and call it from three different tests. In the first part, you'll pass data to the User Functions through an input terminal on the Sequencer. In the second part, you'll modify the program to use a global variable instead of an input terminal. This will give you a chance to call a function in EXEC mode rather than TEST mode. In the third part, you'll learn how to test a waveform output against a mask.

To Pass Data Using an Input Terminal

First, you'll create the User Function Rand, which will simulate a measurement procedure. Rand( ) willsimply add an input parameter to the output of the Random Number object, and put this result on the output pin. Rand( ) will be called from three different tests.

1. Select **Device => UserObject** and place it in the center of your work area. Change the name from **UserObject** to **Rand**.

2. Select **Device => Random Number** and place it in **Rand**. Select **Math => + - * / => +** and place it to the right of **Random Number**. Connect the output of **Random Number** to the upper left input of the + object.

3. Add a data input terminal to **Rand**. Connect the input terminal **A** to the lower left input terminal of the + object.

4. Add a data output terminal to **Rand**. Connect the output of the + object to the **Rand** output terminal.

Your UserObject Rand should look like the figure below.

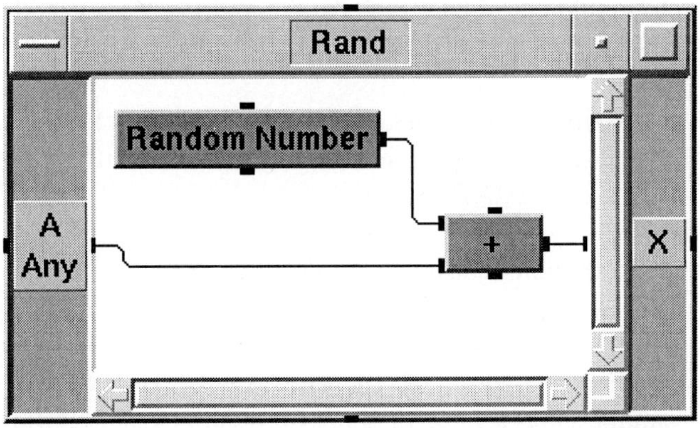

Fig. 9-5. The Rand UserObject

5. Open the **Rand** object menu and click on **Make UserFunction**. When the **Call Function** object appears calling **Rand**, delete it, since you'll be calling **Rand** from the **Sequencer** object.

   Deleting the Call Function object does not remove the User Function. If you want to check this, just click on Edit => Edit UserFunction and you'll see Rand come up in a list box of User Functions to edit.

Now you'll set up three tests in the Sequencer to call Rand using a Sequencer input pin to feed the input parameter to Rand.

6. Select **Device** => **Sequencer** and place it in the upper-center work area.

   Click the transaction bar to get the **Sequence Transaction** dialog box. Change the **FUNCTION** field from **testFunc(a)** to **rand(a)**. Click **OK** to get back to the **Sequencer** open view.

   To reproduce this test two more times you'll have to cut it to put it in a buffer, then paste it back in three times.

Make sure your transaction is highlighted, place the cursor on the transaction bar, press **Ctrl-k** to cut the test, then press **Ctrl-y** three times to paste the test back into the Sequencer. (You could also do the same thing with object menu selections.)

The default test names will be **test1x2**, **test1x1**, and **test1**. Open the three **Sequence Transaction** dialog boxes and change these names to **test1**, **test2**, and **test3** for clarity.

Add an input terminal to the **Sequencer**.

7. Select **Data => Real Slider** and place it to the left of the **Sequencer**. Change the name to the prompt **Select Num:**, size the object to be smaller, and connect it to the **Sequencer** input terminal.

   Tip: You can size an object as you place it by clicking and dragging using the left mouse button.

8. Select an **AlphaNumeric** display, place it below the **Sequencer**, enlarge it to be wider, and connect it to the **Log** output terminal on the **Sequencer**.

9. Save your program as **seqdat1**. Select a number on the **Real Slider** object and run **seqdat1**. It should look like the figure below.

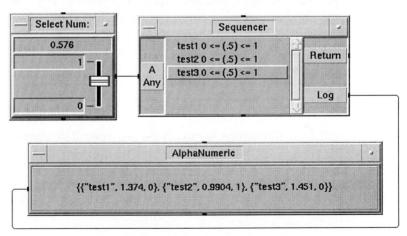

Fig. 9-6. Passing Data Using an Input Terminal

Note that you have used an input terminal name to pass parameters into the User Function Rand. You could also use input terminal names for any of the expression fields in the Sequence Transaction dialog box.

If you have a lot of tests, this method could get awkward with too many input pins. One way to reduce the number of input pins would be to pass records to input terminals, and then use individual fields within the records for the separate tests. Another solution is to use a separate User Function to set up global variables, which can then be called by other User Functions or any expression field within your program. That's exactly what you'll do in the following exercise.

To Pass Data Using a Global Variable

Let's modify the program in the first part to use a global variable to pass the parameter *a* to your User Function Rand.

1. Delete the **Real Slider** object labeled **Select Num**. Delete the **A Any** input terminal on the **Sequencer**.

2. Highlight the **test1** transaction bar, open the object menu, and click **Insert Trans...** . When the **Sequence Transaction** box appears, click **TEST** to toggle the selection to **EXEC** and change the name to **Setup**.

   You'll use EXEC mode, since the User Function will just set up a global variable and will not yield a result that needs to be tested against a specification.

3. Change the **FUNCTION** field to **global( )** and click **OK** to close the dialog box.

You'll now create the User Function global( ).

4. Select **Device => UserObject** and place it in the center of your work area. Change the name **UserObject** to **global**.

CUTTING YOUR TEST DEVELOPMENT TIME WITH HP VEE

Select **Data => Real Slider** and put it in the **UserObject**, change the name to **Select Num:**, and size it to be smaller vertically.

Select **Data => Globals => Set Global** and place it to the right of the **Real Slider**.

Change the global variable from **globalA** to **a**. Connect the **Real Slider** to the **Set Global** object.

You want this function to appear on the screen long enough for the user to select a number, so you need a pop-up panel view. You'll also need an OK button, so that the panel remains on the screen until the user has made a selection.

5. Select **Flow => Confirm(OK)** and place it above the **Real Slider** object. Connect the **OK** data output pin to the **Real Slider** sequence input pin.

   *Note: Instinctively, most people want to place the OK button below the Set Global object, which will lead to an error, because HP VEE will take the existing value of **a** and pause until the OK button is pressed. By placing OK above the Real Slider, HP VEE waits to set the global variable **a** until after the OK is pressed, so the new global value will definitely be used. (Edit => Show Exec Flow will illustrate this very well.)*

6. Select **Display => Note Pad** and place it to the right of the **OK** button. Enter the following user prompt in the **Note Pad**:

   Please select a number for this run of tests 1, 2, and 3.

7. Select the **Note Pad**, the **Real Slider**, and the **OK** button by pressing **Ctrl** and clicking on those objects. Each object will now have a shadow indicating that it's been selected. Now open the object menu and click **Edit => Add To Panel**.

   When you get the **Panel** view, size it to be smaller, and position the **Note Pad** on top, the **Real Slider** in the middle, and the **OK** button on the bottom. You can position the objects in any way you want without altering the Detail view.

9 - 16

Test Sequencing

Open the object menu and click next to **Show Panel on Exec**. See the figures below.

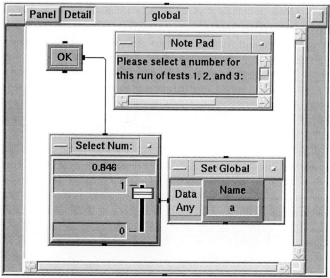

Fig. 9-7. The Global UserObject (Detail)

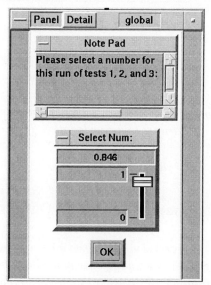

Fig. 9-8. The Global UserObject (Panel)

CUTTING YOUR TEST DEVELOPMENT TIME WITH HP VEE

7. Open the object menu and click **Make UserFunction**. Delete the **Call Function** object that appears. You won't need it, because you've called the global function from the Sequencer.

8. Save your program as **seqdat2** and run it. It should look like the figure below.

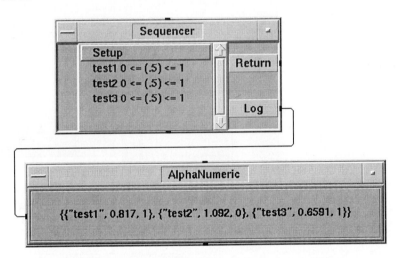

Fig. 9-9. Passing Data Using a Global Variable

Note: *The pop-up panel will appear where you last placed it. Simply drag it to a new location, if you don't like where it appears.*

To Compare a Waveform Output with a Mask

In this exerercise you'll create a User Function called noisyWv and call it from a single transaction bar in the Sequencer. The user will be able to vary the amplitude of the wave from 0 to 1. This function simulates a test result that returns a noisy waveform. You'll use the Coord object in the Data =>

Constant menu to create a straight line mask at 0.6, which the Sequencer will use to test the noisy waveform.

1. Create the **UserObject** called **noisyWv,** as shown below in the **Detail** view.

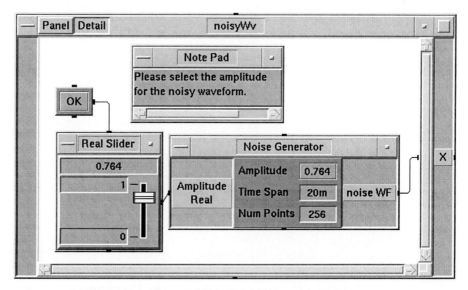

Fig. 9-10. The noisyWv UserObject (Detail)

2. Press **Ctrl** and click on the **OK** button, the **Real Slider**, and the **Note Pad** to highlight them for creating a Panel view. Open the object menu and select **Edit => Add To Panel**.

When you get the **Panel** view, rearrange the objects to your taste, and size the window.

Open the object menu and click next to **Show Panel on Exec**.

Your Panel view should look like Figure 9-11.

CUTTING YOUR TEST DEVELOPMENT TIME WITH HP VEE

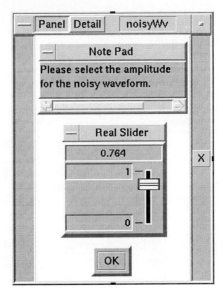

Fig. 9-11. The noisyWv UserObject (Panel)

3. Open the object menu and click **Make UserFunction**. When the **Call Function** object appears, delete it, since you'll call this function from the **Sequencer**.

4. Select **Device => Sequencer** and place it left-center of the work area.

   Add a data input terminal and name it mask.

   Click the transaction bar to get the **Sequence Transaction** dialog box. Type **noisyWv( )** in the **FUNCTION** field. Click **RANGE** and select **LIMIT** from the pop-up menu. Type the terminal name **mask** in the **LIMIT** field. All of the other defaults are fine, so click **OK**.

   This means that test1 will get a result from noisyWv( ) and test it against the limit specified at the terminal named mask. If the noisy wave is less than or equal to the mask at all points, it will pass; otherwise, it will fail.

5. Select **Data => Constant => Coord** and place it above the **Sequencer**. Connect its output to the **Sequencer** input terminal **mask**.

   Open the **Coord** object menu and click **Config...** . Enter **2** in the **Array Elements** field. (You'll only need two pairs of coordinates to specify a straight line.)

   You'll now see two indices for pairs of coordinates. Click the first index, **0000:** and a cursor will appear. You only need to type the coordinates separated by a comma, because HP VEE will add the parentheses automatically. Type **0, 0.6** <Tab> **20m, 0.6** <Enter>.

   The x axis (time axis) for a default waveform in HP VEE goes from 0 to 20 milliseconds; hence, the two x values of 0 and 20m. The two y values are both 0.6, since you want a straight line mask. You can create any mask waveforms you like by configuring the proper number of coordinate pairs and filling them in. The Sequencer comparison mechanism operates just like the Comparator object, which accepts the Coord data type to test waveforms. Of course, you could also compare two Waveform data types. Notice that you should press Tab to move between coordinate pairs, and that pressing Enter tells HP VEE you are done with your input.

6. Select an **AlphaNumeric** display, increase its width, and connect it to the **Log** output from the **Sequencer**.

7. Save your program as **seqdat3** and run it. It should look like Figure 9-12.

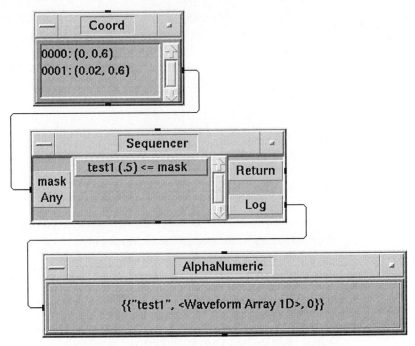

Fig. 9-12. Comparing a Waveform to a Mask

You have now done three exercises focused on passing data with the Sequencer. You used an input terminal and a global variable to pass scalar values, and then you learned how to work with waveform comparisons. In the next lab exercise, you'll focus on accessing and analyzing data from several iterations of the Sequencer object.

Lab 9 - 3: Analyzing Data from the Sequencer

As we mentioned earlier in the chapter, Sequencer data comes out as a record of records. In many cases, however, the Sequencer may run through a series of tests several times. This would generate an array of records. Each record would represent one run through the Sequencer and would hold other records representing each test within a run. The easiest way to visualize this is to imagine a cube of data in memory, as shown in the following figure.

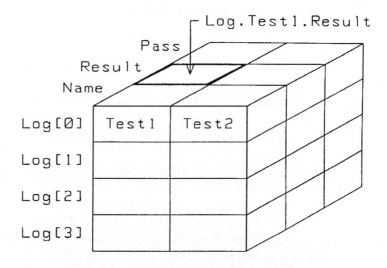

Fig. 9-13. A Logged Array of Records of Records

The array or records is called Log, because that's the name associated with the Sequencer output pin. To access a particular run you use array indexing with the bracket notation. So, Log[0] is the first run through the Sequencer, Log[1] is the second run, and so forth. The main record for each run has two fields, Test1 and Test2. Within the record Test1 there are three fields: Name, Result, and Pass. The same holds for the record Test2. Therefore, Log.Test1.Result gives an array of 4 values, each one representing one of the four runs. Log[0].Test1.Result outputs a scalar value, the Result of Test1 in the first run (Log[0]).

The implications for analysis are that you can think of your data in a simple manner, and you can investigate it in a number of ways. For example, you might want to know how many tests passed in a particular run. Or you might want to average the results of Test2 in all runs. Or you might want to all of the data on Test1 in the fourth run. All of these are possible with this data structure. Let's perform some analysis operations on data from the seqdat1 program. Clear your screen and open this file.

To Analyze Several Runs of Data from the Sequencer

You'll modify the seqdat1 program to run through the Sequencer three times. Then you'll perform some analysis operations on the data.

1. Select **Flow => Repeat => For Count** and place it above the **Real Slider** object. Change the number of iterations to **3**, and connect the data output pin to the sequence input pin of the **Sequencer**.

2. Delete the data line between the **Sequencer Log** pin and the display. Select **Data => Collector** and place it to the right of the **Sequencer**. Connect its upper left data input pin to the **Sequencer Log** pin and its **XEQ ANY** pin (lower left) to the sequence output pin on the **For Count** object. Connect the **Collector** data output pin to the **AlphaNumeric** display. Enlarge the display vertically somewhat to accomodate an array with three elements.

   The Sequencer will now run through test1 and test2 three times and collect the data into an array with three elements, each one holding a record of records for each run. (Refer to the cube of data in the figure above to visualize this.)

   Run your program at this point to see the display of the Sequencer data.

   Now you'll use the Formula object to extract part of this data to analyze. We'll use the results of test1 for all three runs as an example, and find the mean of that array.

3. Select **Math => Formula** and place it below the display. Connect the **Formula** input pin to the output of the **Collector**.

   Change the **Formula** input field to read: **a.test1.result**.

   The **a** refers to the array on the input terminal A Any. Test1.result accesses the proper field. All runs will be shown in an array, since no particular run was designated. (A[0].test1.result would refer to the first run only, for example.)

4. Run your program. It should look like the figure below.

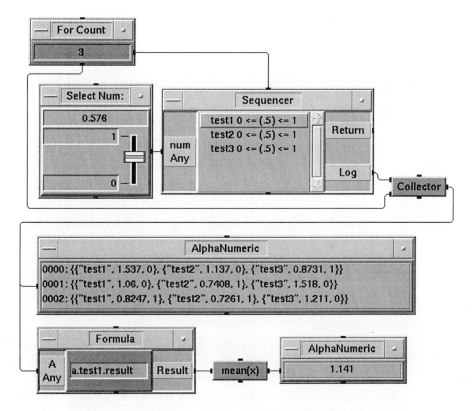

Fig. 9-14. Analyzing Several Runs of Sequencer Data

CUTTING YOUR TEST DEVELOPMENT TIME WITH HP VEE

You have only accessed a single array, but the principle is the same for extracting other arrays of data from the Sequencer output. Note that you can easily change which fields are saved for each test with the Logging Config... selection in the Sequencer object menu.

Lab 9 - 4: Storing and Retrieving Logged Data

We'll modify your seqdat2 program for an example. The first part will use the To/From File objects for data storage, and the second part will use the To/From DataSet objects. First, open the **seqdat2** file and delete the data line to the display.

Using the To/From File Objects with Logged Data

1. Select **Flow => Repeat => For Count** and place it to the left of the **Sequencer**. Change the **For Count** number to **3**, and connect its data output pin to the sequence input pin on the **Sequencer**.

2. Enlarge your work area vertically and place the **AlphaNumeric** display near the bottom. Select **Data => Collector** and place it in the left work area. Connect the **Sequencer Log** pin to the **Collector** data input pin. Connect the **For Count** sequence output pin to the **Collector XEQ** pin.

The Collector will create an array of records of records from the Sequencer. Using the WRITE CONTAINER transaction in the To File object you can write any HP VEE data container to a file quite easily.

3. Select **I/O => To => File** and place it to the right of the **Collector**. Select **I/O => From => File** and place it below the **To File** object. Connect the **Collector** output to the **To File** input. Connect the **To File** sequence output to the **From File** sequence input pin. Connect the **From File** data output to the display.

Check **Clear File At PreRun & Open** in **To File**, and configure a **WRITE CONTAINER a** transaction. Configure a transaction in the **From File** object like the following: **READ CONTAINER x** .

You can use the default data file for storage.

4. Run your program. It should look like the figure below.

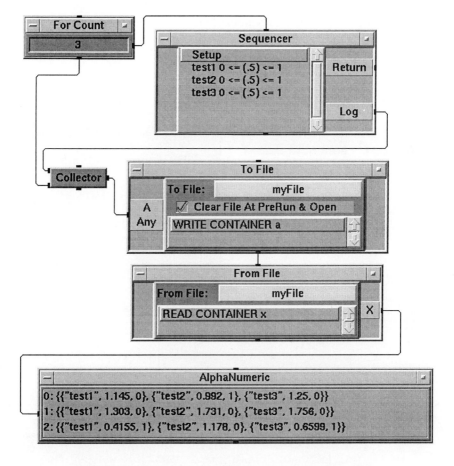

Fig. 9-15. Storing Logged Data with To/From File

Using the To/From DataSet Objects with Logged Data

Since you are storing test data as records, you may prefer to use the To/From DataSet objects. In this case you won't need a Collector, because you can append each run of the Sequencer to the end of the DataSet.

Modify the last program to look like the figure below. The **To/From DataSet** objects are in the **I/O** menu. Notice the sequence line going into From DataSet. Can you explain why? (Ans: You want to wait for all three runs to be appended to the DataSet, before you trigger From DataSet.) Did you remember to change the *Get records* field in From DataSet to *All*?

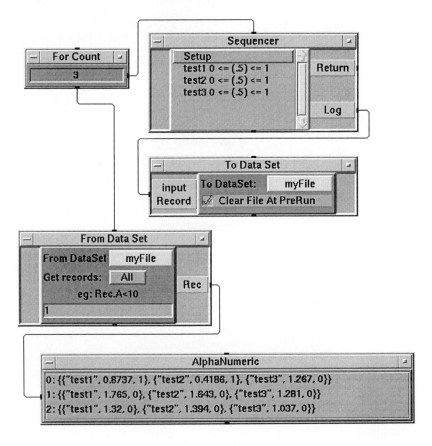

Fig. 9-16. Storing Logged Data with To/From DataSet

Chapter 9 Checklist

Use the following checklist to determine whether there are topics you need to review before going to the next chapter.

- Describe the Sequencer object conceptually.
- Configure a test for the Sequencer.
- Add, insert, and delete operations for a Sequencer test.
- Access logged data from the Sequencer.
- Use Sequencer input terminals to pass data to tests.
- Use Global variables to pass data to tests.
- Compare a waveform output to a mask.
- Analyze several runs of data from the Sequencer.
- Store data using the To/From File objects.
- Store data using the To/From DataSet objects.

Using Operator Interfaces

10

Average Time To Complete: 90 min.

Overview

You have already created a number of operator interfaces and pop-up panels. In this chapter we'll expand upon what you already know, and teach you how to add menus, customize interfaces, add warning signals, and import bitmaps.

Some benefits of using HP VEE operator interface features are:

- Maximum ease of use for the operator
- Improved program performance
- Security from unauthorized changes
- Clarity through visual aids

In this chapter you'll learn about:

- Building operator interfaces
- Using menus for your operator
- Importing bitmaps to add clarity
- Securing your test programs
- Creating high-impact warning signals

Key Points Concerning Operator Interfaces

- **Process for Creating an Operator Interface**

    1. Select the object or objects that you want in the panel view (i.e., click each object to create a shadow).

    2. Select **Edit => Add To Panel**.

    Note: While editing UserObjects or User Functions you can open the Edit menu in the work area by placing the mouse pointer on the background and clicking the right mouse button. You can also locate the Edit menu in the object menu as a submenu.

- **Moving Between Panel and Detail Views** From the main work area or UserObjects click the Panel or Detail buttons on the title bar. For User Functions you open the object menu and select To Panel or To Detail.

- **Customizing** Once you have a panel view, you can change the size of objects, change their placement, and alter the features of display objects without affecting the same objects in the detail view. For example, you could remove the title bar and the scales from a Waveform (Time) display. However, if you delete an object in the detail view, it will also be deleted in the panel view. Notice that there are less menu selections available in a panel view to prevent you from altering the program in any way. You can also clarify the panel view by editing title bars, using the Note Pad object, and using Show Description in the object menus.

- **Importing Bitmaps** You can import bitmaps into the panel view by clicking Select Bitmap in the object menu. The UNIX versions of HP VEE import *.xwd or *.GIF files to serve as the background for your UserObject. HP VEE for Windows imports *.bmp and *.icn files. (You can also find Select Bitmap in any icon pop-up menu.)

- **Securing Panel Views** Securing a panel view means that the user will not be able to access the detail view or be able to change the panel view. There is no "UnSecure" command, so you should save the original program and the secured program in separate files. To secure a program select File => Secure in the main work area. For UserObjects, open the object menu and select Secure.

- **Pop-up Panels** You can cause a panel to pop up at the execution of the UserObject or User Function by selecting Show Panel on Exec in the object menu. Since the panel will also disappear when the UserObject is done executing, you should also use the Confirm (OK) object in your panel to keep the panel on the screen until the user wants to proceed.

- **Constants, Sliders, Toggles, and Enum Objects** These objects are most commonly used for operator input. They all have an Auto Execute selection in their object menus that will automatically executes the object after any operator input. So you'll be able to input values without having to restart your program. You're already familiar with constants and sliders. Toggles send out either a 1 or a 0. They can be formatted as a check box or a button. They are often used with the If/Then/Else object to determine what course of action the user wants to take. Enum objects are used for menus and can be formatted as list boxes, cyclic buttons, or button menus, as the upcoming examples will show.

Common Tasks In Creating Operator Interfaces

The following examples will give you experience implementing the many features associated with panel views in HP VEE. Specifically we'll focus on creating menus, using effective warnings, and importing bitmaps to add more visual impact to your programs. All of the labs will give you a chance to customize the interfaces.

Lab 10 - 1. Using Menus

You'll create an operator interface that includes a menu with three choices: die1, die2, and die3. When the operator selects one, a function by the same name will be called that displays a die (dice is the plural) with one, two, or three dots on its top face. This program serves no practical purpose, but it does simulate a situation where the operator must choose which test to run from a menu. You'll also learn how to import a bitmap to change the appearance of an icon.

First, let's create the three User Functions.

1. Select **Device => UserObject** and place it in the center of your work area. Expand it to a full screen view.

Although we could use any icon to display the imported bitmap, we'll use the Note Pad object, because it has no pins.

2. Select **Display => Note Pad**, place it in the **UserObject**, and iconize it.

3. Open the pop-up menu for the **Note Pad** by placing the mouse pointer over the icon and clicking the right mouse button. Click **Layout => Show Label** to deselect the **Show Label** command.

   Notice the Note Pad label is now removed from the icon.

Using Operator Interfaces

Open the **Note Pad** object menu again and click **Layout => Select Bitmap**. Choose **die1.bmp** (**die1.xwd** in UNIX) in the list box presented and click **OK**.

Although HP VEE automatically goes to the bitmaps subdirectory, you could get your bitmap from any directory. You should now have a colorful picture of a die with one dot on its top.

4. Select **Flow => Confirm (OK)** and place it below the die.

   Select the **Note Pad** and the **OK** objects (press **Ctrl** and click the objects to create a shadow). Open the pop-up Edit menu by placing the mouse pointer on the background and pressing the right mouse button. Select **Add to Panel**.

5. Change the UserObject title to **die1**. Arrange the objects and size them to suit your taste. Open the object menu and select **Show Panel on Exec**.

   Now open the object menu and select **Make UserFunction**. Leave the **Call Function** object on the screen when it appears. You'll use it to call the function your user selects from the menu you'll create shortly.

6. Now create two more **User Functions** in the same way you did for **die1** called **die2** and **die3**. Make sure to select the **die2.bmp** and **die3.bmp** (a **.xwd** extension is used for UNIX) files for the appropriate bitmap.

   In the process of creating these two additional User Functions for die2 and die3 a Call Function object will appear for each one. Just delete them when they appear. The new User Functions will still be available to you, and you only need one Call Function object for this program.

   To check each User Function click Edit => Edit UserFunction and select the function you want from the list box presented.

Now you'll create a menu to select one of these three functions to call.

7. Select **Data => Enum** and place it to the left of **Call Function**.

10 - 5

Enum is an object that outputs an enumerated value from a user-defined list. For example, the user might define the list: Monday, Tuesday, Wednesday, Thursday, Friday. The user could then select one of these from a menu, and Enum would then output that day. The first item in the list is assigned the ordinal position 0; the nth item in the list is assigned ordinal position n-1. For instance, Monday in the list above has an ordinal position of 0, and Friday has an ordinal position of 4. The ordinal position can be extracted from an Enum value by using the ordinal( ) function in a Formula object.

Read the Help entry in the object menu for a more detailed explanation.

8. Open the **Enum** object menu and select **Edit Enum Values...** .

   Click the **Edit Enum Values** dialog box next to **0000:** to get a cursor. Then type in the names of your functions -- **die1, die2, die3** -- pressing the **Tab** key between each entry. When you're done click **OK**.

   There are three formats you can use for your menus. The default one is the List format. Enum will display your first entry as a button. When you click it, HP VEE presents a list box of all your choices. The choice the user selects will be output. A second format is Cyclic, which cycles through your enumerated values one at a time as you click the Enum button. The third format is called Buttons, which displays all of the enumerated values with a button next to each one. The user makes a selection by clicking a button. We'll use the button format for this example.

9. Open the **Enum** object menu and click **Format => Buttons**.

   Now you'll add the Function Name control pin to the Call Function object, which will accept an Enum value as input. Therefore, whatever value your user selects on the Enum object will become the function name that the Call Function object calls. This will become clear as you proceed.

10. Open the **Enum** object menu and select the check box next to **Auto Execute**.

    This will propagate the chosen data value as soon as it's selected.

Using Operator Interfaces

11. Open the **Call Function** object menu and select **Terminals => Add Control Input**. Select **Function Name** and click **OK**.

    Connect the **Enum** data output pin to the **Function Name** input terminal on the **Call Function** object. Connect the **Enum** sequence out pin to the sequence in pin of **Call Function**.

    Note: *The Call Function input terminal requires a Text Scalar, so HP VEE converts the Enum Scalar to a Text Scalar.*

    Remember the dotted line indicates a control pin. When Auto Execute is turned on, Enum executes whenever you make a change to it and sends your selection to Call Function. The control pin on Call Function will replace the function name as soon as the pin receives data. But the Call Function object does not call the specified function until its sequence input pin is fired. (Using Auto Execute and the sequence pins means that the user doesn't have to click Run to begin the program.)

12. Select **Display => Note Pad** and place it in the upper-left work area.

    Type in the user prompt: **Select the desired function:**

    Open the object menu and deselect **Show Title** by clicking the check box. (The check mark will disappear.) This will remove the title bar from the Note Pad and make your program more readable.

Now you need an operator interface that just shows the prompt, the menu, and the Start button.

13. Select your prompt (Note Pad) and the **Enum** objec by pressing **Ctrl** and clicking on the desired objects. Then select **Edit => Add To Panel**. Arrange the icons and size them to suit your taste.

14. Run your program by making a selection. (Don't use the **Run** button, because it will simply use the selection that's already made on the menu.)

    Your program should look like Figure 10-1.

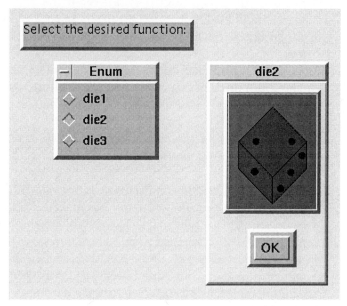

Fig. 10-1. Operator Interface Menus

There are a few things to note, before we move on to the next lab exercise:

- You can use the same techniques in the exercise above to create menus for any program.

- Enum could also be used to select a compiled language program by using the Execute Program object with a control pin that indicated which program to call. If you had imported a library of compiled functions, you could also use the Call Function object to run a function from your library.

- If you have more choices than you can comfortably display on your screen, you should use the list box format in Enum.

Using Operator Interfaces

Lab 10 - 2: Importing Bitmaps for Panel Backgrounds

In the last exercise, you imported a bitmap for an icon. In this exercise you'll import a bitmap for a panel background. Icons in the panel view will be superimposed on this image. Bitmaps are not essential to your programs, but they can add clarity and impact to your tests. For example, you might want to import a schematic to better illustrate what's being tested. In this exercise, we'll show you how to import bitmaps with colorful images.

Bitmaps can only be imported for icons or for the panel view backgrounds in UserObjects or User Functions, so you'll create a User Function called win that will import a graphic saying "Big Winner!" with a hand of cards. A simple Confirm (OK) object will be superimposed on the image to hold the graphic on the screen until you click the OK button.

1. Select **Device => UserObject** and place it in the work area.

2. Select **Flow => Confirm (OK)** and place it in the work area of the **UserObject**.

3. Change the name of the **UserObject** to **win**.

4. Select the **OK** object (highlight it with a shadow). Open the pop-up **Edit** menu by placing the pointer on the **UserObject** work area and clicking on the right mouse button. Select **Edit => Add to Panel**.

5. Open the **UserObject** menu and select **Show Panel on Exec**.

6. Open the **Panel** view **UserObject** menu and click on **Select Bitmap**. Choose **win.bmp (win.gif** in UNIX) and click **OK**. You can move your **OK** button to suit your taste.

   The panel will be sized to hold the *.bmp (or *.gif) file showing the hand of cards. Notice the OK button is superimposed on the image. Any icons in the panel view would also be superimposed on the graphic.

   Note: The Select Bitmap choice is only available from the Panel view of the UserObject or User Function.

CUTTING YOUR TEST DEVELOPMENT TIME WITH HP VEE

7. Open the **UserObject** menu and select **Make UserFunction**. When the **Call Function** appears, run your program. It should look like the figure below. (The black-and-white format below partially obscures the red text below that says "Big Winner!", but you will see the text clearly on your screen.)

   Note: *The pop-up window containing the win function will appear wherever you want it to. Just click-and-drag the image to the new location.*

Fig. 10-2. Importing a Bitmap for a Panel Background

Note on Securing Program: *To secure this program from alteration: (1) create a panel view for the program, (2) save it so that you can alter it, (3) save it again under another name for its secured form, and (4) select File => Secure from the panel view.*

Lab 10 - 3: Creating a High Impact Warning

In this example we'll nest User Functions. One function will be the alarm itself, which will display a big red square and beep. The second function will call the alarm repeatedly creating a blinking light effect and a pulsing sound, until the user turns the alarm off.

First, you'll program the alarm function.

1. Select **Device => UserObject** and expand it to full screen. Change the name to **alarm**.

2. Select **Display => Beep** and place it in the upper-left of the **UserObject**. Adjust the settings so that you have a loud beep that lasts a second. Change the **Duration (sec)** field to **1**. Change the **Volume (0-100)** field to **100**. (These instructions assume your computer has the hardware to support a beep.)

   You don't need to attach the Beep object to anything. It will activate when the function executes.

To create a big red square, you'll use a Waveform display and a Coord constant that simulates a straight line wave. Let's build it and you'll see how it works.

3. Select **Data => Constant => Coord** and place it to the left. Open the object menu and select **Config...** . Type **2** for the number of **Array Elements** and click **OK**.

   Double-click the **0000:** field to select the first entry. Then enter the coordinates **(0,1)**. Double-click the **0001:** field and enter **(20m,1)**. Recall that you only have to enter the pairs; HP VEE will put the parentheses in for you.

4. Select **Display => Waveform (Time)** and place it to the right of **Coord**. Connect the Coord data output to the Waveform (Time) data input. Change the **y** range fields to **0** and **1**.

You will now get a straight line wave at the maximum value. If you now select the display feature that fills in the graph under the line, you'll produce a square, which will be the color of the trace.

5. Open the **Waveform (Time)** object menu and select **Traces & Scales...** . Click the **Color:** field and select the **Pen 2** (red). Keep clicking the **Points:** field until you get the option that looks like a small hill that's completely filled in below the top line. Click **OK**.

6. Open the **Waveform** menu and select **Panel Layout => Graph Only**. Open the object menu again and deselect **Show Title**.

You want the display to stay on the screen for one second to synchronize with the **Beep** object, so you'll use a **Delay** object set to **1** second.

7. Select **Flow => Delay**, set it to **1**, and connect its sequence input pin to the **Waveform (Time)** sequence out pin. The alarm will then last 1 second.

8. Select **Display => Note Pad** and add the message: **TURN OFF INSTRUMENTS!**. Size the **Note Pad** to your taste. Your detail view of the **UserObject alarm** should look like the figure below.

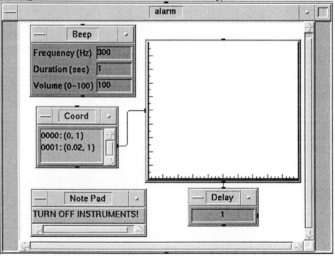

Fig. 10-3. The UserObject Alarm (Detail View)

Using Operator Interfaces

9. Select the **Waveform (Time)** display and the **Note Pad**. Open the pop-up **Edit** menu and select **Add To Panel**. When you get the **Panel** view, size and arrange the objects to your taste. Open the **alarm** object menu and select **Move**. Move the panel view to the center of your work area. Open the **Note Pad** object menu and deselect **Show Title**.

10. Open the **alarm** object menu and select **Show Panel on Exec**.

11. Open the **alarm** object menu again and select **Make UserFunction**. When the **Call Function** object appears, delete it.

    HP VEE will still hold the function alarm in memory. If you want to edit the function again, select Edit => Edit UserFunction.

You will now create the function that repeatedly calls the alarm function.

12. Select **Device => UserObject** and expand it to full screen size.

    Change the name of the **UserObject** to **warning**.

13. Select **Flow => Repeat => Until Break** and place it in the upper-left work area.

14. Select **Device => Function => Call**, edit the **Function Name** field to **alarm**, and connect its sequence input pin to the **Until Break** data output pin.

You'll now use the **Toggle** object to ask the user, if he or she wants to turn off the alarm.

15. Select **Data => Toggle**, expand it to its open view, change its name to: **Turn off alarm?**, and iconize it. Open the **Toggle** object menu, select **Initialize => Initial Value...** , and make sure it's **0**. Open the object menu again and select **Initialize => Initialize at PreRun**. Connect the **Call Function** sequence out pin to the **Toggle** sequence in pin.

    This will give you an input object that uses a check box. If the user checks the box, the object outputs a 1; otherwise, the object outputs a 0.

CUTTING YOUR TEST DEVELOPMENT TIME WITH HP VEE

The output can be tested with an If/Then/Else object to tell HP VEE what to do next.

16. Select **Flow => If/Then/Else** and place it to the right of the **Toggle**. Connect the **Toggle** data output to the data input **A** of the **If/Then/Else** object. Edit the expression in the **If/Then/Else** object to: **a == 1**. (Recall that the symbol for "equals" is ==, not =.)

   If the terminal A holds a 1, the Then output will fire; otherwise, the Else output fires.

17. Select **Flow => Repeat => Break** and connect it to the **Then** output on the **If/Then/Else** object. Your UserObject should look like the figure below.

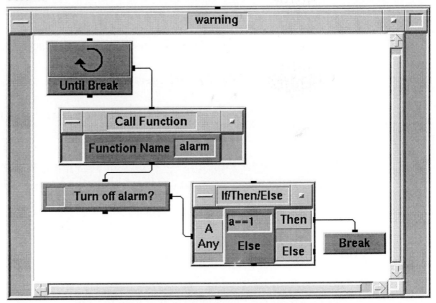

Fig. 10-4. The Detail View of the Warning UserObject

18. Select the **Toggle** object (**Turn off alarm?**). Open the pop-up **Edit** menu and select **Add To Panel**. Size the panel view to surround the **Toggle** and place the **warning UserObject** at the bottom-center of the work area.

19. Open the **warning UserObject** menu and select **Show Panel on Exec**. Open the object menu again and deselect **Show Title**, since the title serves no purpose to the operator. The **alarm User Function** is labeled.

20. Open the **warning UserObject** menu. (Place mouse pointer over the data input area and press the right mouse button.) Select **Make UserFunction**. Move the **Call Function** object to the top center of your screen.

21. Run your program. (Stop the program by clicking the box next to the **Turn off alarm?** prompt. It should look like the figure below.

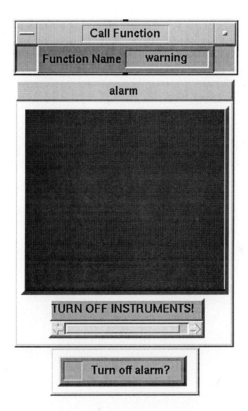

Fig. 10-5. The Warning Program

Note: Position the pop-up panels so that they don't hide each other.

Chapter 10 Checklist

You should now be able to perform the following tasks. Review, if necessary, before moving on to the next chapter.

- Summarize the key points concerning operator interfaces.

- Use a menu to select tests on an operator interface.

- Import a bitmap for an operator interface.

- Import a bitmap for an icon.

- Secure a program.

- Create a high impact warning.

Optimizing HP VEE Programs

11

Average Time To Complete: 2 hrs.

Overview

There are three basic components to performance in test programs: the speed of taking the measurement, the rate at which the data is transferred to the computer, and the speed at which your program processes the data. This chapter will focus solely on the execution speed of your HP VEE program, which can be improved as much as two orders of magnitude by using the best programming techniques.

In the first section, you'll learn the basic principles for optimizing any HP VEE program. The second section will cover optimizing parts of your programs by linking compiled functions in other languages on UNIX platforms.

In this chapter you'll learn about:

- Basic techniques for optimizing programs

- Using compiled functions in other languages on UNIX platforms

Basic Techniques for Optimizing Programs

This section covers the techniques that can improve program performance up to two orders of magnitude.

Perform Math on Arrays Whenever Possible

Performing mathematical operations on arrays is not always the most intuitive approach, but it will improve program performance greatly. For example, suppose your test must find the square root of measurements you're taking. The most traditional way to program this would be to make a measurement and calculate the square root within a loop. The optimized technique in HP VEE would store all the measurements in an array, and then calculate the square root of the array in one step.

Consider the example on the next page. The program on top iterates 1024 times. Each iteration calculates a square root and throws the result away. (This program is for illustration purposes only, and does not do any useful work.) The program on the bottom creates an array of 1024 elements, calculates the square root of the array yielding an array of square roots, and throws the result away. Although they both yield the same results, the bottom program executes 166 times faster than the one on top.

You could increase your program performance by two orders of magnitude just using this one technique. The basic principle behind this is simple. There is a fixed amount of overhead whenever an object executes, so you reduce the number of times an object executes by using arrays rather than scalar values.

Optimizing HP VEE Programs

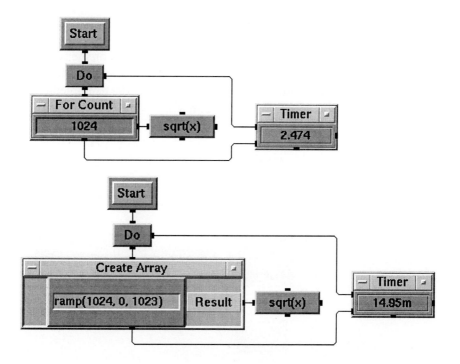

Fig. 11-1. Optimizing With Array Math

The object labeled Create Array is just a Formula object renamed. The ramp function generates an array with 1024 elements starting at 0 and ending at 1023.

Make Objects into Icons Whenever Possible

The more information HP VEE has to maintain on the screen the more time it will take your program to run. Using iconic views instead of open views will optimize your program several times. The example in the figure below operates 4.9 times faster using an iconic view for the Counter object.

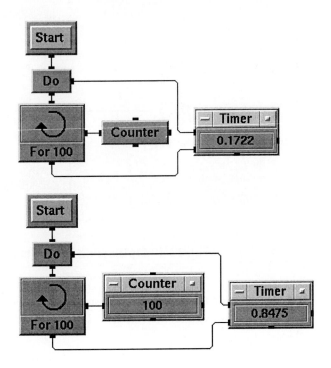

Fig. 11-2. Optimizing Your Programs Using Icons

Reduce the Number of Objects in Your Programs

As you become more experienced you will automatically use less objects, but there are two areas that lead to significant optimization.

- First, try to use a single equation in a Formula object instead of using separate mathematical objects. For example, put the equation ((a + b) * c)/d into a Formula object instead of using separate objects for addition, multiplication, and division.

- Second, nest function calls within other function parameter lists. For instance, in the next two figures the function randomize uses the array generated by the function ramp. In the second program the function call to ramp is nested in the call to randomize resulting in faster program execution.

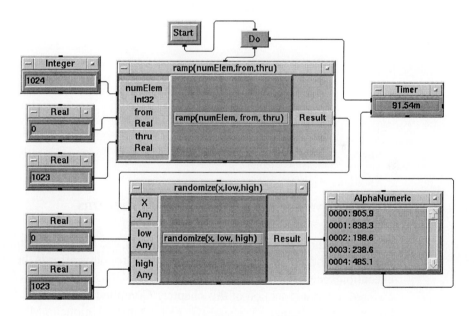

Fig. 11-3. Function Calls Without Optimization

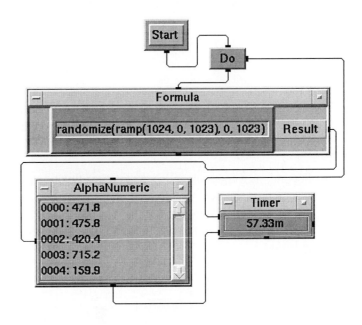

Fig. 11-4. Function Calls with Optimization

Other Ways to Optimize HP VEE Programs

Besides the three techniques mentioned already, the linking of compiled functions in other languages to your HP VEE programs affords the greatest execution speed gains. Compiled functions on UNIX platforms will be covered in the last section of this chapter. Compiled functions on PCs will be covered in Chapter 13: Using HP VEE Features Unique to MS Windows. Below we have listed a variety of other optimization techniques that you can use in your applications, when appropriate.

- Run your program from the panel view instead of the detailed view. HP VEE will have less objects to maintain on the screen.

- Collect data for graphical displays and plot the entire array at once rather than plotting each individual scalar point. If the X values of a plot are regularly spaced, use an XY Trace display rather than an X vs. Y Plot.

- Use one If/Then/Else object with multiple conditions instead of multiple If/Then/Else objects.

- Set graphical displays to be as plain as possible. The settings that allow the fastest update times are Grid Type => No Grid and Panel Layout => Graph Only.

- When reading data from a file use the ARRAY 1D TO END: (*) transaction instead of performing READ transactions on one element at a time.

- Use the Sequencer to control the flow of execution of several User Functions instead of separate Call Function objects.

- When using the Sequencer, only enable logging for transactions where the Log record is required.

Optimizing With Compiled Functions (HP-UX and SunOS)

The process of using compiled functions in other languages involves shared libraries on UNIX platforms and Dynamic Link Libraries (DLLs) on PC platforms. Shared libraries are discussed in this section; DLLs are covered in Chapter 13.

You can dynamically link a program written in C, C++, Fortran, and Pascal with your HP VEE programs on HP-UX workstations. Although all the languages mentioned should work on SunOS, only C is supported there at this time. Note that Pascal compiled functions are only supported on the HP 9000, Series 700 workstations.

Benefits of Using Compiled Functions

- Faster execution speed

- Leveraging your current test programs in other languages

- Developing data filters in other languages and integrating them into your HP VEE programs

- Securing proprietary routines

For these benefits you will add complexity to your development process. Only use a compiled function when the capability or performance that you need is not available using an HP VEE User Function or an Execute Program escape to the operating system.

Optimizing HP VEE Programs

The Process of Integrating Compiled Functions (HP-UX and SunOS)

The following is only the outline of the process. We will explain how to integrate compiled functions in detail shortly.

Outside HP VEE:

1. Write functions in C, C++, Fortran, or Pascal and compile them (Only C is supported on SunOS currently).

2. Write a definition file for the functions.

3. Create a shared library containing the compiled functions.

Inside HP VEE:

1. Use an Import Library object to bind the shared library to your program at run time. Within this object you will specify that you're calling a library containing Compiled Functions, the file that contains the shared library, and the definition file.

2. Call any functions in the shared library as you would any internal HP VEE function using a Call Function object or a function call from an expression field within an object such as the Sequencer or the Formula object.

3. (optional) You may also delete the library to free up memory using a Delete Library object.

Design Considerations

- You can use any facilities available to the operating system including math routines, instrument I/O, and so forth. However, you cannot access any HP VEE internals from within the program to be linked.

- You need to provide error checking within your compiled function, since HP VEE cannot trap errors in an external routine.

- You must deallocate any memory you allocated in your external routine.

- When passing data to an external routine, make sure you configure your Call Function input terminals to the type and shape of data that your routine requires.

- System I/O resources may become locked, so your external routine should be able to handle this type of event.

- If your external routine accepts arrays, it must have a valid pointer for the type of data it will examine. Also, the routine must check the size of the array. If the routine changes the size, you need to pass the new size back to your HP VEE program.

- The compiled function must use the *return( )* statement as its last statement, not *exit( )*. If the compiled function exits, then so will HP VEE, since a compiled function is linked to HP VEE.

Compiling Functions and Creating a Shared Library (HP-UX)

To create a shared library, your function must be compiled as position-independent code. It must then be linked with a special option to create a shared library. The first step is to compile your function using a **+z** compiler option to create position-independent code and a **-c** option, which prevents the compiler from performing the link phase. The commands for compiling are:

For c functions: **cc +z -c filename.c**

For FORTRAN functions: **f77 +z -c filename.f**

For PASCAL functions: **pc +z -c filename.p**

For c++ functions: **CC +z -c filename.c**

In each of the above cases, you would produce an output file *filename.o*. You would then link this file to be a shared library with the following command:

ld -b -o filename.sl filename.o

The **-b** option tells the linker to generate a shared library from your position-independent code. The **-o** option tells the linker to call your output file filename.sl instead of using the default name a.out.

The use of a makefile (consult HP-UX documentation for more information) simplifies things greatly, particularly if your function depends on routines from multiple files. The examples shown later will use these makefiles.

Compiling Functions and Creating a Shared Library (SunOS)

Use the following command to compile a C program on SunOS:

cc -pic -c <filename.c>

Any file holding your C source code for your function may be substituted for <filename.c>.

Use the following command to create a shared library on SunOS:

ld -assert pure-text -o <filename.so> <filename.o>

Use the object code created by compiling for <filename.o>, and substitute the appropriate shared library name for <filename.so>.

Creating a Definition File

The Call Function object determines the type of data it should pass to your function based on the contents of the definition file you provide.

The function definition defines the type of data the function returns, the function name, and the arguments the function accepts. The function definition is of the following general form:

\<return type\> \<function name\> (type parameter1, type parameter2, ...)

Valid return types include character strings, long integers, and double-precision floating point real numbers. These correspond to the HP VEE data types String, INT32, and REAL respectively. Parameters may be passed by value or by reference. Only parameters that are passed by reference will have both an input and output pin on the Call Function object. This will become clear in the coming examples. Passing data by value tells HP VEE to send a copy of the data to your function; passing by reference tells HP VEE to send the address of the data. You pass data by reference if your data will be sent back to the HP VEE program after the function alters it. You must also pass data by reference when sending arrays. HP VEE allows up to 20 reference parameters to be passed to a Compiled Function. For parameters passed by value, HP VEE allows up to 20 long integer parameters, or up to 10 double precision floating point parameters.

Importing and Calling a Compiled Function (HP-UX)

Once you have created the shared library and definition file outside of HP VEE, you can integrate the library into your HP VEE program. The process is similar to importing and calling User Functions. First, you use an Import Library object found in the Device => Function menu. You can change the Library Type field to Compiled Function (the default is User Function). You will then see a fourth field added to indicate the definition file. See the figure below.

Optimizing HP VEE Programs

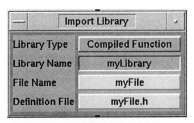

Fig. 11-5. Importing a Library of Compiled Functions

The Library Type can only be one of three choices: User Function, Compiled Function, or Remote Function. The Library Name field is simply the name HP VEE uses to identify your library, in case you would like to delete it later in the program. The File Name field will signify the file that holds the shared library.

Once you have imported the library with Import Library, you can call the Compiled Function by specifying the function name in the Call Function object. For example, the Call Function object below calls the Compiled Function named myFunction.

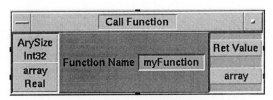

Fig. 11-6. Using Call Function for Compiled Functions

You can call a Compiled Function just as you would call a User Function. You can either select the desired function using Select Function from the Call Function object menu, or you can type in the name. In either case, provided HP VEE recognizes the function, the input and output terminals of the Call Function object will be configured automatically for the function. The necessary information is supplied by the definition file. Or you can reconfigure the Call Function input and output terminals by selecting Configure pinout in the object menu. Whichever method you use, HP VEE will configure the Call Function object with the input terminals required by the function, and with a Ret Value output terminal for the return value of the function. In addition, there will be an output terminal corresponding to each input that is passed by reference.

You can also call the Compiled Function by name from an expression in a Formula object, or from other expressions evaluated at run time. For example, you could call a Compiled Function by including its name in an expression in a Sequencer transaction. Note, however, that only the Compiled Function's return value (Ret Value in the Call Function object) can be obtained from within an expression. If you want to obtain other parameters from the function, you will have to use the Call Function object.

You may also delete the library of Compiled Functions by using the Delete Library object in the Device => Function menu. Using the Import Library, Call Function, and Delete Library objects you can shorten your load time and conserve memory by importing and deleting libraries only when they're needed.

Compiled Function Example Using C (HP-UX and SunOS)

The following C function accepts a real array and adds 1 to each element in the array. The modified array is returned to HP VEE on the Array terminal of the Call Function object, while the size of the array is returned on the Ret Value terminal. This function, once linked into HP VEE, becomes the Compiled Function called in the HP VEE program shown in the next figure. This example is located in the ~installDir/examples/concepts directory (/usr/lib/veetest/concepts using the full path on UNIX platforms, or C:\vee\examples\concepts on MS Windows). The .ex extension indicates the program; the .c extension is the C source code; the .h extension is the definition file; and the .sl extension indicates the shared library file.

```c
/*
        C code from manual49.c file
        This file is used to create a shared library.

        To make a shared library on HP-UX:
        cc -Aa +z -c manual49.c
        ld -b -o manual49.sl manual49.o

        To make a shared library on SunOS:
        cc -pic -c manual49.c
        ld -assert pure-text -o manual49.c manual49.o
*/


#include <stdlib.h>


double dummy( )
{
        return 0.0;
}

long myFunc(long arraySize, double *array)
{
        long i;

        dummy( );      /* workaround for Sun C compiler bug */
        for (i=0; i<arraySize; i++, array++){
                *array += 1.0;
        } /* for */

        return(arraySize);
} /* end myFunc( ) */
```

The definition file for this function is as follows:

```
/*
            definition file for manual49.c
*/

long myFunc(long arraySize, double *array);
```

(This definition is exactly the same as the ANSI C prototype definition in the C file.)

Although this example is simple, it illustrates some important points. First, you must include any header files on which the routine depends. In this case, the stdlib.h file isn't necessary; it is there to illustrate the point. The example program uses the ANSI C function prototype. The function prototype declares the data types that HP VEE should pass into the function. The array has been declared as a pointer variable, which means that the variable holds the address of the array, not the array itself. HP VEE will put the addresses of the information appearing on the Call Function data input terminals into this variable. The array size has been declared as a long integer. HP VEE will put the value (not the address) of the size of the array into this variable. The positions of both the data input terminals and the variable declarations are important. The addresses of the data items (or their values) supplied to the data input pins (from top to bottom) are placed in the variables in the function prototype from left to right. See the figure on the next page.

Note that one variable in the C function (and correspondingly, one data input terminal in the Call Function object) is used to indicate the size of the array. The arraySize variable is used to prevent data from being written beyond the end of the array. If you overwrite the bounds of an array, the result depends on the language you are using. In Pascal, which performs bounds checking, a run-time error will result, stopping HP VEE. In languages like C, where there is no bounds checking, the result will be unpredictable, but intermittent data corruption is probable.

This example program has passed a pointer to the array, so it is necessary to de-reference the data before the information can be used. The asterisk before the variable array in the For loop indicates that the operation should be performed on the value at that address. Since array has been passed by reference, HP VEE automatically creates both an input and output pin on the Call Function object.

The arraySize variable has been passed by value, so HP VEE only creates an input terminal. However, here we've used the function's return value to return the size of the output array to HP VEE. This technique is useful when you need to return an array that has fewer elements than the input array.

Note that the C routine is a function, not a procedure. The Compiled Function requires a return value, so if you use a language that distinguishes between procedures and functions, make sure you write your routine as a function.

The HP VEE program in Figure 11-7 on the next page calls the Compiled Function created from our example C program.

CUTTING YOUR TEST DEVELOPMENT TIME WITH HP VEE

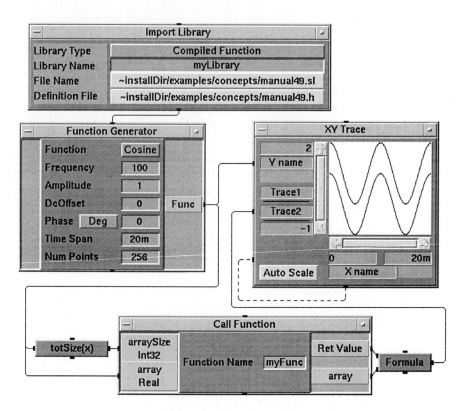

Fig. 11-7. Program Calling a Compiled Function

There are a few things to note about this program. First, the Import Library object executes before the Call Function object in the program. If you have any doubts about the order of execution regarding these two objects, use the sequence pins to assure the right order. Secondly, notice that the parameter variable *array* passed by reference to your function has both input and output terminals, but the variable *arraySize* passed by value has only an input terminal. Thirdly, the Formula object uses the size of the array in the Ret Value terminal to send the correct number of array elements to the display. Finally, the XY Trace uses a control pin to Auto Scale after it has received the two waveforms (note the dotted line from the sequence out pin to the control input pin).

C++ Dependencies

The definition file for C++ is the same format as for C. You must use the same calling conventions as you would with C. You also need a return( ) statement. The main difference when programming in C++ is that you need to put extern "<identifier>" before your function definition. For example:

extern "C" double foo(long, *double)

{
    ...
    return(...);
}

We have defined the function foo with the phrase extern "C". C++ needs to be able to resolve function names that may have the same names but belong to different classes. It does this by adding information before and after the function definition. So, two functions named foo, belonging to different classes, would actually have different names associated with each when C++ gets finished with compilation. This prevents HP VEE from using the function named in the compiled function object, because the function named foo doesn't show up in the compiled code. Using the C definition syntax, though, prevents the C++ compiler from adding information before and after the function name, then HP VEE can find it. This means that HP VEE cannot call class member functions directly. It can only dynamically link functions that have not been declared as part of class definitions.

Compiled Function Example Using PASCAL (HP-UX)

The following code is an example Pascal function that accepts a long integer and a pointer to a floating point array. The function adds the value 3 to every element in the array. This function is for instructional purposes only.

```pascal
module myFunc;

export
 type
  fArray = array [1..262144] of longreal;
  pArray = ^fArray;

 var
  i: integer;

 function add3(waveForm: pArray; arraySize: integer): integer;

implement

 function add3(waveForm: pArray; arraySize: integer): integer;
  begin
      i := 1;
      add3 := 0;
          while ((i <= arraySize) and (arraySize <= 262144)) do
            begin
              waveForm^[i] := waveForm^[i] + 3;
              i := i + 1;
            end;
          add3 := i - 1;
  end;

end.
```

Notice a few things about this function. The first item deals with the need to make visible the symbols HP VEE needs. HP VEE needs the name of the shared library file and the name of the function. Pascal doesn't make its symbols visible (the symbolic references to functions, procedures, variables, etc.) unless you specifically export them. So, we have created a Pascal module, exporting the name of the function we want to make visible. We also need to export the variable type declarations and variables the exported function will use.

The type section of this module contains two entries.

fArray = array [1..262144] of longreal;

This statement declares a new data type called fArray. It is an array containing 256k long reals. Long reals are 64-bit floating point numbers on HP-UX.

pArray = ^fArray;

This declaration creates a data type called pArray. A variable of this type would be a pointer to a variable of type fArray.

These two new data types represent the information our function will need to accept. The HP VEE program passes us a pointer to a floating point array and a long integer. The integer will hold the size of the array, and we use this information to create the function prototype:

function add3(waveForm: pArray; arraySize: integer): integer;

This function returns an INT32 value representing the size of the array.

Note that we declared the array data type to be 256k elements. Notice also that the array bounds are [1..262144]. We did this because Pascal has very strong array bounds and type checking. You can't simply perform mathematics on the pointer variable to index to the next element in the array, as you can do in C and C++. You must use a subscripted variable. So, if we declared a variable as a pointer to a scalar real we would only be able to access the first element in the real array.

We declared a fixed array size and used the integer variable as the subscript index into the array. Make certain that your function doesn't try to index beyond the array boundaries. Most Pascal arrays start at 1 not 0, as they do in C.

Pascal shared libraries are supported on the HP 9000, Series 700 workstations at revisions 8.05 and greater of HP-UX, and on Series 300/400 workstations at revisions 9.0 and greater of HP-UX. The makefile and definition file are listed below:

```
add3.sl:  add3.o
        ld -b add3.o -o add3.sl
add3.o:  add3.p
        pc +z -c add3.p

/*
        definition file for add3.p
*/

long add3(double *array, long arraySize)
```

Compiled Function Example Using FORTRAN (HP-UX)

The following example code is a FORTRAN program that accepts a floating point array and an integer. The integer represents the number of elements in the array. The function adds the value 5 to every element in the array.

```
        integer*4 function add5(wave, size)

        real*8 wave
        dimension wave(1:*)
        integer*4 size
        integer*4 i
        do 10 i = 1, size
           wave(i) = wave(i) + 5
   10   continue
        add5 = size

        return
        end
```

Optimizing HP VEE Programs

The function prototype is very similar to the equivalent C function. We declare the return type, followed by the function name and its parameters. The parameter types are declared after the function declaration and before the function body.

Notice the array declaration.

> **real*8 wave**
> **dimension wave(1:*)**

We declare a variable of type **real*8**, which is a 64-bit floating point real, or the equivalent of a **double** in C. We then dimension the variable to be an "assumed size" array. This is done with the **(1:*)** syntax. FORTRAN, unless you tell it otherwise, assumes all array bounds start at 1.

By also passing in the size of the array, we can use the variable named **size** to check the bounds on our array subscript.

FORTRAN assumes all parameters passed to a function are passed by reference. This means that the address of the variable, as opposed to the value that the variable holds, is given to the called function. This makes our coding task easy, because we can declare variables without the need for pointer de-referencing.

The make and definition files are as follows:

```
add5.sl: add5.o
 ld -b -o add5.sl add5.o
add5.o: add5.f
 f77 -c +z add5.f

/*
         definition file for add5.f
*/

long add5 (double *wave, long *size)
```

Execute Program Object vs. Compiled Functions (HP-UX)

When you're deciding which method to use to integrate your compiled language programs with HP VEE, you should consider the following distinctions:

Execute Program

- Longer start-up time

- Communication through pipes

- Protected address space

- Continuous execution

- Service of asynchronous events

Compiled Function

- Short start-up time

- Communication by passing on the stack

- Memory space shared with HP VEE

- Synchronous execution

- Signals not blocked or caught

Continuous data acquisition is better done with the Execute Program object.

Chapter 11 Checklist

You should now be able to perform the following tasks. Review topics, if necessary, before proceeding.

- Explain three basic techniques for optimizing HP VEE programs and give examples of each.

- Explain at least two more techniques in addition to the three above.

- If you have a UNIX platform, create a shared library and import a Compiled Function into an HP VEE program.

Writing Instrument Drivers

12

Average Time To Complete: 1 hr.

Overview

You don't need an instrument driver to talk to an instrument. HP VEE has the Direct I/O object that allows communication with an instrument over any of the supported interfaces. However, an instrument driver (ID) provides greater ease of use with a soft front panel for an instrument. You don't need to know the instrument command strings, and you can control the instrument from HP VEE.

Using the Driver Writer's Tool you can create most customized drivers in less than a day. This chapter will give you an overview of this tool and how you should use it. In some cases, you'll want to create a more advanced driver. We will clarify what these conditions are, and direct you to additional documentation on the HP VEE instrument driver language.

In this chapter you'll learn about:

- Instrument drivers for HP VEE

- The key features of the Driver Writer's Tool

- Using Learning and Expert Modes in the Driver Writer's Tool

- Creating a front panel for an instrument

- When to use the instrument driver language.

Using the Driver Writer's Tool

The Driver Writer's Tool (DWT) is a separate application from HP VEE that comes with the product. It is located in your HP VEE home directory, and is installed automatically with the rest of HP VEE. On PCs you click the DWT icon to run the application; on UNIX platforms you enter *dwt* at a prompt while in your HP VEE directory. You then see a driver development environment like the one in the figure below.

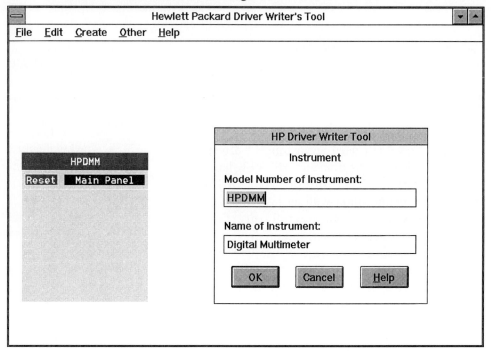

Fig. 12-1. The Driver Writer's Tool

The DWT has all of its documentation online, so there are no manuals or installation guides that come with the product. There is also a tutorial when Learning Mode is selected in the Other menu (a checkmark toggles on and off). This chapter will give an overview of that tutorial using some of that documentation. You'll also be guided through a simple example outside of the tutorial. In the Learning Mode you make selections in the interactive

Writing Instrument Drivers

dialog boxes on the right to create the ficticious instrument driver named HPDMM you see on the left. The tutorial automatically takes you through most of the DWT features by providing defaults for the fields in the dialog boxes. Click Help on the main menu bar to access DWT documentation.

Benefits of the Driver Writer's Tool

- Instrument Drivers (IDs) written with DWT work with HP VEE on each of its platforms or the HP Interactive Test Generator.

- Supports any programmable instrument equipped with the IEEE-488 interface.

- Lets you create specific IDs for special applications.

- Saves time, letting you create a simple ID in about a day.

- Provides ASCII source file, letting you edit the ID code (using the ID language) created with HP DWT to add more functionality.

  Note: *You cannot use DWT to modify IDs supplied by HP.*

The Driver Development Process

1. Run the DWT application, as described above.

   Make sure there is a checkmark next to **Learning Mode** in the **Other** menu. If there is no checkmark, then you are in **Expert Mode,** which is used to develop drivers on your own.

2. Work through the tutorial by editing entries in the dialog boxes on the right and clicking **OK** when you're done.

   - OR -

CUTTING YOUR TEST DEVELOPMENT TIME WITH HP VEE

Once you are familiar with the DWT, you'll want to change to Expert Mode by selecting Other => Learning Mode to remove the checkmark. In this mode, you have full control over the order you use to create and edit an ID. DWT uses the same dialog boxes as in Learning Mode to create the ID's panel. All of the DWT commands are available to you. However, commands remain dimmed if they are not allowed. You can rearrange controls on the panel, add or delete controls and subpanels (any extra panel added to the ID using the Panel dialog box), and change specifications.

Use the Help button on the main menu bar to get an overview of what you're doing and to learn how to use the Help facility. The Help button at the bottom of the Instrument dialog box will give complete instructions on the details of the fields you see in that particular box.

In both Learning and Expert Modes the ficticious driver HPDMM starts with the name, the reset button, and the panel button already created. In the Learning Mode the dialog boxes will prompt you for any changes you want. In the Expert Mode, you just click the control you want to edit and the appropriate dialog box will appear.

The predefined sequence in **Learning Mode** prompts you to include the following features common in most IDs:

Reset Button	**Numeric Display**
Discrete Controls	**Continuous Controls**
String Input Controls	**Toggle Buttons**
Push Buttons	**Subpanels**
Status Panel	**Couplings**
Auto Update	

As you complete dialog boxes, features appear on the ID panel at the left side of the DWT window.

In Expert Mode all of the above controls may be found in the Create and Other menus or by clicking on the particular control on the ID panel.

3. Save your ID.

Writing Instrument Drivers

When you finish creating an ID in Learning Mode, DWT asks if you want to save it. To save the ID, click **Yes**. Another dialog box appears that lets you accept or change the current path and file name. You should save IDs in a common driver directory so all drivers are in the same location. Click **OK** when you are ready.

DWT creates two files in the following formats:

» **yourfile.dwt** (DWT internal), readable only by DWT.

» **yourfile.id** (ASCII), ready to compile.

You can edit the ASCII file, but the changes cannot be read by DWT. To make changes to the ID, you should do so in DWT. Both files are updated when you resave existing IDs.

4. Debug the ID.

    When you load your ID into HP VEE, it will automatically compile the ASCII file creating yourfile.cid. Simply configure and add the ID file to the list of instruments available to your HP VEE program. Then open the object in the HP VEE work area as a State Driver. See Chapter 3: Two Easy Ways to Control Instruments or HP VEE documentation for detailed configuration information.

    Once the ID appears in the HP VEE work area, exercise the controls to change the settings. This is how you can debug the driver, and verify that it operates in the way you intended.

    Note: *ID panels should work as intended whether an instrument is connected or not. If your ID is to control a real instrument, connect that instrument to the interface to debug I/O communications.*

    a) **Exercise each ID control.**
    b) **Note problems that need changing.**
    c) **If the ID requires modification, return to DWT.**
    d) **Enter DWT's Expert Mode and edit the ID.**

12 - 5

CUTTING YOUR TEST DEVELOPMENT TIME WITH HP VEE

Note: *Although HP VEE will compile the ID automatically, you can run the ID compiler outside of HP VEE. See DWT's online documentation for instructions, if you would like to do this.*

DWT Dialog Boxes

- The **Instrument Dialog Box** identifies the model number and name. The model number will appear in the panel title bar, and is used as the default ID filename.

- The **Reset String Command Dialog Box** creates a Reset button that lets the user put the instrument into a reset or preset condition. This is usually similar to its power-on condition.

    Note: *You should always provide a reset button in an ID. The default entries specify a reset command string, and that HP VEE should send a Selected Device Clear (SDC) command to the instrument at the start of the reset cycle. You can accept the default entries or modify them for your instrument.*

- The **Numeric Display Dialog Box** creates a way for you to display measurement data. Instruments that analyze inputs such as multimeters, counters, and power meters use such displays. The default entries for this dialog box let you create a display for a voltmeter. You can accept the default entries or modify them to create a display for other instruments. You can set an error checking option as well as the size of the display.

- The **Discrete Dialog Box** creates a function selector control in the form of a submenu. The discrete control provides several different values for an instrument feature. For example, you can use this control to let an ID user select sine, square, or triangle wave output on a function generator. The default entries for this dialog box let you create a function selector for a voltmeter. You can accept the default entries or modify them to create a different discrete control. The output and query strings should be listed in the instrument's programming manual.

- The **Continuous Dialog Box** creates a control that provides a range of values -- you need to define maximum, minimum, and initial values) -- for an instrument feature. For example, a function generator ID includes continuous controls to adjust frequency and amplitude. The default entries for this dialog box let you create a frequency control for a function generator. You can accept the default entries or modify them to create a different continous control. The control has a name and input field where the user may type in a value.

- The **String Input Dialog Box** creates a control providing a field on the panel, in which the ID user can enter text. This is useful for instruments that can accept string inputs over the bus, or to display messages on the ID panel. The default entries let you create a display area on the panel called String containing the initial value of BUSY. The maximum number of Characters allowed is 256. You can accept the defaults or modify them to suit your needs.

- The **Toggle Button Dialog Box** creates a button that sets an instrument to one of two conditions. Such buttons are used to turn filters on or off, change modulation between AM or FM, or switch amplitude range between automatic or manual. The default entries for this dialog box let you create an on/off button for a voltmeter filter. You can accept the default entries or modify them to create a different toggle button.

- The **Push Button Dialog Box** creates a button that initiates an immediate action when pushed. For example, such buttons are used for resets and calibrations. The default entries for this dialog box let you create a calibration button for a voltmeter. You can accept the default entries or modify them to create a different push button.

- The **Panel Dialog Box** lets you add more panels to the ID as existing panels fill up or to organize controls into logical groups. You can also rename panels you have already added.

- The **Status Panel Dialog Box** allows you to provide instrument status information to the ID user. You can specify an error query string, a serial poll, an SRQ mask, SRQ status, self test, or instrument identification.

CUTTING YOUR TEST DEVELOPMENT TIME WITH HP VEE

- The **Couplings Control Box** lets you specify which controls interact with each other. For example, in a function generator, the frequency might interact with the function. So, when the function changes, the frequency may change to an allowed value. For IDs with frequency and function coupled, HP VEE queries the frequency so that the stored state and display are correct. Correct use of couplings is crucial for state drivers.

- The **State Recall Dialog Box** allows you to configure your ID to recall predefined instrument states (a collection of values for each ID control). When the ID user recalls a state, HP VEE programs the ID and instrument values for each control in the order you select in this dialog box. State Recall is an advanced feature and should be implemented by programmers familiar with the instrument driver language. (More information on this in a later section of this chapter.)

- The **Create XY Display Dialog Box** provides a way to display a waveform or a spectrum. Instruments that analyze inputs such as oscilloscopes, sprectrum analyzers, and network analyzers use such displays. The default entries let you create a simple display for an oscilloscope or a spectrum analyzer. Note that creating an XY display is complicated even when using DWT. Only programmers familiar with the instrument driver language should do this. (The ID language is discussed in a later section of this chapter.)

The figure below contains an ID panel illustrating some of the DWT controls.

Writing Instrument Drivers

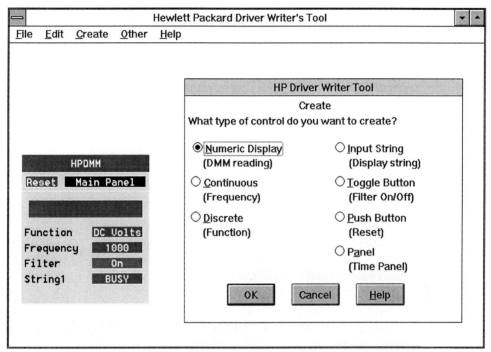

Fig. 12-2. An ID Panel Showing Some of DWT's Controls

Lab 12 - 1: Creating a Simple Customized Driver

This exercise will give you some practice using the Driver Writer's Tool. Suppose you would like to create a customized driver for the HP3314A Function Generator. A driver for this instrument is supported by HP VEE, so you can compare your results to a standard HP driver when you're done. If you don't have the instrument, you can do this exercise anyway. You just won't be able to verify communication with the instrument.

Let's say that your application only requires the following functions:

    Reset
    Function
    Frequency

12 - 9

CUTTING YOUR TEST DEVELOPMENT TIME WITH HP VEE

        Amplitude
        Offset
        Symmetry
        Number
        Mode

You'll use the DWT to create an ID that implements these functions.

1. In MS Windows, click the **Driver Writer Tool** icon.

   Note: On UNIX *platforms, enter* ***dwt*** *at a prompt.*

2. DWT begins in **Learning Mode**. In the **Instrument** dialog box, double-click the **Model Number of the Instrument** field to highlight the default entry, and type **FG3314A**. Click and drag the **Name of the Instrument** field to highlight the default entry, and type **Function Generator**. Click **OK**.

   Notice that the name on the title bar of the ID on the left side changes to FG3314A.

3. You now see the **Reset String Command** dialog box on the right with the **Send Device Clear?** button selected. From the instrument documentation, you find out that the **Device Clear** message will configure the HP3314A to its initialized state, so you leave the button pushed down. You don't need any additional string to reset your instrument, so delete the default entry ***RST** in the **Enter string to Reset Instrument** field. Click **OK**.

   The ID doesn't change, since a Reset button is already on the default ID panel. However, now it will simply send the Device Clear message over the HP-IB bus, instead of adding the *RST command as well.

4. Next you see a **Numeric Display** dialog box asking if you want to create a **Numeric Display**. You don't need one, so you click the **No, do not create Display** button, then click **OK**.

Writing Instrument Drivers

5. You now see a **Function Selector** dialog box. Leave the default: **Yes, create Function Selector**, and click **OK**. You will then see something like the figure below.

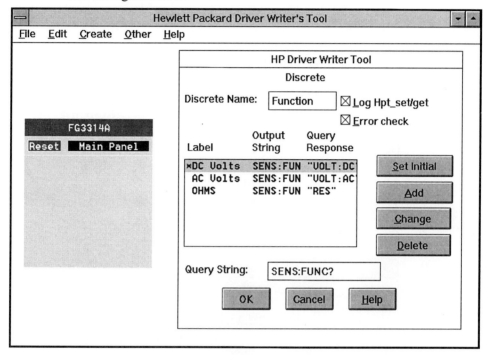

Fig. 12-3. DWT with the Discrete Dialog Box

You now edit the **Discrete** dialog box to match the various function choices of the HP 3314A.

Leave the default name **Function** in the **Discrete Name** input field, because the HP 3314A instrument documentation uses that term. From the **HP-IB Programming Summary** in the back of the **HP3314A Operating Manual** you find that the format for the output string and the query response string is: **FUd**, where **d = {0 for AC Off (DC only), 1 for Sine, 2 for Square, 3 for Triangle}**. The query string is **QFU**. The query response strings are simply **FU0, FU1,...** .

CUTTING YOUR TEST DEVELOPMENT TIME WITH HP VEE

The defaults need to be edited. You highlight a line, then click on one of the four buttons to the right: **Set Initial**, **Add**, **Change**, or **Delete**. If appropriate, another dialog box appears. **Set Initial** chooses the default selection for **Function** indicated by an asterisk. The other buttons are self-evident.

Change the input fields to:

Label	Output String	Query Response
DC Only	FU0	FU0
*Sine	FU1	FU1
Square	FU2	FU2
Triangle	FU3	FU3

Query String: QFU

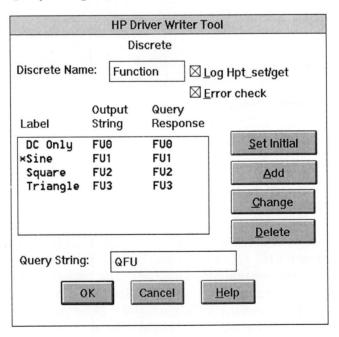

Fig. 12-4. The Edited Discrete Dialog Box in the DWT

Writing Instrument Drivers

Click **OK** when you're done, and compare it to Figure 12-4.

6. Select **Create more Controls/Panels**, then click **OK** from the **Create Controls/Panels** dialog box.

7. Click **Continuous (Frequency)**, then **OK**, since you want to add a continuous range control next called **Frequency**.

   Edit the **Continuous** dialog box to look like the figure below. The values come from the **Function Generator Operating Manual (HP3314A)**.

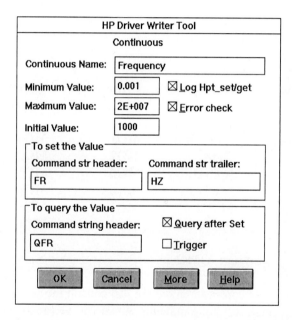

Fig. 12-5. The Edited Continuous Dialog Box

7. Add the following continuous controls using the information provided:

Name	Min	Max	Init.	Hdr	Trail.	Query
Amplitude	0	10	.001	AP	VO	QAP
Offset	-5	5	0	OF	VO	QOF
Symmetry	5	95	50	SY	PC	QSY
Number	1	1999	1	NM	EN	QNM

8. Add the following **Discrete** control, **Mode**, using the information provided:

Name	Label	Output String	Query Response
Mode	*Free Run	MO1	MO1
	Gate	MO2	MO2
	N Cycle	MO3	MO3
	1/2 Cycle	MO4	MO4
	Fin*N	MO5	MO5
	Fin/N	MO6	MO6

Query String: QMO

If you get confused anywhere just consult the online Help system, which explains everything in detail. When you've finished adding the Mode control, tell DWT that you don't want to create any more controls in the **Create more Controls/Panels** dialog box. Your panel on the left of the DWT should look like Figure 12-6.

Writing Instrument Drivers

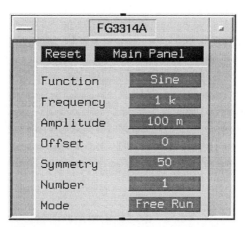

Fig. 12-6. The FG3314A Instrument Driver

9. Click **Done**, then **OK** on the **Status/Couplings** dialog box.

10. Save your ID by following the instructions on the remaining dialog boxes, start HP VEE, configure the ID, then select it and try out the controls. (Consult Chapter 3 if you need a review of configuring.)

    Note: *On PCs the driver is automatically saved in C:\VEE_USER. On UNIX platforms the driver is saved in your home directory. If you want to put it in another directory, just use the whole path when specifying the filename for the driver. When you are configuring your ID in HP VEE, you will have to specify where it's located.*

    Note: *Your driver is saved in an ASCII format designated by the *.ID extension. This file can be ported to other HP VEE platforms; the source code will automatically be compiled on the UNIX platforms. The DWT will also compile the ID for you on the PC, where the file will be designated with a *.CID extension. (Or you can use the HP ID Compiler, which also comes with HP VEE.)*

Compare your driver with the Main Panel of the HP3314A driver provided with HP VEE. This will help you to understand the boundaries of the DWT. More advanced drivers can be written using the ID language, as explained in the next section.

The online tutorial will also give you examples filling out the Status Panel, specifying Couplings, and adding Auto Update. You should go over these before writing your own drivers.

When You Need the Instrument Driver Language

As you can see, the DWT will serve most of your ID development needs, but there are instances when you would want to extend your power using the Instrument Driver Language, such as:

- Implementing advanced DWT features such as state drivers using Learn strings or XY displays.

- To add functionality to an ID such as a control that only appears under certain conditions or using different units of measurement (Hz or kHz, for example).

DWT will give you and *.id file that may be edited using the ID language, so you can implement most functionality with the DWT and then add to it with the ID language. To order the language documentation *HP Instrument Driver Language Reference*, call your local HP Sales Representative and ask for part number E2001-90004.

Chapter 12 Checklist

You should be able to perform the following tasks before proceeding. Review the appropriate topics.

- Explain what an HP VEE instrument driver does.

- Give the distinguishing features of the Driver Writer's Tool.

- Explain the difference between Learning Mode and Expert Mode. How can you switch back and forth between these two modes?

- Create an instrument driver using the instrument documentation and the DWT.

- Describe the circumstances under which you would want to use the Instrument Driver Language.

Using HP VEE Features Unique To MS Windows

13

Average Time To Complete: 2 hrs.

Overview

In general, HP VEE programs will port between the supported platforms, but there are some features that are unique to particular operating systems that you need to understand. For example, when using compiled functions on the UNIX platforms, HP VEE uses shared libraries; however, on the PC platform HP VEE uses Dynamic Link Libraries, since shared libraries are only implemented in the UNIX operating systems. On a PC running MS Windows, Dynamic Link Libraries provide similar functionality to the shared libraries in UNIX. We will describe the key differences between HP VEE on different operating systems in this chapter, and show you how to use the features that are unique to HP VEE for Windows.

In this chapter you'll learn about:

- The differences between HP VEE for Windows and HP VEE on UNIX platforms

- Using Dynamic Data Exchange (DDE)

- Using Dynamic Link Libraries (DLLs)

Differences Between HP VEE for Windows (Version B.02.00) and HP VEE on UNIX Platforms

Note: The HP-UX and SunOS versions of HP VEE (versions B.00.01 and B.01.00 respectively) will be synchronized with the B.02.00 version in late 1994. The differences between these versions are very slight, and do not affect portability issues. The differences noted below will be true regardless of the HP VEE version you have.)

Programs

In general, HP VEE programs will port between the UNIX platforms and HP VEE for Windows with the following exceptions:

- **Named Pipes**

    The To/From Named Pipe (Unix) object in the I/O menu won't operate using HP VEE for Windows, since named pipes don't exist in MS Windows. Instead, you use Dynamic Data Exchange (DDE) with the To/From DDE (PC) object, which we'll discuss in the next section of this chapter.

- **HP BASIC/UX**

    Since HP BASIC/UX isn't available on a PC, the Initialize HP BASIC/UX (Unix) and To/From HP BASIC/UX (Unix) objects don't operate on the PC version of HP VEE. (Nor do they exist on the SunOS.)

- **The Execute Program (Unix) Object**

    The UNIX version of Execute Program is replaced with the Execute Program (PC) object. HP VEE loads a program using the Execute Program (Unix) object, but gives you an error message explaining the incompatibility, if you try to run it on a PC.

- **Remote Functions**

    When you are configuring the Import Library object, Remote Function (HP-UX only) is not available, since Remote Procedure Calls (RPCs) used to implement Remote Functions aren't available on a PC platform.

- **To/From Stdin, Stdout, Stderr**

    Although these objects do work on a PC, they are implemented with files and are not recommended for general programming. You should only use them when porting an HP VEE program from a UNIX platform to the PC.

    Note: *You can create programs that will port easily by using either the whichOs( ) object or the whichPlatform( ) object in the Math => String menu. The first will identify the operating system; the second identifies the platform. The program can then choose a path appropriate for the operating system running the program. These objects will only be available on the PC version B.02.00 until late 1994.*

Bitmap Formats Supported

	PC	Workstations
Gif		X
X11 Icon	X	X
xwd		X
MS Windows Bitmap (*.BMP)	X	

There are many commercial applications available that will translate one format into another such as *Image Alchemy* (available for PCs) from:

Handmade Software, Inc.
15951 Los Gatos Blvd., Suite 17
Los Gatos, CA 95032
+1 408 358-1292
+1 408 356-4143 fax
+1 408 356-3297 BBS

Internet: hsi@netcom.COM
CompuServe: 71330,3136

With the bitmap formats supported and an application like the one above, you should be able to get whatever format you need. Using HP VEE for Windows, you can also press Print Screen, which puts the screen image on the Clipboard. Then you can move the image into Paintbrush (in the Accessories Group) using the Paste command. After editing the image to your taste, you can then save it in *.bmp or *.pcx format.

Fonts and Screen Resolutions

HP VEE for Windows chooses a font size that looks good with your screen resolution. (You can override this choice by editing the V.INI file.) If you create a program on a low resolution screen, and then port to a high resolution screen, text may be clipped, since HP VEE autoscales the boxes to fit around the text. When porting programs, make sure the screen resolutions are similar to avoid problems.

Data Files

ASCII data files constructed with the **To File** object should be readable with the **From File** object on either the workstation or the PC platform. No binary files will work across platforms, since the byte ordering is reversed between workstations and PCs.

Memory Usage

You can configure an HP-UX system to handle processes larger than 16 MB for your large HP VEE programs. However, MS Windows only allows up to 16 MB for each process. Therefore, there may be some HP VEE programs that will not run on HP VEE for Windows due to this memory allocation limitation. You can try rewriting any UserObjects as User Functions to reduce the memory usage, but after that you are limited by your PC. In practice, smartdrive software and networking might subtract 3 MB each from the 16 MB leaving you with about 10 MB of memory for your HP VEE program.

> **Note:** *You can only run one copy of HP VEE at a time in MS Windows.*

Using Dynamic Data Exchange (DDE)

DDE is a message-based protocol for exchanging information between Windows applications. A DDE conversation takes place between a DDE client and a DDE server. The DDE client is the program that makes the request for a connection in a conversational mode with a DDE server. Once this link is established, the client can then request data and services from the server application. An MS Windows application supporting DDE may act as a client, a server, or both. HP VEE only supports DDE as a client application. You implement DDE with the To/From DDE (PC) object in the I/O menu. It offers similar functionality to the To/From Named Pipe (Unix) object on UNIX platforms. The DDE objects operate by sending transactions in much the same way a To/From File object works.

The most common terms associated with DDE are Application, Topic, and Item. When a client such as HP VEE wants to have a conversation with a DDE server, it must do so through an identification process using a server name, a topic name, and an item name. These three values get defined as strings in a DDE conversation.

The application name identifies a server in a DDE conversation. In most cases, the name of the application's .exe file is also the DDE server name. The topic name is a string that identifies a category of data. For example, if the server is a spreadsheet, a topic would be the name of a spreadsheet file. In general, most applications also support a topic by the name of "System". This topic is typically used to get more information on the application's available items. The item name usually refers to the data transmitted in the DDE conversation.

The client application starts a conversation by posting a message that includes the server's name (the application's name, such as a name of a spreadsheet program) and a name of a topic of its interest. If the server acknowledges this request positively, a link is established between the two. The client can then request data from the server. The server provides the data, if it has access to the data requested; otherwise, it replies negatively. The client can also "poke" (write) data items to the server. The conversation stops when the client and the server send termination messages to each other.

Using HP VEE Features Unique to MS Windows

The HP VEE for Windows DDE Object uses four types of transactions:

- **READ (REQUEST)** will read data from a DDE transfer.

- **WRITE (POKE)** will write (poke) data to a DDE transfer.

- **EXECUTE COMMAND:** "*<some command>*" sends the command to the DDE server and executes the command.

- **WAIT** waits for a specified amount of time.

    Note: Experienced DDE users will notice the absence of DDEInitiate and DDETerminate commands in HP VEE for Windows implementation of the DDE object. You don't need to use them, because HP VEE automatically performs the DDEInitiate and DDETerminate statements before and after any transaction statements.

Lab 13 - 1: Building a Simple DDE Object

In the following exercise, you build a DDE object that communicates with the MS Windows Program Manager to create and delete a workgroup, workgroup item, and icon.

1. Select **I/O => To/From DDE (PC)** and place it in the left work area.

2. Change the **Application** input field to **progman**; change the **Topic** input field to **progman**.

    The application name progman identifies the MS Windows Program Manager application. Progman is the topic name too.

Now that you've identified the application and topic, you want to send a command to the Program Manager to create a Work Group.

13 - 7

3. Click the transaction bar to get the **I/O Transaction** dialog box. Click **READ (REQUEST)** to get the menu of DDE actions, highlight **EXECUTE**, then click on **OK**.

4. In the **I/O Transaction** dialog box, double-click the **COMMAND** input field to highlight the default quotation marks, type the command **"[CreateGroup(DDE Test)]"**, then click on **OK**. (You can also click in the COMMAND input field to get a cursor, then type between the quotation marks.)

   CreateGroup is the Program Manager command that creates a program group, and DDE Test is the title of that group.

   Your To/From DDE object should look like the figure below.

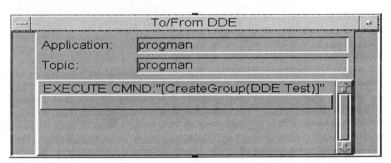

Fig. 13-1. The DDE Object With the First Transaction

Now that you've created a group with the Program Manager, let's add an item to that group.

5. Double-click just below the first transaction bar to get another **I/O Transaction** dialog box and configure it to execute the command:

   "[AddItem(C:\\WINDOWS\\NOTEPAD.EXE, Note Pad)]"

   (The double backslash is an escape character in HP VEE indicating a single backslash in the text. Refer to Chapter 6: Generating Reports Easily for a complete list of escape characters.)

Using HP VEE Features Unique to MS Windows

AddItem is the Program Manager command, and C:\\WINDOWS\\NOTEPAD.EXE is the program that will be assigned to the new icon. Note Pad is the title that will appear under the icon. The icon bitmap is embedded in the NOTEPAD.EXE file.

The second transaction bar should now read:

EXECUTE CMND: "[AddItem(C:\\WINDOWS\\NOTEPAD.EXE, Note Pad)]"

6. Configure the next transaction bar to read:

WAIT INTERVAL: 5

7. Configure the fourth transaction to read:

EXECUTE CMND: "[DeleteGroup(DDE Test)]"

Your DDE object should now look like the figure below.

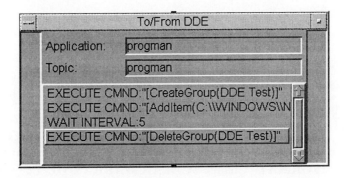

Fig. 13-2. DDE Object With 4 Transactions Configured

Now you can test your DDE object.

13 - 9

CUTTING YOUR TEST DEVELOPMENT TIME WITH HP VEE

8. Run your HP VEE program. Your DDE object should produce something similar to the figure below. (You'll need to have your Program Manager window open to see the DDE Test window appear.)

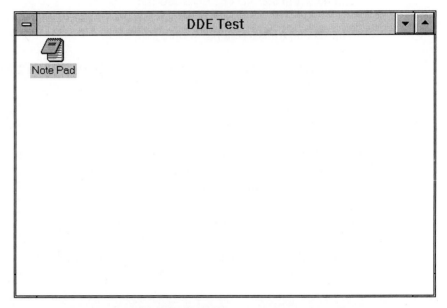

Fig. 13-3. Your DDE Object Creating a Workgroup

Now let's read data from the Program Manager.

9. Add another transaction to your DDE object. In the **I/O Transaction** dialog box, leave **READ (REQUEST)**. Change the **ITEM** input field to **"progman"**. Leave the **TEXT** input field at **X**. Leave **STRING FORMAT**. Change **SCALAR** to **ARRAY 1D**. Leave the default array size at **10**. Click **OK**.

X is the name of the data output pin, which will hold the contents of the data you read from the Program Manager. So you now have to add this pin to the DDE object.

10. Add a data output pin to the DDE object. The default will be labeled **X**.

13 - 10

Using HP VEE Features Unique to MS Windows

11. Select a **Logging AlphaNumeric** display and connect it to the **To/From DDE** object output pin **X**.

12. Run your program. It should look similar to the one below. (You will have to put your HP VEE window on top of the Program Manager window after your program runs to see the results shown below.)

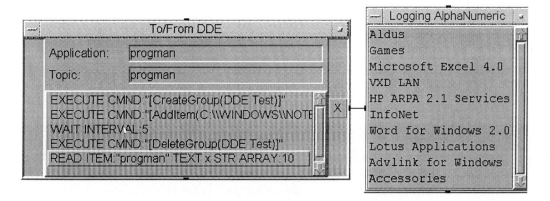

Fig. 13-4. The DDE Program

The workgroup named DDE Test with the Note Pad icon in Figure 13-3 has already been created and deleted in Figure 13-4 above. The text in the display will vary depending on the workgroups your Program Manager is displaying.

Note: *There is an excellent DDE program example in C:\VEE\EXAMPLES\ESCAPES\DDEPROGMN.VEE that demonstrates the use of the To/From DDE object to query the MS Windows Program Manager groups. If you study this example, it will increase your ability to utilize DDE.*

Using Dynamic Link Libraries (DLLs)

Complete documentation for writing DLLs is contained in the Microsoft Windows Software Developer's Kit. The following is meant to be a primer in writing DLLs for HP VEE with a simple example in the lab exercise.

Conventional C programs contain statements in one source program that call functions in other source programs or libraries of compiled programs. A linker connects external calls from compiled objects to entry points in other compiled objects or library routines. In a traditional "static" environment, linking a compiled object to a library routine results in compiled code from the library being added to the execution module by the linker.

The Microsoft Windows Software Development Kit (SDK), however, introduced a new form of linking that delays the linking of some libraries until run time. This dynamic technique allows these library execution routines to be shared, since the object code is not bound with individual software packages.

By inventing Dynamic Link Libraries (DLLs), the developers of MS Windows created a new form of execution object. The DLL resembles a conventionally linked program, but has additional information providing entry points for the individual functions.

DLLs are supported by a new type of library called an import library (IMPLIB). You use an IMPLIB like a conventional library, except the linker simply adds a reference to an entry point in a DLL, instead of adding compiled code to the executable. The DLL is typically linked when the main program is loaded. However, your program can also load a DLL at run time and call one of its functions.

DLLs are at the core of most MS Windows applications. DLLs have a default extension .DLL. MS Windows itself consists of a set of DLLs using a .EXE extension: USER.EXE, GDI.EXE, and KRNL286.EXE or KRNL386.EXE. In HP VEE for Windows, you can access functions in DLLs using the Call Function object and expression fields.

Note: Only DLL's specifically written for HP VEE will work with the Call Function object and expression fields. This is because HP VEE does not support 8-bit characters, 16-bit integers, or 32-bit reals.

The Development Process Using the DLL

The following process is an overview. We'll discuss each of these steps in more detail after you understand the process overview.

Outside of HP VEE for Windows:

1. Create your DLL.

2. Create your definition file holding the prototypes of the DLL functions.

Inside HP VEE for Windows:

3. Use the **Import Library** object in the **Device => Function** menu to load the DLL.

4. Call a function in the DLL using a **Call Function** object or an expression.

5. **(optional)** Use a **Delete Library** object in the **Device => Function** menu to free up memory while your program is running.

Creating a DLL for HP VEE for Windows

The complete documentation for creating DLLs is in the Microsoft Windows Software Development Kit. The following comments include special considerations for creating a DLL for HP VEE.

Before an HP VEE program is created, the DLL and definition file should be created first. The DLL is created like any other DLL with two exceptions.

First, only a subset of the C data types are allowed (see the definition file section below for a description of supported types). Second, the DLL functions must be declared as _far _cdecl (not _far _pascal) in the source code and with an underscore in the .DEF file (MS Windows definition). For example, if your function looked like this in the .DLL file:

```
long _far _cdecl genericFunc(long a)
{
   return(a * 2);
}
```

Then the .DEF file would contain:

    EXPORTS _genericFunc

Creating the Definition File for HP VEE for Windows

The definition file is a file which contains a list of prototypes of the imported functions. HP VEE uses this file to configure the Call Function objects and to determine how to pass parameters to the DLL function. The format for a prototype is:

    <type> <name>([[<type> <pointer> [<name>]][,<type> <pointer> [<name>]]*])

where --

    <type> := 'long'|'double'|'char*'|'*veedata'
    <name> := a blank delimited string
    <pointer> := '*'|''

and --

    long = 4 byte signed long integer
    double = 8 byte double precision floating point number
    char* = far pointer to a null terminated string

veedata = pointer to a struct that contains information about the HP VEE container

The veedata data type completely defines the state of an HP VEE container (the number of dimensions, the size, the shape, the type, and so forth). This makes it easy to pass an HP VEE data container directly to a DLL function and for the function to pass data back in an HP VEE format as a return value.

Examples of DLL Function Prototypes:

long aFunc(double *, long param2, long *param3, char *)
    This function passes in 4 parameters and returns a long.

double aFunc( )
    This function has no input parameters and returns a double.

long aFunc(char *aString)
    This function passes in a string and returns a long.

char* a StrFunc(char **aString)
    This function passes in an array of strings and returns a string.

Importing a DLL

Once your DLL and definition file are written, you import the DLL in a way that's similar to importing a shared library in UNIX.

1. Select **Device => Function => Import Library**.

2. Change the **Library Type** input field to **Compiled Function**.

    The **Import Library** object automatically adds a fourth field for the **Definition File**.

3. The **Library Name** field is arbitrary, since HP VEE uses it to keep track of this library in case you want to delete it later. You can use the default name, **myLibrary,** or type in a new name. Change the **File Name** input field to the name of the file that holds the DLL, and the **Definition File** input field to the appropriate definition file name.

   Note: Remember that you can load a library manually during your development phase by selecting Load Lib from the Import Library object menu. This will enable you to see what functions are available by choosing Select Function in the Call Function object menu.

   You can see an example of a configured Import Library object in An Example Using a DLL later in this chapter.

Calling a Function from a DLL

- **Using a Call Function Object**

1. Select **Device => Function => Call**.

2. After you have loaded the DLL library by selecting **Load Lib** in the **Import Library** object menu, choose **Select Function** from the **Call Function** object menu, then choose the desired function from the list box presented.

   HP VEE automatically configures the Call Function object with the function name, and the proper number of input and output pins. Notice that the input pins have default names of A, B, C, ... that map to the first, second, third, ... parameters. The top output pin is the return value from the function. The second, third, ... output pins map to any parameters passed by reference to the function. If you've entered the function name, you can also configure the object by selecting Configure Pinout in the object menu.

- **Calling a Function from an Expression**

You can also call a DLL function from an expression field provided the library has been loaded. When used in this way, you must enclose the parameters in parentheses after the function name, and the function only sends back its return value. Any parameters passed by reference can only be retrieved by using the Call Function object. For example, you might use the following expression in a Formula object:

$$2 * yourFunc(a,b)$$

The *a* and the *b* would refer to two input pins on the Formula object, and the return value of yourFunc would be multiplied by *2* and placed on the output pin.

Deleting the DLL

Use the **Delete Library** object in the **Device => Function** menu to delete a DLL. While developing your program you can also select **Delete Lib** from the object menu. Deleting the library conserves memory.

An Example Using a DLL

In this exercise you will import a DLL and call a function from the DLL. You'll use a DLL that comes with HP VEE for Windows. This HP VEE program is located in C:\VEE\EXAMPLES\ESCAPES\MANUAL49.VEE. (The same program is designed to work on HP-UX, SunOS, or MS Windows NT.) Open this file in HP VEE.

Examine this example closely. It should look like Figure 13-5 on the next page.

CUTTING YOUR TEST DEVELOPMENT TIME WITH HP VEE

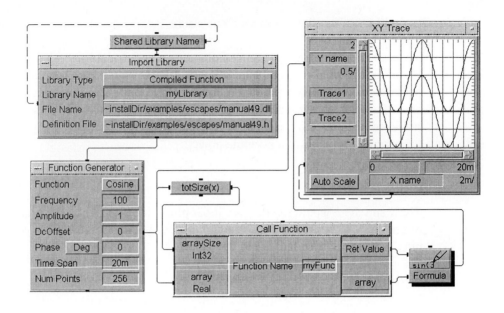

Fig. 13-5. A Program Using a DLL (MANUAL49.VEE)

Specifically, MANUAL49.VEE calls a compiled function called myFunc. MyFunc requires a C datatype called *long*, which is the same as an HP VEE Real. This number specifies the size of an array and a pointer to an array of reals. The definition file is located in MANUAL49.H, and the source file for the C code is located in MANUAL49.C. MyFunc adds 1 to every element of the array.

Before the first call to the compiled function, the DLL must be loaded using the Import Library object (in the Device => Function submenu). The Function Generator is used to create a waveform, which is output to the array input pin on the Call Function object. The totSize object (in the AdvMath => Array submenu) is used to determine the size of the waveform, which is output to the arraySize input pin on Call Function. The XY Trace object displays both the original and the new waveforms.

> *Note:* The Call Function output pin labeled Ret Value holds the size of the returned array, so the expression B[0:A-1] in the Formula object will send the entire array to the display object.

13 - 18

Run the program and notice that the second trace is one greater than the first trace at all points on the waveform.

Another key point to notice in the program is the method used for making it portable to all HP VEE platforms. The UNIX platforms use shared libraries compiled on either HP-UX or SunOS indicated by the filename extensions *.sl or *.so respectively. The MS Windows DLL uses a Microsoft C 16-bit compiler; whereas, the MS Windows NT uses a Microsoft C 32-bit compiler. These DLLs are both indicated using a *.dll extension.

The UserObject called Shared Library Name identifies which operating system you're using, then transmits the correct library name to the Import Library object, as shown below.

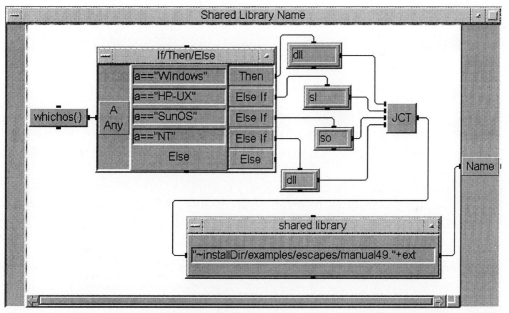

Fig. 13-6. The Shared Library Name UserObject

The whichos( ) function has been used in a renamed Formula object to identify the operating system. An expanded If/Then/Else object examines the output of the whichos( ) function, then triggers the appropriate text constant. This filename extension is then added to the MANUAL49 file using a renamed Formula object. (The input terminal on the Formula object labeled *shared library* has also been changed to *ext*.)

A control pin for a File Name has been added to the Import Library object; hence, you see a dotted line between the UserObject and the Import Library object.

> **Reminder:** *The whichos( ) function is only available on HP VEE for Windows at the release of this book in Jan. 1994. Whichos( ) will also be available on the UNIX versions of HP VEE in late 1994.*

Chapter 13 Checklist

You should now be able to perform the following tasks:

- Explain the key differences between HP VEE for Windows and HP VEE on the UNIX platforms.

- Explain what DDE means and where you would use it.

- Explain the differences between a DDE client and DDE server using HP VEE as an example.

- Use the To/From DDE object to send commands to a DDE server application, wait for a specified interval, and read data from the server application.

- Explain the basic concepts of a DLL.

- Explain the key points in creating a DLL for HP VEE.

- Import a DLL, call a function within it, then delete the DLL.

Using HP VEE Features Unique to HP-UX

14

Average Time To Complete: 2 hrs.

Overview

When you use HP VEE on an HP-UX platform, there are certain unique features that you might want to use: integrating HP BASIC/UX programs with your HP VEE programs and utilizing the remote test capabilities in HP VEE.

This chapter first explains the process of initiating an HP BASIC/UX program from HP VEE. Then you'll do an exercise that utilizes what you've learned.

The last section will explain the benefits of remote testing and show how easily you can set up a remote test station with HP VEE.

In this chapter you'll learn about:

- Communicating between HP VEE and HP BASIC/UX programs

- Using remote test capabilities

Communicating with HP BASIC/UX Programs

The Initialize HP BASIC/UX and To/From HP BASIC/UX objects are used to communicate with your HP BASIC programs, and are only supported on the HP 9000, Series 300/400 computers.

Using the Initialize HP BASIC/UX Object

The Init HP BASIC/UX object, as shown in the figure below, has a single field, in which you specify the HP BASIC program you'd like to run.

Fig. 14-1. The Init HP BASIC/UX Object

Enter the entire path, filename, and any options for the program you'd like to run. Here we've used /usr/lib/veetest/examples/rmb/man34a.bas as an example. The program may have been stored or saved in HP BASIC. The object will spawn the HP BASIC/UX process and run the program. You can also use relative paths from the present working directory to specify the program, if you desire. This object doesn't provide any data path to or from HP BASIC/UX; use the To/From HP BASIC/UX object for that purpose. You can use more than one Init HP BASIC/UX objects in an HP VEE program.

Note that there is no direct way to terminate an HP BASIC/UX process from an HP VEE program. Instead, you should use a QUIT statement in your HP BASIC program when it receives a certain data value from your HP VEE program. You could also use an Execute Program object to kill the HP BASIC process using a shell command, such as *rmbkill*. When you exit HP VEE, any HP BASIC/UX processes still attached are terminated automatically.

Using Unique HP-UX Features

Using the To/From HP BASIC/UX Object

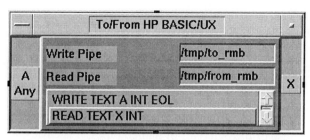

Fig. 14-2. The To/From BASIC/UX Object

The To/From HP BASIC/UX object that you see in the figure above located in the I/O => HP BASIC/UX menu facilitates data transfer to and from HP BASIC programs. This object creates and uses named pipes for interprocess communication. For simplicity HP VEE implements one pipe for READ transactions and another pipe for WRITE transactions. We have included two transactions writing and reading an integer as an example. You can use the default pipes or create your own by typing in new paths and filenames for Write Pipe and Read Pipe. Transactions are configured the same way as other transaction objects you've used in HP VEE. Note that the Write Pipe and Read Pipe fields can be added to the object as control inputs.

All To/From HP BASIC/UX objects contain the same default names for read and write pipes. Therefore, be sure that you know which pipe you really want to read or write. Make sure that pipes to different programs have unique names. In your HP BASIC program make sure you address OUTPUT and ENTER statements to the correct pipe. Refer to the example in the next section and the lab exercise to see how you can do this in HP BASIC.

If the pipes do not exist before To/From HP BASIC/UX operates, then they are created. However, there are some overhead costs; if the pipes exist beforehand, the program runs more quickly. These pipes are created for you automatically if they do not already exist:
   /tmp/to_rmb
   /tmp/from_rmb

14 - 3

To create additional pipes, use the operating system command *mknod*.

HP BASIC/UX pipes (which are simply named pipes) are opened when the first READ or WRITE transaction to that pipe operates after PreRun. All named pipes are closed at PostRun. (See HP VEE documentation for a detailed description of PreRun and PostRun.) The EXECUTE CLOSE READ PIPE and EXECUTE CLOSE WRITE PIPE transactions allow the named pipes to be closed at any time.

Because of the behavior of named pipes, it is easiest to structure your transactions to transmit known or easily parsed data blocks. For example, if you are transmitting strings, determine the maximum length block you wish to transmit and pad shorter strings with blanks. This avoids the problems of trying to read more data from a pipe than is available and of leaving unwanted data in a pipe.

To help prevent a READ transaction from hanging until data is available, use a READ IOSTATUS DATA READY transaction in a separate TO/FROM HP BASIC/UX object. This transaction returns a 1 if there is at least one byte to read, and a 0 if there are no bytes to read.

To read all the data available on the read pipe until the read pipe is closed, use a READ ... ARRAY 1D TO END: (*) transaction.

If you're running diskless, be certain you WRITE and READ to or from uniquely named pipes. Otherwise, several workstations on the same diskless cluster may attempt to read/write from/to the same named pipe, which will cause contention problems.

A Simple Example Using To/From HP BASIC/UX

The following HP BASIC program is the target of the To/From HP BASIC/UX object in Fig. 14-2. It simply receives an integer from the HP VEE program, increments it by one, and returns the new number to HP VEE.

```
10          INTEGER Number
20          ASSIGN @From_vee TO "/tmp/to_rmb"
30          ASSIGN@To_vee TO "/tmp/from_rmb"
40          !
50          ENTER @From_vee;Number
60          OUTPUT @To_vee;Number+1
70          QUIT
80          END
```

Note how the code keeps the pipes straight by assigning clear functional names.

Lab 14-1: Communicating with HP BASIC, Case #1

You'll create an HP VEE program that communicates with the HP BASIC program above. The user selects an integer, then clicks the Start object. The HP BASIC program is initiated; it receives an integer from HP VEE, increments it by one, and sends the result back. HP VEE displays this result. The program will be timed, so that you can compare performance with a similar program in Lab 14-2.

Reminder: *You must have HP BASIC/UX installed to run this program.*

1. Select **Flow => Start** and place it in the upper-left work area.

2. Select **I/O => HP BASIC/UX => Initialize HP BASIC/UX**, place it below the **Start** object, and connect their sequence pins.

   Enter the HP BASIC program you want to initiate:
   /usr/lib/veetest/examples/rmb/man34a.bas
   (This file contains the HP BASIC program above.)

3. Select **I/O => HP BASIC/UX => To/From HP BASIC/UX**, place it below **Init HP BASIC/UX**, and connect their sequence pins.

CUTTING YOUR TEST DEVELOPMENT TIME WITH HP VEE

You can use the default pipes. Add a data input and a data output pin.

Configure two transactions to pass the integer value to the HP BASIC program and read a new one back:

> **WRITE TEXT a INT EOL**
> **READ TEXT x INT**

4. Select **Data => Integer Slider**, place it to the left of the **To/From HP BASIC/UX** object, and connect their data pins. Change the title of **Integer Slider** to **Int Slider**. Size the object to your taste.

5. Select **Display => Logging AlphaNumeric**, place it to the right of the work area, and attach it to the data output of the **To/From HP BASIC/UX** object.

6. Select **Device => Timer**, place it to the right of the **Init HP BASIC/UX** object.

   Attach the **Timer** upper data input pin to the **Start** sequence out pin. Connect the **To/From HP BASIC/UX** sequence output pin to the lower data input pin on the **Timer**.

7. Select a number using the **Int Slider** and run your program. It should look like Figure 14-3. Save your program as **rmb1.vee**.

Using Unique HP-UX Features

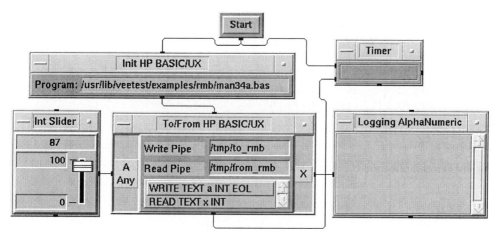

Fig. 14-3. Communicating with HP BASIC, Case #1

Notice how long it takes to initiate the HP BASIC/UX process. If you can, design your programs to initiate the HP BASIC program just once to save on overhead, and then you can communicate with it by using the To/From HP BASIC/UX object one or more times, as the following lab exercise does.

Lab 14-2: Communicating with HP BASIC, Case #2

This program is very similar to the last lab. This program illustrates how to use HP BASIC/UX by running a program that executes and remains active.

Reminder: *You must have HP BASIC/UX installed to run this program.*

The HP BASIC/UX program reads a number and determines its sign. If the number is positive, the program adds 1 to the number, returns the incremented value, and remains active. If the number is negative, the program returns -1 and terminates using the QUIT command. The HP BASIC/UX program listing follows:

```
10         INTEGER Number
20         ASSIGN @From_vee TO "/tmp/to_rmb2"
```

14 - 7

CUTTING YOUR TEST DEVELOPMENT TIME WITH HP VEE

```
30        ASSIGN @To_vee TO "/tmp/from_rmb2"
40        !
50        LOOP
60          ENTER @From_vee;Number
70          IF Number >0 THEN
80            OUTPUT @To_vee;Number+1
90          ELSE
100           OUTPUT @To_vee;-1
110           GOTO Done
120         END IF
130       END LOOP
140       Done: !
150       QUIT
160       END
```

For the HP VEE program, use **rmb1.vee** that you created for Lab 14-1, make the following changes, and save it under a different name.

1. Change the **Program** field in the **Init HP BASIC/UX** object to:

    /usr/lib/veetest/examples/rmb/man34b.bas

    You can examine this file, if you wish, to make sure the code is the same as above.

2. Change the **Write Pipe** field to: **/tmp/to_rmb2**.

    Change the **Read Pipe** field to: **/tmp/from_rmb2**.

3. Run your program several times. It should look like Figure 14-4.

Using Unique HP-UX Features

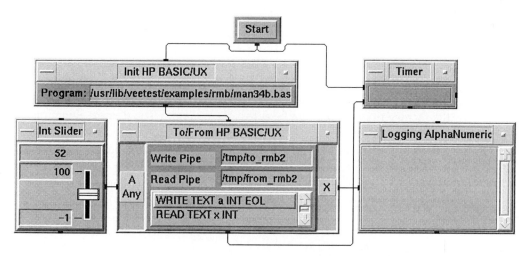

Fig. 14-4. Communicating with HP BASIC, Case #2

Note that the first time you click Start, the program takes a considerable amount of time to run, because it's initiating the HP BASIC/UX process. As you enter new positive numbers, the run time is greatly reduced, because the HP BASIC/UX program is already running.

Both of these lab exercises are included as examples with HP VEE for HP 9000, Series 300/400 workstations in:

/usr/lib/veetest/examples/rmb/manual34.vee

Examine **manual35.vee** in the same directory for more techniques on communicating with HP BASIC programs.

Using Remote Test Capabilities

You have the power to run HP VEE User Functions on remote computers that are networked together. The other HP-UX workstation might be across the factory floor, or it might be across the country. The Remote Functions, as they are called, are like local User Functions except they do not allow any views or user interaction on the remote "host". For example, they could be used to gather test data and send it back to you, but nothing would be displayed on the remote computer screen. You import a library and make function calls just like you would for local User Functions, but you do need to do some system administration work to set up the communication links.

Benefits of Remote Functions

- Allows you to supervise several test stands from a single program on the factory floor in a distributed test environment.

- More efficient use of networked system resources.

- Facilitates the creation of an I/O server.

System Administration Tasks

HP VEE performs a number of tasks automatically when you installed the product, but here are a few things you need to do:

- The two machines must be networked together, so that one can communicate with the other. You must set up an entry on the remote system in either the /etc/hosts.equiv or the $HOME/.rhosts file. The etc/hosts.equiv file can be modified only by a system administrator, while the $HOME/.rhosts can be modified by the user. It is common practice that the /etc/hosts.equiv file have all machines in a particular subnet as

Using Unique HP-UX Features

entries. In other words, the file is the same on all machines. The entry in the /etc/hosts.equiv field on the remote host is simply the local host name, or the entry in the $HOME/.rhosts file is the local host name followed by the user name.

- The user on the local system must have a valid login on the remote system that specifies the same user name.

- The user must have a home directory on the remote system.

Using Remote Functions in Your Program

1. Import the **Remote Functions** using the **Import Library** object in the **Device => Function** menu, as shown in the figure below.

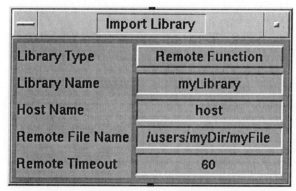

Fig. 14-5. Importing a Remote Function Library

You import Remote Functions just as you would User Functions. Just select Remote Function for the Library Type field and the Import Library object will show five fields, as shown above, for you to fill in. The three new fields are:

- **Host Name**: The name of the remote workstation in symbolic form, such as *remhost*, or the actual IP address of the host -- 12.14.22.93, for example.

- **Remote File Name**: The name of the file that holds the Remote Function library specifying the full path.

- **Remote Timeout**: The timeout period in seconds for communication with HP VEE. If your Remote Function does not return the expected data in this time period, an error occurs.

2. Call a **Remote Function**, either by using the **Call Function** object or by specifying the function in an expression field.

   When the Import Library object is executed (either by selecting Load Lib from the object menu, or during normal program execution), a "service" HP VEE process is started on the remote host specified in the Host Name field. The local HP VEE process is called the "client" process. The client process and the service process are connected over the network, and are able to communicate. When a Call Function object in the client HP VEE calls a Remote Function, the arguments (the data input pins on the Call Function object) are sent over the netework to the remote service, the remote function is executed, and the results are sent back to the Call Function data output pins. If your program deletes the library of Remote Functions with the Delete Library object, the service HP VEE process is terminated and the connection is broken.

3. (optional) Delete the library of Remote Functions using the **Delete Library** object in the **Device => Function** menu.

See the figure below for the entire process of importing a Remote Function library, calling one of its functions, and deleting that library.

Using Unique HP-UX Features

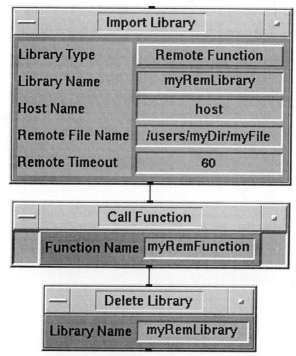

Fig. 14-6. Using Remote Functions

Errors

There are two classes of errors that can occur in a remote HP VEE service:

- **Fatal Errors** mean you cannot use your remote HP VEE service. For example, a timeout occurs. In most cases, something has gone wrong with the network or in calling the remote service, not in the remote service itself. You will get a fatal error message. HP VEE will attempt to terminate the remote service, and you'll need to import the Remote Function library again.

- **Non-Fatal Errors** usually occur in the Remote Function itself (a divide-by-zero error, for example). A normal error message is displayed giving the name of the Remote Function, where the problem occurred.

14 - 13

Chapter 14 Checklist

You should be able to perform the following tasks before proceeding to the next chapter:

- Communicate with an HP BASIC/UX program using the Initialize HP BASIC/UX and To/From HP BASIC/UX objects.

- Optimize the communication with HP BASIC/UX programs by keeping the HP BASIC program active during several data transfers.

- Explain the system administration tasks involved in setting up remote test capabilities.

- Import Remote Function libraries, call Remote Functions, and delete Remote Function libraries.

15

Data Acquisition With PC Plug-in Cards

Average Time To Complete: 2 hrs.

Overview

DT VEE (sold by Data Translation) is a customized version of HP VEE. DT VEE adds a data acquisition menu that enables you to use PC plug-in cards for your measurements. You'll learn how easy it is to set up your data acquisition application using a data acquisition board, familiar Windows dialog boxes, and DT VEE objects. You'll set up both simple and complex applications, and cover in detail the flexibility and power available to you through the data acquisition objects. You'll need to have DT VEE installed, a data acquisition board in your computer (such as a DT2801, DT2821, or DT2831), and a general knowledge of data acquisition concepts to do the labs. (At the release of this book in Jan. 1994, DT VEE did not include HP VEE features used to control HP-IB instruments.)

In this chapter you'll learn about:

- Data acquisition in DT VEE
- Using data acquisition objects
- Advanced topics using DT VEE
- An example application

Data Acquisition Using DT VEE

Data acquisition using DT VEE allows you to use the computer's power to aid in your scientific application. Although the scientific fields where data acquisition is used can vary from biomedical to sound to rotating machinery, the basic need to convert data from sensors to data that the computer can process is the same.

With DT VEE and a data acquisition board, you can run many scientific applications on your PC. The scope of your application in terms of data acquisition revolves around a number of issues: the type of sensors you need to extract data; the signals you need to count; time voltage values for stimulus; or control signals to start, stop, or control digital devices. One example of a data acquisition application is a research environment studying photosynthesis in cells. This application needs to get data characterizing a cell's reaction to light (as monitored by a sensor). The cells are exposed to light several times within a certain time period; this requires start signals from the computer at timed intervals. The analysis of the signal requires filtering out noise, linear curve fitting, display of the signal during the acquisition and after the analysis, and storing the data for later reference.

Since data acquisition is an integral part of your application, it is also an integral part of DT VEE. You've been learning how HP VEE can accomplish the analysis, display and storage of your data. DT VEE provides all the power of HP VEE for Windows plus a data acquisition menu for PC plug-in cards.

Data Acquisition Subsystems

Data acquisition boards are the interface between real world data and your PC. In DT VEE, the data acquisition objects have the capability to work with the four subsystems on a data acquisition board. Subsystems are the functional sections of the board. You can have any of the following capabilities at your disposal in DT VEE: analog to digital inputs (A/D),

Data Acquisition with PC Plug-in Cards

digital to analog outputs (D/A), counter/timers (C/T), and digital input and output (Digital I/O). See the table below.

DATA ACQ. BOARD SUBSYSTEMS	PURPOSE
Analog Input (A/D)	Inputs data from sensors
Analog Output (D/A)	Outputs waveforms for stimulus or control
Digital I/O	Inputs or outputs digital signals (TTL)
Counter Timers (C/T)	Are used for the timing or generation of digital waveforms (TTL)

Table 15-1. Data Acquisition Board Subsystems

Each subsystem is treated separately and has a unique identifier, called a subsystem handle. By passing the subsystem handle, the data acquisition objects in DT VEE know which board and subsystem to access.

The Data Acquisition Menu

In DT VEE, data acquisition is done through the DataAcq menu (Figure 15-1). The first five entries -- A/D Config, D/A Config, C/T Config, Digital In Config, and Digital Out Config -- are the main objects for doing data acquisition. Each of these five objects controls the subsystem indicated by its name. The Data objects control the data flow between DT VEE and a subsystem. The Control objects are used to start or stop a subsystem and to monitor its status. The Get Config and Set Config objects allow you to get or set subsystem parameters individually.

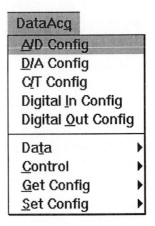

Fig. 15-1. The Data Acquisition Menu

Using the Data Acquisition Objects

The Subsystem Configuration Objects

The subsystem configuration objects (A/D Config, D/A Config, C/T Config, Digital In Config, and Digital Out Config) set up and initialize the entire subsystem. They can be used any time a constant configuration is required. To configure a subsystem at runtime, use the Control, Get Config, and Set Config objects.

The subsystem configuration objects are always the first objects used in any data acquisition application. They initialize the subsystem and output the subsystem handle. This handle is used by all other data acquisition objects to identify and communicate with that subsystem.

All of the subsystem configuration objects come up in an open view with a Configure button. The Configure button accesses a dialog box. The A/D Config object dialog box (Figure 15-2) is used for A/D setup. It allows you to specify the channels from which you need to acquire data as well as the rates and gains associated with each channel. Other options let you specify sampling duration, external timing, and files for the incoming data.

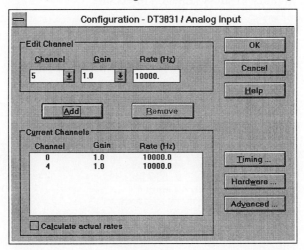

Fig. 15-2. The Analog Input Object Dialog Box

CUTTING YOUR TEST DEVELOPMENT TIME WITH HP VEE

The D/A Config dialog box (Figure 15-3) is used for D/A setup. Options for this object let you specify the channel and rate as well as external timing and information files.

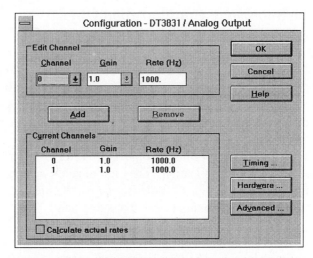

Fig. 15-3. The D/A Config Object Dialog Box

The Digital In Config and Digital Out Config objects (Figure 15-4) configure the digital I/O subsystems on the board.

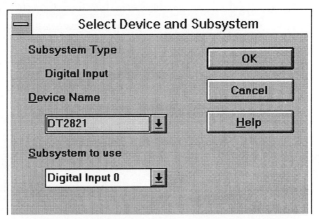

Fig. 15-4. The Digital In Config Dialog Box

Data Acquisition with PC Plug-in Cards

The C/T Config dialog box (Figure 15-5) configures the counter/timer mode, its clock input or source, and the gate type and shape. Functions for the counter/timer include: Count Events, Measure Frequency, One Shot, and Generate Rate. More information on each counter/timer function can be found by selecting Help in the C/T Config object menu.

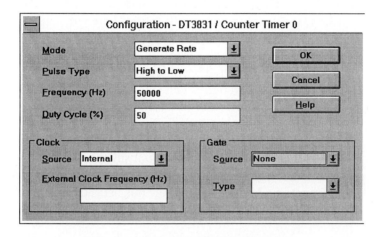

Fig. 15-5. The C/T Config Dialog Box

Lab 15 - 1: Configuring a Subsystem

This lab exercise teaches you the fundamentals of using the subsystem configuration object dialog boxes. You'll learn how to select a channel and choose the gain and rate associated with that channel. Although the lab uses the A/D Config object, the skills learned here will apply to all other subsystem configuration objects.

To set up an analog input operation using the A/D Config object, you'll select channels 0 through 3 with gains of 1.0, 2.0, 4.0, and 8.0 respectively. The acquisition rate will be 1200 Hz for each channel.

The actions above produce a channel list. This list specifies the sampling order of the channels on the data acquisition board along with the corresponding gain and acquisition rate. The A/D Config subsystem configuration object lets you create this list and view it in the Current Channels list box.

> *Note:* *If the data acquisition board you are using does not have gain, the option will be grayed.*

1. Select **DataAcq => A/D Config** and place it on the left side of the work area.

2. Click the **Configure** button.

   > *Note:* *If you have more than one board installed, the Configure button will ask you to specify which board's subsystem you want to set up.*

3. The default channel and gain are **Channel 0** at a **Gain** of **1.0**. Keep the default settings. In the **Rate** box, type **1200**.

4. Click **Add**. Notice the channel, gain, and rate in the **Current Channels** list box. This box shows you your channel list as you build it.

5. In the **Channel** box, channel 1 should already be listed because the channel number is incremented automatically. In the **Gain** box, type or select a gain of **2**. Keep **1200** for the **Rate** box setting. Click **Add**.

Data Acquisition with PC Plug-in Cards

Repeat step 5 to configure channels **2** and **3** with the gain of **4.0** and **8.0** respectively and a rate of **1200** for each channel. The **Current Channel** list box should look like that shown in Figure 15-6.

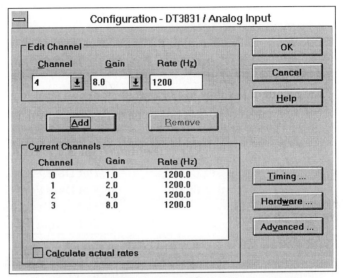

Fig. 15-6. The Current Channels List Box

6. Click the check box next to **Calculate actual rates**.

   This option determines if the subsystem can actually achieve the current acquisition rates you have selected. The Current Channels list box is updated to reflect the actual settings achievable.

7. Click **OK** to close the dialog box.

The Data Objects

The Data objects control flow of data acquisition data to or from DT VEE. See Figure 15-7.

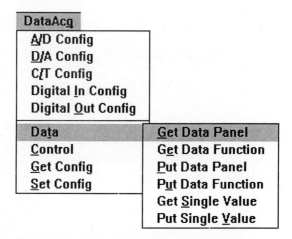

Fig. 15-7. The Data Objects in the DataAcq Menu

Data Acquisition with PC Plug-in Cards

The Get Data Panel and Put Data Panel objects receive or send data, any number of points or samples at a time. The Get Data Function and Put Data Function objects serve the same purpose as their counterparts, but allow the channel number and the number of points to be input pins. See Figure 15-8.

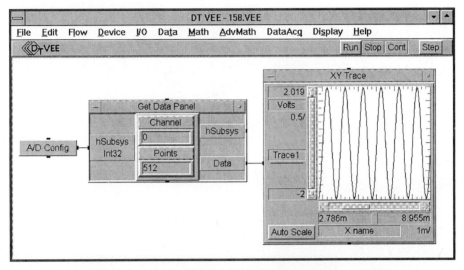

Fig. 15-8. A/D Transfer of 512 Samples into DT VEE

The Get Single Value and Put Single Value objects transfer one point or sample at a time. See Figure 15-9 below. With all data objects, the channel you want to get data from or put data to must be specified.

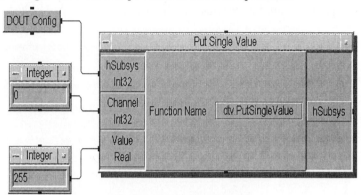

Fig. 15-9. Digital Output

For each channel of data you want to use in DT VEE, use a Data object from the DataAcq menu. See Figure 15-10.

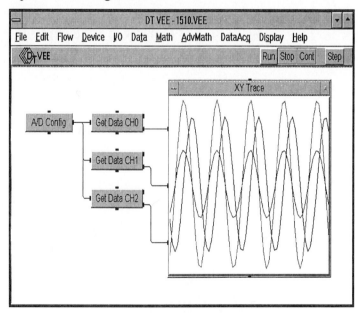

Fig. 15-10. Transferring Data Into DT VEE

To transfer data from multiple analog input channels into DT VEE, configure the A/D Config object for three channels, and then add more data objects. In Figure 15-10 we are transferring three channels to a display object using Get Data Panel.

Connecting Data Objects

Since the subsystem configuration object initializes the subsystem and returns the subsystem handle, any other object that operates on a subsystem (Data, Control, Set Config, and Get Config) has to be connected to the right of the subsystem configuration object. The subsystem configuration object's data output terminal contains the subsystem handle. In Figures 15-8 through 15-10, you can see that all the Data objects are connected to the right of the subsystem object. Figures 15-8 and 15-10 show programs using analog input. The Get Data Panel object receives data from the requested channel.

The analog output program looks similar (see Figure 15-11 later in this chapter). The D/A Config object initializes the subsystem. The data from the Put Data Panel object is used for output. Take a moment to consider the connection from the D/A Config object. Although at first it may seem counter-intuitive, the Put Data Panel object is connected to the right of the D/A Config object because it needs the subsystem handle of an initialized subsystem. Initialization is accomplished by the D/A Config object.

Figure 15-16 (later in this chapter) shows the subsystem/data relationship while describing how to start two subsystems simultaneously. Starting the analog input subsystem happens before the Get Data object executes, because the analog input section starts first and then passes data to DT VEE. For analog output, data must be received before the subsystem can start, so the Put Data object is placed before the Start Acq object.

Lab 15 - 2: Using the D/A Config Object

This exercise teaches you the fundamentals of using subsystem configuration objects with data objects to perform data acquisition. You will use the D/A Config object and the Put Data Panel object to output 2000 voltage values on analog output channels 0 and 1 at a rate of 50 Hz. The sampling relationship between the D/A Config object and the Function Generator object is also explored.

1. Select **DataAcq => D/A Config** and place it to the left on your work area.

2. Click on **Configure**. Keep the current channel and gain entry. In the **rate** box, type **2000**. Click **Add**. In the **channels** box, select or type **1**, keep the **rate box** entry of **2000**. Click **Add** again to enter channel one with the same gain and rate. Click **OK** to close the dialog box. Iconize the **D/A Config** object.

   Note: The D/A Config object dialog box is configured to start automatically when given data using the Put Data Panel object. You can change this using the advanced option. For this lab, use the default setting.

3. Select **DataAcq => Data => Put Data Panel** and place it to the right of the **D/A Config** object. Change the title to Put Data/CH0. Iconize the **Put Data Panel** object and connect its **hSubsys** input to the output of the **D/A Config** object.

4. Clone the **Put Data Panel** object and change the title to **Put Data/Ch1**. Change the **Channel** selection to **1**. Iconize the **Put Data Panel** object and connect its **hSubsys** input to the output of the **D/A Config** object.

5. Select **Device => Virtual Source => Function Generator** and place it below **D/A Config**. Change the title to **Function 0**. Change the **Function** field to **Sine**; the **Frequency** field to **50**, the **Amplitude** to **2.5**, the **DC Offset** to **2.5**, the **Time Span** to **1**, and **Num Points** to **2000**. Connect the output to the **Put Data Panel** object for input to **channel 0**.

Note: *The Num Points field in the Function Generator times 1/time span should match the sampling rate specified in the D/A Config object (2000) to achieve the time span specified (1 second) and the frequency specified (50Hz).*

6. Clone the **Function Generator** and place it below **D/A Config**. Change the title to **Function 1**. Change the **Function** field to **Triangle**, and the **Amplitude** to **1.5**, and the **DC Offset** to **1.5**. Connect the **Function 1** output to the **Put Data Panel** object for **channel 1**.

7. Select **Display => XY Trace** and place it to the right of the **Put Data Panel** objects. Add a data input terminal to the **XY Trace** and connect the data inputs to the outputs of **Function 0** and **Function 1**.

8. Hook up an oscilloscope to the output of **channel 0** and/or **channel 1**, if desired. Run your program. It should look like the one below.

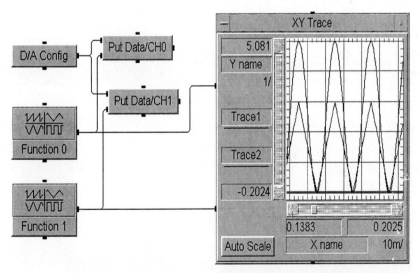

Fig. 15-11. Using Analog Output and Put Data

The output to the oscilloscope from channel 0 should be a sine wave with an amplitude of +5V and a frequency of 50Hz. The output to the oscilloscope from channel 1 should be a triangle wave with an amplitude of +3V and a frequency of 50Hz.

Continuous Analog Input or Output

To do continuous analog input or output over a period of time, you use a Flow object. The Flow object loops on the Data objects to continuously transfer data. Using Get Data Panel and Put Data Panel allows gap-free data transfers to and from A/D and D/A Subsystems. For example, using the Until Break object, we can acquire the specified number of points of data -- or a buffer of data -- repeatedly and gap-free. See the figure below.

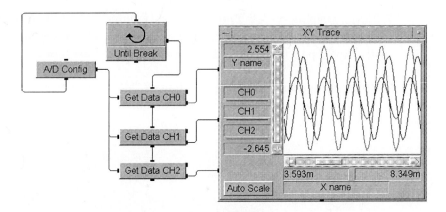

Fig. 15-12. Continuous Analog Input

Data Acquisition with PC Plug-in Cards

Putting an Until Break object in an analog output program allows you to output data values until a toggle is pressed. See Figure 15-13 below.

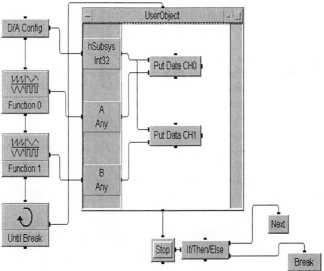

Fig. 15-13. Continuous Analog Output

On Your Own

Use the D/A Config and two Put Data Panel objects to output a sine wave over two channels continuously.

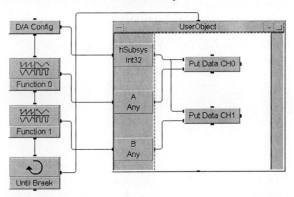

Fig. 15-14. Solution to the On Your Own Exercise

The Control Objects

Control objects allow you to control starting, stopping, closing, and getting the status for a given subsystem. See Figure 15-15 below.

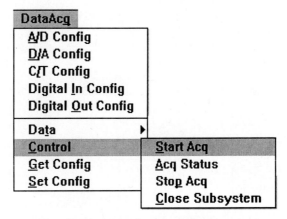

Fig. 15-15. The Control Objects in the DataAcq Menu

Start Acq is used to specify when in the program you want your subsystem configuration object to start. It can also be used after the Stop Acq object to restart a subsystem. Situations where you need to use the Start Acq object include restarting a subsystem because an error occurred in your program, using a Set Config object, and synchronizing the start of two or more subsystems, as shown in Figure 15-16.

Data Acquisition with PC Plug-in Cards

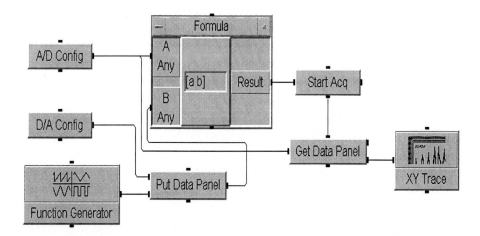

Fig. 15-16. Starting Two Subsystems Together

Note: To pass two subsystem handles to Start Acq, the Formula object takes two inputs and outputs a one-dimensional array with two elements.

The Stop Acq object allows you to stop a subsystem that is in progress. Stop Acq stops the subsystem and flushes any data in progress. Starting acquisition with the Start Acq object after the Stop Acq object starts the subsystem over again.

The AcqStatus object reports the state of a subsystem as well as information about the data. For an A/D subsystem, AcqStatus reports how many samples are waiting to be read by a Get Data Panel or Get Data Function object. For a D/A subsystem, the AcqStatus object reports how many samples can be written by a Put Data Panel or Put Data Function object.

The Close Subsystem object closes a subsystem and releases its subsystem handle. It also frees any system resources being used. To access the subsystem after a Close Subsystem object, you must use one of the subsystem configuration objects to re-initialize it and get a new subsystem handle. When using two data acquisition board subsystems that share system resources such as a DMA channel or interrupt level (consult your hardware manual for more information), you must use the Close Subsystem object to release the resources of one subsystem before initializing a subsystem dependent on the same resources.

Connecting Control Objects

Control objects require the subsystem handle as a data input and have to execute after (to the right) of a subsystem configuration object.

Lab 15 - 3: Stopping After an Error

This section teaches you how to use the Control objects Stop Acq and Close Subsystem. The program will generate an error by attempting to get data from a channel that is not configured. You'll learn how to handle the error at runtime by stopping the acquisition and closing the subsystem.

1. Select **DataAcq => A/D Config** and place it to the left in your work area. Leave the default settings.

2. Select **Device => UserObject** and place it to the right of the **A/D Config** object.

3. Select **DataAcq => Data => Get Data Panel** and put it in the **UserObject**. Edit the channel to **1**. Keep the default number of points.

    Note: Since our A/D Config object is configured for channel 0 only, data from channel 1 will not be available, causing an error.

4. Add three terminals to the **UserObject**: **Data Input**, **Data Output** and **Error Output**.

Data Acquisition with PC Plug-in Cards

Note: An error terminal cannot be added to the Get Data Panel object, so we add one by placing it in a UserObject.

5. Connect **A/D Config** to **Get Data Panel**. Connect the data output of **Get Data Panel** to the data output of the **UserObject**.

6. Select **DataAcq => Control => Stop Acq** and place it below the **UserObject**. Connect the **Stop Acq** sequence input pin to the error output pin of the **UserObject**. Connect the output from the **A/D Config** object to the input of the **Stop Acq** object.

7. Select **DataAcq => Control => Close Subsystem** and place it to the right of **Stop Acq**. Connect the **Stop Acq** output pin to the **Close Subsystem** input pin.

8. Run your program. It should stop without an error dialog box and look like Figure 15-17.

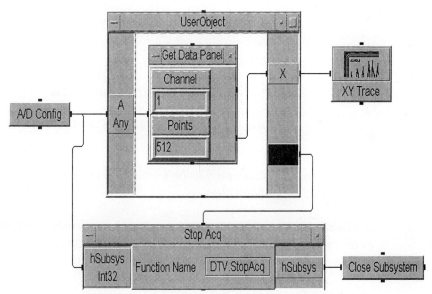

Fig. 15-17. Stopping and Closing a Subsystem

15 - 21

The Get Config and Set Config Objects

The Get Config and Set Config objects allow you to get and set subsystem parameters at run time. See the figure below.

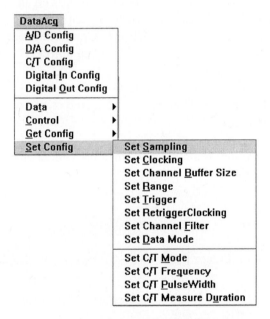

Fig. 15-18. The Set Config Objects

The Set Config objects override the existing value for a parameter set in the subsystem configuration objects.

In Figures 15-19 and 15-20, parameters are changed using Set Config objects as the result of a calculation and input from a user respectively. Get Config objects are used in both programs to pass current parameter settings.

Data Acquisition with PC Plug-in Cards

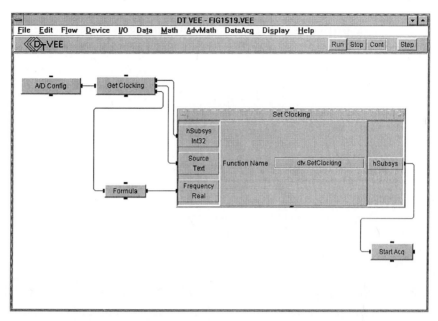

Fig. 15-19. Setting the Clock Rate From a Calculation

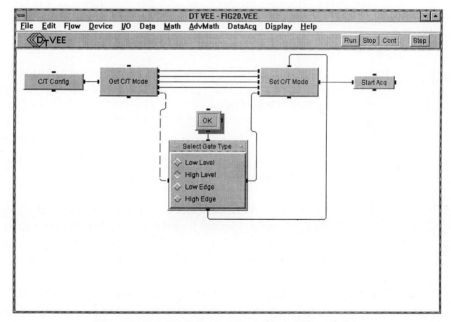

Fig. 15-20. Setting the Gate from User Input

15 - 23

CUTTING YOUR TEST DEVELOPMENT TIME WITH HP VEE

Connecting the Get Config and Set Config Objects

Like the Data and Control objects, the Get Config and Set Config objects require the subsystem handle as a data input. In a program, they have to execute after (to the right) of a subsystem configuration object. Since the Set Config objects change parameters of the subsystem, they should execute before the subsystem has started (Start Acq). Executing a Set Config object when a subsystem is running causes an error.

Lab 15 - 4: Using the Config Objects with the D/A Subsystem

In this section you'll learn how to use Get Config and Set Config objects in a data acquisition program. You will output data on channel 0 of the analog output subsystem, stop the operation, and start it again using channel 1. Use a Set Config object to select the output channel of the analog output subsystem. Because the Set Config object executes after the D/A Config object, the new value set by the Set Config object overrides the other channel setting.

1. Select **DataAcq => D/A Config** and place it to the left in your work area. Click on **Configure**. Use the default setting of **channel 0**. Type **2000** in the rate box. Click **OK**.

2. Select **DataAcq => Data => Put Data Panel** and place it to the right of the **D/A Config** object. Connect the **D/A Config** object to the **Put Data Panel** object's **hSubsys** input.

3. Select **Device => Virtual Source => Function Generator** and place it below **D/A Config**. Set the frequency to **20 Hz**, the time span to **.5 seconds**, and the NumPoints to **1000**. Connect the output of the **Function Generator** to the data input of the **Put Data Panel** object.

4. Select **DataAcq => Control => Stop Acq** and place it to the right of the **Put DataPanel** object. Connect its input pin to the output pin of **Put Data Panel**.

5. Select **DataAcq => Get Config => Get Sampling** and place it to the right of **Stop Acq**. Connect the output of **Stop Acq** to the input of **Get Sampling**.

6. Select **Data => Constant => Integer** and place it below the **Function Generator**. Set the value to one.

7. Select **DataAcq => Set Config => Set Sampling** and place it to the right of the **Integer** object. Connect the output of **Integer** to the **Channel** input pin of **Set Sampling**. Connect the other input pins on **Set Sampling** to the corresponding output pins on **Get Sampling**.

8. Select **DataAcq => Data => Put Data Function** and place it to the right of **Set Sampling**. Connect the output of **Set Sampling** to the **hSubsys** input pin, the output pin of **Integer** to the **Channel** input pin, and the **Function Generator** to the data input pin.

   Note: To see the output of the D/A, connect channels 0 and 1 to an oscilloscope.

9. Run your program. It should look like Figure 15-21.

CUTTING YOUR TEST DEVELOPMENT TIME WITH HP VEE

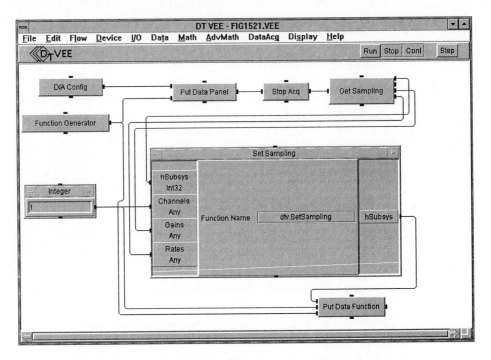

Fig. 15-21. Using Config Objects with a D/A Subsystem

Advanced Topics

Handling Errors

Many of the DataAcq objects are actually secured UserObjects; therefore, you cannot add an error terminal. However, in some cases, you will want to add an error terminal to handle errors at run time. To do this, simply place the DataAcq object inside a UserObject. You can add an error terminal to the UserObject. Because of the rules of propagation, any error produced inside the UserObject will propagate out the error pin. See Figure 15-17 or Lab 15-5 for an example.

External Timing

Many of the subsystems can be externally timed for applications that need to synchronize data acquisition with physical events. The signals needed for external timing are described in the hardware manual for your data acquisition board. External timing for the analog input and analog output subsystems can be an external clock or an external trigger. An external clock is used to time the acquisition or output of each voltage value or point, and a trigger is used to start the acquisition or output. For the Counter Timer subsystem, external signals can be used to provide the source and gate.

Lab 15-5: External Clocks and the A/D Subsystem

In this exercise, you'll learn how to set up an external clock to time the conversions of the analog input subsystem. You will monitor the status of the acquisition to make sure that the external timing is being received. If the external timing is not received, you will stop the program.

CUTTING YOUR TEST DEVELOPMENT TIME WITH HP VEE

Note: An external clock is recommended for this lab. If you do not have an external clock, the program will detect this and terminate with the error message "External Clock Not Working".

1. If you have an external clock source, connect it to the **A/D external clock input** for your board. Consult the hardware manual for your board for connection and external clock requirements.

2. Select **DataAcq =>A/D Config**. Click the **Configure** button. Keep the default channel, gain, and rate. Click the **Timing** button. Select **external clock**. Type in the rate of the external clock. Click **OK**. Click **OK**. Iconize the **A/D Config** object.

3. Select **Device => UserObject** and place it to the right of the **A/D Config** object. Change the title to **Time-out**.

4. Select **DataAcq => Data => Get Data Panel** and put it inside your **UserObject**. Keep the default entries and iconize the **Get DataPanel** object. Connect the **Get Data Panel** object to the **A/D Config** object.

5. Select **Flow => Delay** and place it in the **UserObject**. Set the delay for **5** seconds.

6. Select **Device => UserObject** and place it to the right of **Delay**. Change the title of the **UserObject** to **Message**. Connect the data output of **Delay** to the sequence input of the **UserObject** entitled **Message**.

7. Select **Display => Notepad** and place it in the **UserObject** entitled **Message**. Type in the message: **External Clock Not Working**.

8. Select **Flow => Confirm (OK)** and place it below **Notepad**. Select both objects and add them to the user panel. Open the **Message** object menu and select **Show Panel on Exec**.

9. Select **Flow => Exit UserObject** and place it in the **UserObject** entitled **Time-out** under the **UserObject** entitled **Message**. Connect the sequence output pin of **Message** to the sequence input pin of **Exit UserObject**.

Data Acquisition with PC Plug-in Cards

10. Select **Display => XY Trace** and place it to the right of the **UserObject** entitled **Time-out**. Connect the data output pin of the **Get Data Panel** object to the data input pin of the **XY Trace**.

11. Run your program, it should look like Figure 15-22. Iconize **Time-out** to simplify the program appearance.

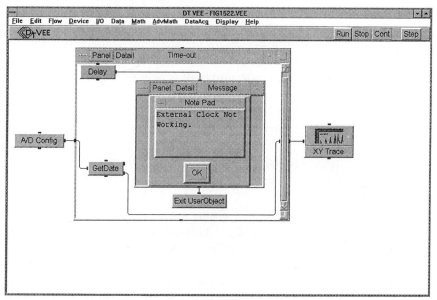

Fig. 15-22. Externally Timed Analog Input

Lab 15-6: Using One Subsystem to Clock Another Subsystem

This section teaches you how to use one subsystem to externally time another. You'll learn how to use the Digital I/O subsystem to provide an external signal for the Counter Timer subsystem.

Counter/timer 1 is configured to generate a rate with external gating. The digital output subsystem 0 is configured to output that gate. An Integer

15 - 29

CUTTING YOUR TEST DEVELOPMENT TIME WITH HP VEE

object will change the digital output state and gate the counter/timer. The appropriate hardware pins must be tied together on the screw terminal panel.

> *Note: Counter/timer and digital I/O subsystems are necessary for this Lab. Not all boards have both subsections. Check your hardware user manual for more information.*

1. Select **DataAcq => C/T Config** and place it to the left of your work area. Click **Configure** for the counter/timer dialog box. Select **counter/timer subsystem 0, generate rate mode, frequency 100 Hz, duty cycle 50**, and **external gate source of type high level**. Click **OK**.

2. Select **DataAcq => Digital Out Config**. Place it below **C/T Config**. Click **Configure** and select **digital output 0**. Click **OK**.

3. Select **DataAcq => Control => Start Acq** and place it to the right of **C/T Config**. Connect the output of **C/T Config** to the input of **Start Acq**.

4. Select **DataAcq => Data => Put Single Value**. Place it to the right of **Digital Out Config**. Change the title to **Put Initial Value**. Connect the **hSubsys** input pin to the output of **Digital Out Config**.

5. Select **Data => Constant => Integer** and place it below **Digital Out Config**. Set the value to **0**. Change the title to **Channel**. Connect its output to the **Put Initial Value** channel input pin

6. Select **Data => Constant => Integer** and place it below Channel. Set the value to 0. Change the title to Initial Value. Connect its output pin to the **value** input pin of the **Put Initial Value** object.

7. Select **DataAcq => Data => Put Single Value**. Place it below **Put Initial Value**. Connect the **hSubsys** output of **Put Initial Value** to the **hSubsys** input pin. Connect the output of **Channel** to the channel input pin.

8. Select **Data => Constant => Integer** and place it to the left of **Put Single Value**. Set the value to **1**. Connect the output of **Integer** to the value input of **Put Single Value**.

Data Acquisition with PC Plug-in Cards

9. Select **Flow => Start**. Place it above **C/T Config**. Connect its sequence output pin to the sequence input pin of **C/T Config**.

10. Connect the **Start Acq** sequence input pin to the sequence output pin of **Put Initial Value**. Connect the **Start Acq** sequence output pin to the sequence input pin of **Put Single Value**.

11. Make the necessary external connections. Tie the **Digital I/O Port 0, bit 0** pin to the **Counter Timer 0 Gate** pin. Connect your oscilloscope to the **Counter Timer 0** ouput to see the waveform.

12. Click **Start**. Your program should look like the one in **Fig. 15-23**. (See Fig. 15-24 for a timing diagram of the signals in this lab.)

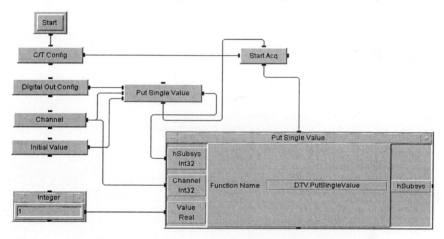

Fig. 15-23. Gating Counter Timer with Digital I/O

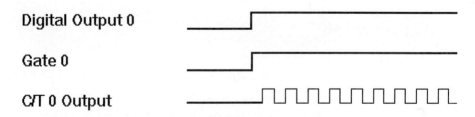

Fig. 15-24. Timing Diagram for Lab 15-6

Direct Disk Access

The A/D Config and D/A Config objects have the ability to communicate directly to disk for optimum performance. Use this option when you have to read and write data at high rates.

The A/D Config object's advanced configuration dialog box has an option called Data Mode. The choices for Data Mode let you indicate how the data gets presented to the Data objects. The data can be gap-free, or the data can have gaps. Gap-free indicates that all data is available, and any data loss will cause an error and stop acquisition. By allowing the data to have gaps, DT VEE can continue to operate, even if it cannot keep up with the incoming data. This mode can be used in applications where it's not critical to process every data sample. When combined with writing data directly to disk, allowing gaps lets you do processing without jeopardizing disk write performance.

> *Note:* Data loss to disk is never acceptable and any gaps will result in an error. The Data Mode option only affects the data available to the Data objects.

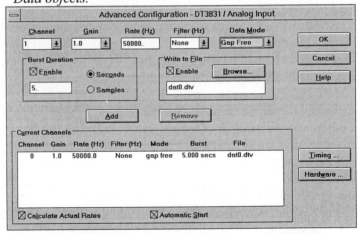

Fig. 15-25. Writing Data Directly to Disk

For the D/A subsystem, the Data Mode choices are the same. Allowing gaps lets DT VEE continue to output old data if new data is not available.

Example Application: Brain Wave Analysis

Application Description

Brain wave analysis looks at information coming from electrodes on a patient's scalp that sense electrical activity in the brain (EEG). In addition, patient vital signs such as blood pressure and heart rate are monitored. In real time, the signals are displayed on the computer monitor. The EEG signals are also saved to disk for further processing.

In this example, 12 channels are being sampled at various rates. Ten of the channels are EEG data with a sampling rate of 10 kHz. Two of the channels measure the heart rate and blood pressure with sampling rates of 1000 Hz and 100 Hz respectively. A push button is used to externally trigger the start of the application. The DT2839 data acquisition board was chosen for this application for its high channel count, high sampling rate, and ability to sample channels at very different rates.

Data Acquisition Profile

- High channel count

- External trigger

- Various sampling rates

- Board used: DT2839

Processing Profile

- Real-time display
    Time domain
    Frequency domain

- EEG data written to disk files

The A/D Config object is set up to sample the heart rate (ECG) on channel 0, the blood pressure (aortal pressure) on channel 1, and 10 EEG sensors on channels 2-11. The heart rate and aortal pressure need to be viewed in real-time, but do not need to be stored in disk files. All of the EEG data needs to be stored for further processing. The Data Mode selected is Allow Gaps. Allowing gaps lets DT VEE continue to display the time domain and frequency domain data even if the display is not keeping up with the acquisition and writing to disk. See Figure 15-26

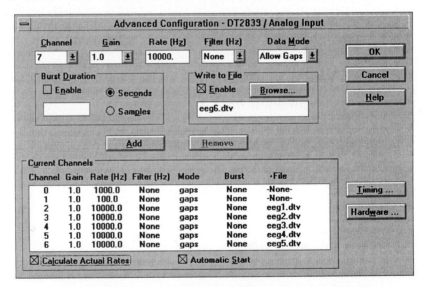

Fig. 15-26. The Advanced Configuration Dialog Box

The timing setup involves an external trigger received from a push button operated by the user. See Figure 15-27.

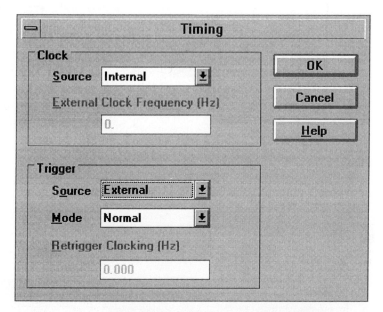

Fig. 15-27. The Timing Dialog Box

The heart rate, blood pressure, and one EEG channel are viewed with XY Trace objects. The Frequency spectrum is viewed with a Magnitude Spectrum object. See Figures 15-28 and 15-29.

CUTTING YOUR TEST DEVELOPMENT TIME WITH HP VEE

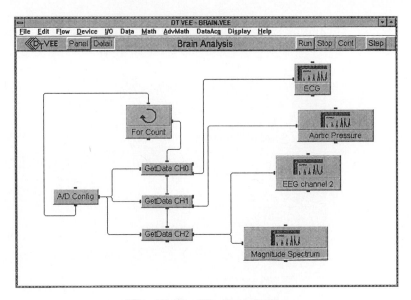

Fig. 15-28. The Detail View

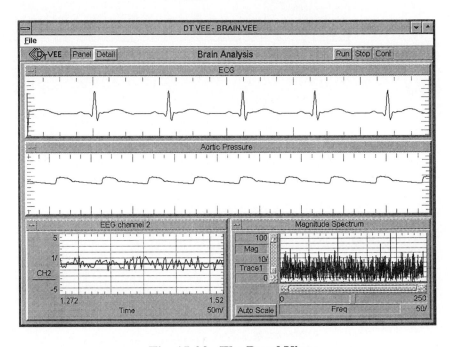

Fig. 15-29. The Panel View

Chapter 15 Checklist

Use the following checklist to determine whether there are topics you need to review:

- Describe the main subsystems of a data acquisition board.

- Describe what a subsystem handle is and how it is used by the data acquisition objects.

- Acquire two analog input channels continuously and display the data.

- Generate a 1 kHz square wave on counter/timer channel 1 (if available).

Appendix A:
Ordering and Configuration Information

HP VEE for Windows (E2120B)

- IBM PC or compatibles ('386DX required, 33MHz '486 recommended)

- Running MS Windows 3.1 or later and MS DOS 5.0 or later (at the printing of this book, HP intended to support MS Windows NT in the near future)

- 8 MBytes RAM (16 MBytes recommended)

- SVGA 800 x 600 monitor (1024 x 768 SVGA monitor recommended)

- IEEE-488 (HP-IB/GP-IB -- either HP or National Instruments cards), RS-232, and VXI (supported through HP-IB)

- Run-Only version available (E2125B)

HP VEE-Test for HP-UX (E2110B - Series 300/400, E2111B - Series 700)

- HP 9000, Series 300, 400, or 700

- Running HP-UX 8.x or later

- X Windows 11.4

- 12 MBytes RAM required (16 to 32 MBytes recommended)

- Video: VGA (Run-Only), 1024 x 768 resolution, or 1280 x 1024 resolution

- IEEE-488.2 (HP-IB/GP-IB), RS-232, GPIO (Series 300 only), MXI (Series 700 only), VXI

HP VEE for Sun (E2112B)

- Sun SPARCstations

- SunOS versions 4.1.2 or 4.1.3 (at the printing of this book HP intended to support the Solaris operating system in the near future)

- Open Windows versions 2.0 or 3.0

- 16 MBytes RAM required (24 to 32 MBytes recommended)

- Video: Any display supported by Open Windows 2.0 or 3.0

- IEEE-488.2 (HP-IB/GP-IB), VXI supported through HP-IB

DT VEE for Windows (SP0900 - CL)

- IBM PC-compatible '386 with math coprocessor (33 MHz, '486 recommended)

- MS Windows 3.1 or later, MS DOS 5.0 or later

- 8 MBytes RAM required (12 to 16 MBytes recommended)

- SVGA 800 x 600 monitor (SVGA 1024 x 768 recommended)

- Appropriate DT Open-Layers hardware driver(s)

- Run-only version available (SP0901 - CL)

Where to Order HP VEE

Call your local HP sales office listed in your telephone directory or an HP regional office listed below for the location of your nearest sales office.

United States of America:

Rockville, MD
(301) 670 4300

Rolling Meadow, IL
(708) 255 9800

Fullerton, CA
(714) 999 6700

Atlanta, GA
(404) 980 7351

Canada:
(416) 678 9430

Japan:
(8113) 3335 8192

Latin America:

Mexico
(525) 202 0155

Brazil
(11) 709 1444

Australia/New Zealand:
(03) 895 2895

CUTTING YOUR TEST DEVLOPMENT TIME WITH HP VEE

Hong Kong:
(852) 848 7070

Korea:
(2) 769 0800

Taiwan:
(2) 717 9524

Singapore:
(65) 291 8554

India:
(11) 690 355

PRC:
(1) 505 3888

In Europe, Africa, and Middle East, please call your local HP sales office or representative:

Austria/South East Area:
(0222) 2500 0

Begium and Luxembourg:
(02) 761 31 11

Denmark:
45 99 10 00

Finland:
(90) 88 721

France:
(1) 69.82.65.00

Germany:
(06172) 16 0

Greece:
(01) 68 28 811

Ireland:
(01) 2844633

Israel:
(03) 5380 333

Italy:
(02) 95 300 930

Netherlands:
(020) 547 6669

Norway:
(02) 87 97 00

Portugal:
(11) 301 73 30

South Africa:
(011) 806 1000

Spain:
900 123 123

Sweden:
(08) 750 20 00

Switzerland:
(057) 31 21 11

Turkey:
(90 1) 4 125 83 13

CUTTING YOUR TEST DEVLOPMENT TIME WITH HP VEE

United Kingdom:
(0344) 362 867

For countries not listed, contact Hewlett-Packard, International Sales Branch, Geneva, Switzerland.

Tel: +41-22-780-7111
Fax: +41-22-780-7535

Where to Order DT VEE

United States or Canada:
1-800-525-8528

United Kingdom:
(0734) 793838

Germany:
(07142) 95 31-0

France:
011.33.69.29.98.88

Italy:
(030) 242 5696

Appendix B:
Additional Lab Exercises

The following exercises should be done to reinforce the HP VEE concepts you've learned in this book. Each programming problem will be classified under the main concept being stressed. You should develop a solution, then compare yours to the programs in this appendix. There are many ways to program any given task, so you have a valid solution if it meets the problem specifications. However, programs that execute more quickly and are easier to use should be considered better solutions. A short discussion of key points will follow each solution.

General Programming Techniques

Apple Bagger

You want to know how many apples it takes to fill a ten pound basket. Create an HP VEE program that counts how many apples it takes to fill the basket. Each apple weighs between 0 and 1 pound.

Suggestions:

This program can be created with 10 or fewer objects. Choose from the following:

    Start
    Until Break
    Random Number
    Accumulator

Break
Real
Conditional (A>=B)
Stop
Counter
If/Then/Else

===

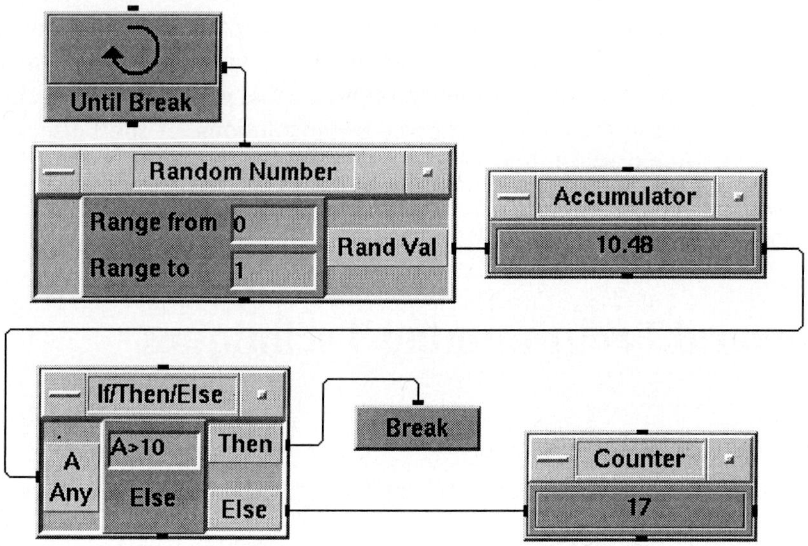

Fig. B-1. Apple Bagger, Solution 1

Key Points:

- **Optimal Solutions:** To optimize the performance of your programs, use fewer objects, if possible. Here we've used 6 objects; the program could also be implemented with 10 objects, as the next figure will show.

- **Until Break and Break Objects:** Use these objects for loops that require testing a condition. Here we want the loop to stop when the total weight of the apples is greater than 10 pounds.

- **Accumulator:** Use the Accumulator to keep a running total.

- **Counter:** Use the Counter to keep a running count. Here we use it to track the total number of apples in the basket. Note that when the total weight is over 10, only the Then pin fires on the If/Then/Else object giving us the correct answer in the Counter.

The following figure gives another solution using more objects:

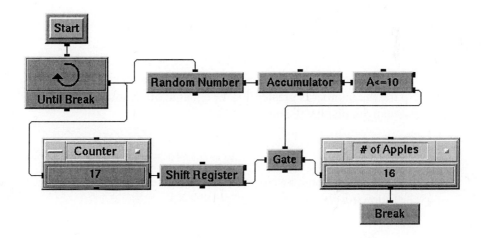

Fig. B-2. Apple Bagger, Solution 2

Key Points:

- **Start:** Using a Start object for this program is redundant, since you can use the Run button on the main menu bar. Start is best used when you have two programs on a screen, and you want to be able to run them independently. Or you have a program with a feedback loop, and you want to define where to initiate execution.

- **Shift Register:** You use a Shift Register to access the previous values of the output. In solution 2 the Counter is keeping a running count of every apple before it's weighed, so the count must be reduced by one when the total weight exceeds 10.

- **Gate:** The Gate is used to hold the output until another action occurs and activates its sequence pin. Here, when the condition A<=10 is no longer true the Else pin on the If/Then/Else object activates the gate.

Testing Numbers

Step 1

Create a program that allows a user to enter a number between 0 and 100. If the the number is greater than or equal to 50, display the number. If it is less than 50, display the message "Sorry."

Suggestions:

This program can be created with 7 or fewer objects. Choose from the following objects:

    Start
    Integer
    Slider
    Real
    If/Then/Else
    Formula
    Gate
    Text
    Junction
    AlphaNumeric

Additional Lab Exercises

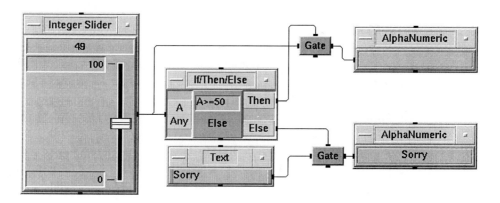

Fig. B-3. Testing Numbers, Step 1

Step 2

After the model is working with 7 objects, try programming it with 5 objects without using the Gate object.

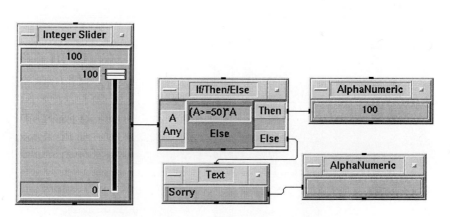

Fig. B-4. Testing Numbers, Step 2

B - 5

CUTTING YOUR TEST DEVELOPMENT TIME WITH HP VEE

Key Points

- **Auto Execute:** All input objects such as the Integer Slider have an Auto Execute selection in the object menu. If chosen, the object operates whenever its value is changed.

- **Eliminating Gates:** The expression (A>=50)*A in the If/Then/Else object evaluates to a 1*A, if A>=50 is true, or 0, if false. So A is put on the Then pin, if the expression is true, and a 0 is put on the Else pin, if the expression is false. (Any expression that evaluates to a non-zero is considered true, and the value is propagated on the Then pin.)

Step 3

Can you now program a solution using only 3 objects?

HINT: Try using a triadic expression in the Formula object. The format is: (<expression> ? <if TRUE,output value> : <if FALSE, output value>). For example, if A < 10 evaluates to TRUE, you want the value of A on the Result pin; otherwise, you want the string "FALSE" on the Result pin. You would use the following triadic expression: (A<10 ? A : "FALSE").

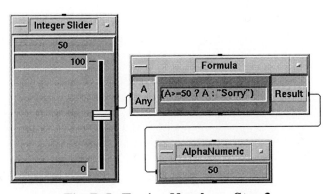

Fig. B-5. Testing Numbers, Step 3

Additional Lab Exercises

Collecting Random Numbers

Create a program that generates 100 random numbers and displays them. Record the total time required to generate and display the values.

Suggestions:

This program can be created with 6 or fewer objects. Choose from the following:

    Start
    For Range
    Until Break
    Random Seed
    Random Number
    Collector
    Formula
    Set Values
    Allocate Array
    Logging AlphaNumeric
    Strip Chart
    VU Meter
    Date/Time
    Timer
    Now( )
    Break
    Do

HINT: To improve performance, send the data to the display only once by first collecting the data into an array using the Collector object. Note the performance differences.

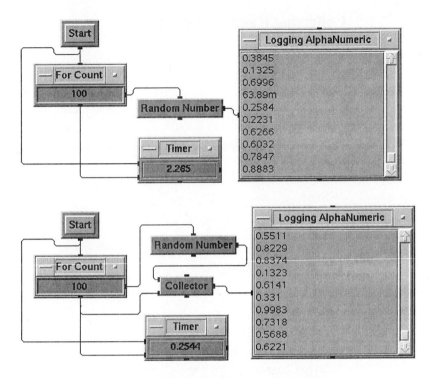

Fig. B-6. Collecting Random Numbers

Key Points

- **Logging AlphaNumeric vs. AlphaNumeric:** Use Logging AlphaNumeric to display consecutive input (either Scalar or Array 1D) as a history of previous values. Use AlphaNumeric to display data as a single value, an Array 1D, or an Array 2D. The Logging display gives you an array without index values; the AlphaNumeric display gives you the same array with index numbers and values.

- **Timing Pins:** Notice that we are timing from the execution of Start to the sequence output pin on For Count, because that pin fires after the thread has executed.

Additional Lab Exercises

Random Number Generator

Step 1

Create a random number generator that requires external inputs. Display the numbers on a strip chart. Inputs should be allowed for:

  Maximum random number
  Minimum random number
  Number of random numbers generated

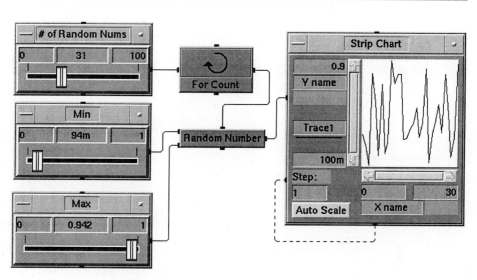

Fig. B-7. Random Number Generator, Step 1

Key Points:

- **Layout of Slider Objects:** You can select either a vertical or horizontal format for the screen image of the slider objects by clicking on Layout in the object menus.

- **Strip Chart:** Use a Strip Chart to display the recent history of data that is continuously generated.

B - 9

CUTTING YOUR TEST DEVELOPMENT TIME WITH HP VEE

- **The Auto Scale Control Pin:** By clicking on Terminals => Add Control Input... in a display's object menu, you can select Auto Scale as a control pin. By connecting it to the display's sequence output pin, HP VEE will automatically autoscale your graph after the data is displayed. Note the dotted line indicating the control pin connection.

Step 2

Collect the random numbers into an array. Find the moving average and display it with the numbers.

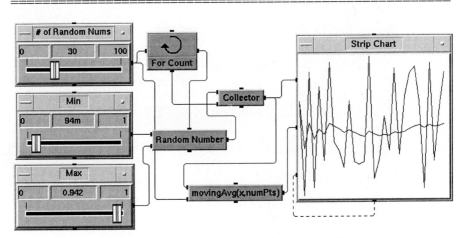

Fig. B-8. Random Number Generator, Step 2

- **MovingAvg(x, numPts):** Use this object located in the AdvMath => Data Filtering menu to smooth the input data using the average of a specified number of data points preceding the point of interest to calculate the smoothed data point.

Additional Lab Exercises

Using Masks

Mask Test

Step 1

Create a 50 Hz sine wave with an adjustable amount of noise. Test the noisy sine wave to be certain that it stays below the following limits:

(0, 0.5)
(2.2m, 1.2)
(7.2m, 1.2)
(10.2m, 0.5)
(20m, 0.5)

If the sine wave exceeds the limits, mark the failing points with a red diamond. HINTS: You can change the format of the displays from lines to dots to diamonds. Select Traces and Scales in the object menu. Also, you may find the Comparator object helpful.

Step 2

Add to your program to calculate and display the percentage of failures.

CUTTING YOUR TEST DEVELOPMENT TIME WITH HP VEE

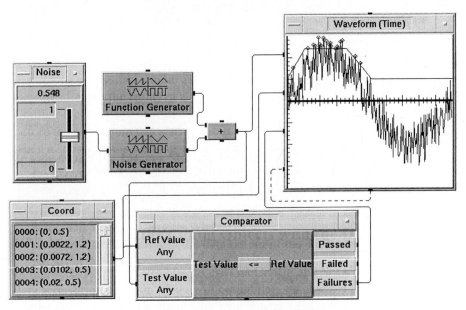

Fig. B-9. The Mask Test, Step 1

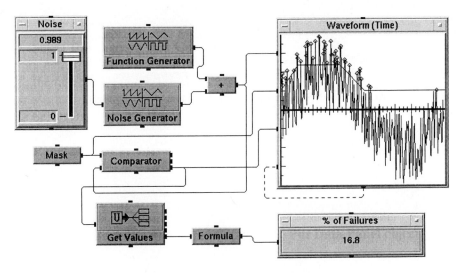

Fig. B-10. Mask Test, Step 2

Additional Lab Exercises

Key Points:

- **Mask:** The mask is created using the Data => Constant => Coord object, then configuring it for 5 array elements. You simply input the coordinate pairs separated by commas and HP VEE will add the parentheses. The x values were chosen knowing that the time span of the waveform was 20 milliseconds. Also, note that the Waveform (Time) display will accept a Coord data type as an input. You could also have used a Data => Build Data => Arb Waveform object, which converts a Coord to a Waveform data type by specifying the number of points in the Waveform.

- **Comparator:** This object compares a test value against a reference value. Once again, you can compare a waveform to an array of coordinate pairs. The Failures pin gives you an array of the data points that failed, which you can send to the display and highlight with a different color or type of line.

- **Get Values:** This object is extremely useful for breaking down the information in an array. In this case, we've simply used the TotSize pin to get the number of failed data points for the percentage-of-failures calculation. (In version B.02.00, you could also use AdvMath => Array => totSize(x) to get the size of the array of Coord from the Comparator. Prior to this version there was a bug in the totSize(x) object when used on a Coord array.)

- **Formula:** *A/256*100* is the formula used to compute the percentage of failures.

Using Strings and Globals

Manipulating Strings and Globals

Using string objects or functions create a program that accepts a user's name in the following format: <space> <firstname> <space> <lastname>. After the user enters their name, have the program strip off the first name and only print the last name. Store the string into a global variable. Retrieve the string using the Formula object.

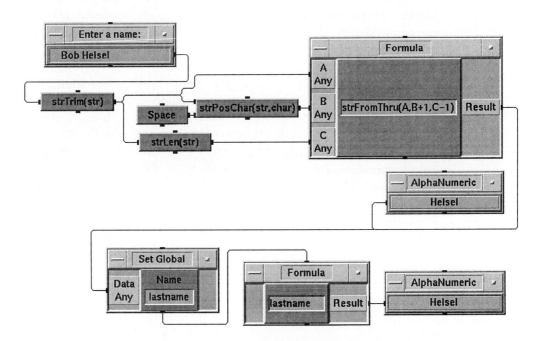

Fig. B-11. Manipulating Strings and Globals

Key Points

- **String Objects and Functions:** StrTrim(str) first strips off any spaces or tabs from the front and back of the name. StrPosChar(str,char) yields the index of the space character between the firstname and lastname. StrLen(str), of course, gives the length of the string. All of these were performed using the string objects, but they could also be done using string functions within a Formula object. StrFromThru(A,B+1,C-1) is used in the Formula object, and the function takes the string from input A, adds 1 to the index of the space from input B, and subtracts 1 from the string length at input C. (Recall that all indexing is zero-based.)

- **Set Global:** Notice how easily you can set a global variable called lastname, which can then be referenced in any expression field, such as the Formula object in this example.

CUTTING YOUR TEST DEVELOPMENT TIME WITH HP VEE

Optimizing Techniques

Optimizing HP VEE Programs

Step 1

For this lab, you will build a simple HP VEE program two ways and note the difference in execution speed. Create a program that sends the range, 0 to 710 step 10, through both a sine function and cosine function. Put the results of the functions on an X vs Y display. Use the Timer object to clock how long the program takes.

Step 2

Clone all of the objects from the first program. Modify the new set to collect the range into an array. Now, the sine and cosine functions are run against an array of points, and only plotted one time. Note the time savings.

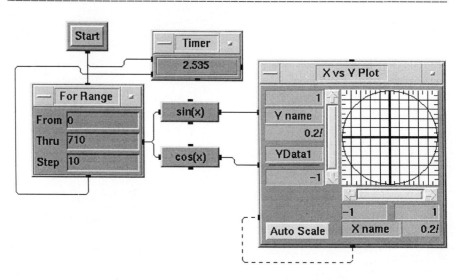

Fig. A-12. Optimizing HP VEE Programs, Step 1

Additional Lab Exercises

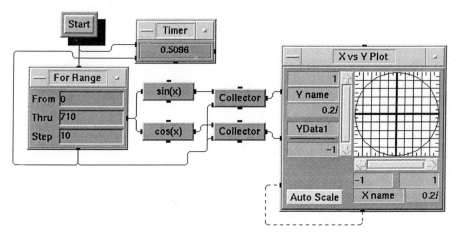

Fig. B-13. Optimizing HP VEE Programs, Step 2

Key Points

- **Optimizing with Arrays:** Note the increase in performance between step 1 and step 2 that comes from using arrays. Whenever possible, perform analysis or display results using arrays rather than scalar values.

- **X vs Y Display:** We used this display instead of the the Waveform or XY displays, because we had separate data for the X and Y data.

B - 17

UserObjects

A Random Noise UserObject

Step 1

Create a UserObject that generates a random noise waveform. Display the noisy waveform and the noise spectrum outside the UserObject. Provide control outside the UserObject for the following: amplitude, number of points, interval (time span), DC offset.

> *Note:* Do not use a virtual source inside the UserObject. Use objects such as Build Waveform and Random Number to create your UserObject.

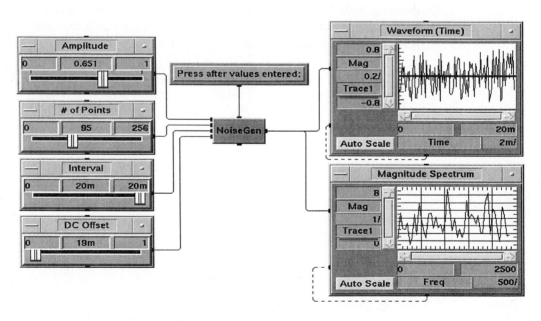

Fig. B-14. A Random Noise UserObject

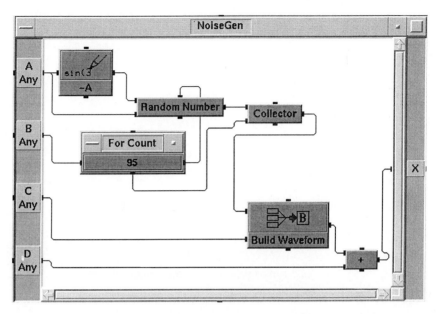

Fig. B-15. The NoiseGen UserObject

Key Points

- **UserObject:** Notice that the UserObjects you build are essentially customized objects that you've added to HP VEE.

- **Build Waveform:** This object creates a Waveform data type from a Real array of amplitude values and a time span (the length of time in seconds over which the y data was sampled).

HP VEE User Functions

Using User Functions

Step 1

Create a function called NoiseGen that accepts an amplitude value (0-1) from a slider and returns a noisy waveform.

Do not use: Virtual Source, For Count, For Range

Do use: Formula, Ramp(), Build Waveform

HINT: Use randomize(array, -a,a) where the array must be 256 points, and a is the amplitude.

Build a simple model to be certain this function works correctly.

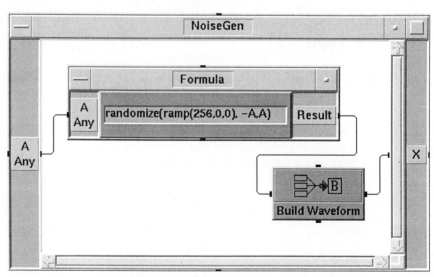

Fig. B-16. The NoiseGen User Function

Additional Lab Exercises

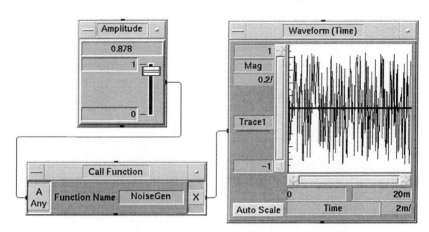

Fig. B-17. Using User Functions, Step 1

Key Points

- **Ramp():** Notice that the ramp( ) function is used to generate an array of 256 points within the parameter list for randomize( ).

- **Build Waveform:** Notice that the default time span here is 20 milliseconds, so that you only need to send an array to this object to build a waveform.

- **No Auto Scale on Display:** You don't need Auto Scale this time, because the amplitude will be no greater than 1, so the default scales are satisfactory.

Step 2

In the same program, create another function called AddNoise that calls the first function, NoiseGen. AddNoise should add the noisy waveform from you NoiseGen function to a sine wave. AddNoise should have two inputs, one for the NoiseGen amplitude and one for the sine wave; it should have one output for the result.

CUTTING YOUR TEST DEVELOPMENT TIME WITH HP VEE

Build a simple model with a slider for the noise amplitude, and the Virtual Source => Function Generator (sine wave, Freq = 100 Hz) for the good waveform to add to the noise. Display the resultant waveform.

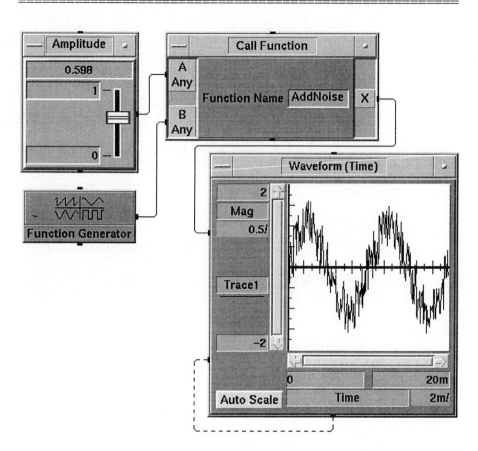

Fig. B-18. Using User Functions, Step 2

Additional Lab Exercises

Step 3

In the same program, call the AddNoise function again, this time from a Formula object, taking the absolute value of the result. Display the absolute value waveform on the same display. Next prepare to edit the AddNoise function. Turn on Show Data Flow. Leave the edit window open and run the program. Notice how useful this capability would be for debugging purposes.

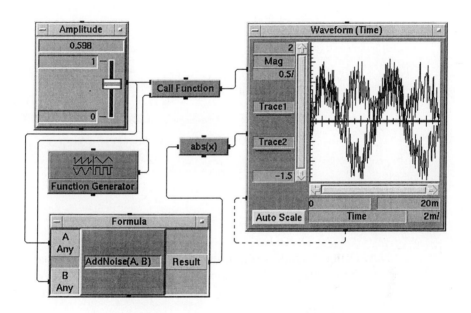

Fig. B-19. Using User Functions, Step 3

B - 23

CUTTING YOUR TEST DEVELOPMENT TIME WITH HP VEE

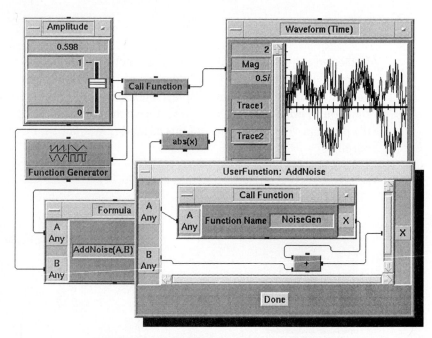

Fig. B-20. Edit Window Feature in Step 3

Step 4

Now change your program so that the slider sets a Global variable called Amplitude. Have the NoiseGen function use that Global (so NoiseGen will no longer require an input pin). Make the program run correctly. Save this file as UFLAB.

Additional Lab Exercises

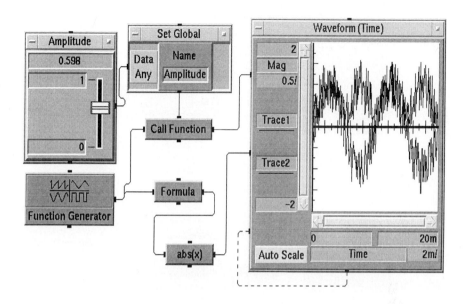

Fig. B-21. Using User Functions, Step 4

Importing and Deleting Libraries of User Functions

Build a simple program to import the UFLAB (Using User Functions, Step 4 program name) functions, call the function that adds the noise, and then delete the functions programmatically. Use the Select Function choice in the object menu of the Call Function object.

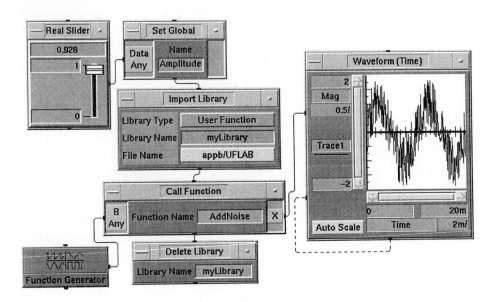

Fig. B-22. Importing and Deleting Libraries (B.00.01)

Note: In versions B.02.00 and later you must use a <library name>.<function name> format in Call Function. In this case it would be **myLibrary.AddNoise** in the Call Function object.

Key Points

- **Load Lib:** You need to click on Load Lib in the Import Library object menu to manually load the library you specified, so that you can use the Select Function feature in Call Function.

- **Select Function:** Notice that this selection will configure the proper input and output pins for the function you select.

- **Editing User Functions:** If you import a library of User Functions programmatically, you will not be able to edit them. If you want to edit the User Functions you import, use the Merge Library command instead.

Additional Lab Exercises

- **Global Variable Caution:** Notice that when you use a global variable in a function, you have to remember that global when using that function in other programs. One of the advantages of explicitly creating inputs and outputs is that they are easier to track.

Operator Panels

Creating Operator Panels and Pop-ups

Step 1

Create a UserObject to interact with an operator. Use two inputs, A and B. If A and B are equal, send A to the output. If A and B are not equal, prompt the operator to select either A or B for the output, while the current value of each is displayed. If the operator does not respond in 10 seconds, generate an error message.

HINT: Each panel that pops up needs to be a separate UserObject. Also, remember to enable Show Panel on Exec when you want a panel to pop up.

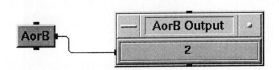

Fig. B-23. Creating Operator Panels Program

Key Points

- **Iconized UserObject:** The entire program is in the iconized UserObject, AorB. When it executes, the appropriate pop-up panels will appear.

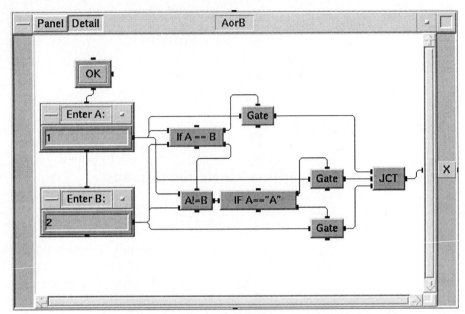

Fig. B-24. The AorB UserObject Detail View

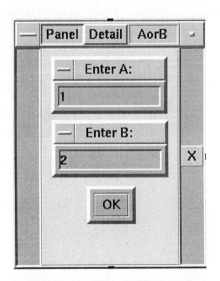

Fig. B-25. The AorB Panel View

Additional Lab Exercises

Key Points

- **Gating Selections:** In the AorB detail view, the If A==B simply gates A to the output, if A and B are equal. If not, then the UserObject AnotB is activated which will ask the user for her choice. The AnotB output is tested and the correct value is gated to the AorB output.

- **AorB Panel View:** The AorB pop-up panel gets the original two values from the user. Note the OK object is above the input boxes. Why? (You want the user to enter values before the input boxes execute.) If the two values are not equal, AnotB has its own pop-up panel for more user input.

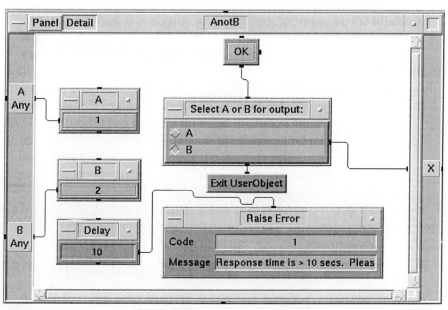

Fig. B-26. AnotB Detail View

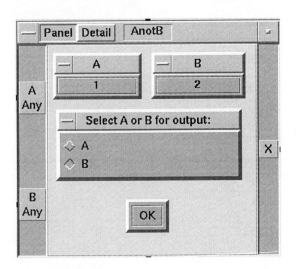

Fig. B-27. AnotB Panel View

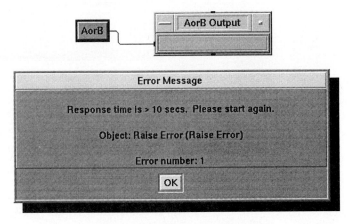

Fig. B-28. AnotB Error Message

Additional Lab Exercises

Key Points

- **Enum Object as a Menu:** Note the use of the Data => Enum object edited for two choices and formatted for buttons. This configuration will output a text A or B. If you need the ordinal value (0 or 1), then put the output through the ordinal(x) function.

- **Exit UserObject:** If the user responds in under 10 seconds, this object will exit the UserObject, even though the Delay object may not have finished executing.

- **Delay and Raise Error:** After 10 seconds the Delay object pings the Raise Error object, which will pause execution of the program and display the Error Message you have typed in. A black outline will also appear around the object that caused the error, which goes away when you click on Stop or Run on the main menu bar.

Step 2

Change the UserObjects into UserFunctions.

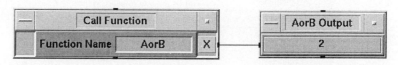

Fig. B-29. Creating Operator Panels Program, Step 2

Working with Files

Moving Data To and From Files

Step 1

Create an HP VEE program to write the time of day to a file. Generate 100 random points and write them to the file. Calculate the mean and standard deviation of the numbers and append them to the file in the following format:

    Mean: xxxxxx
    Std Dev: yyyyyy

Next, read only the mean and standard deviation from the file.

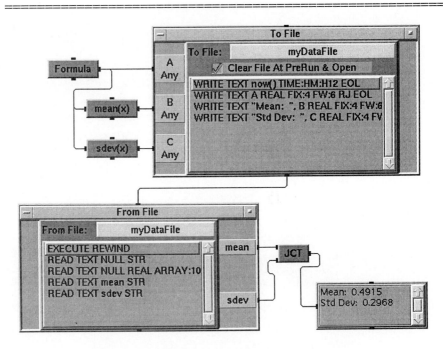

Fig. B-30. Moving Data To and From Files

Additional Lab Exercises

Key Points

- **Generating an Array:** Use randomize(ramp(100,0,1), 0, 1) in the Formula object to create an array of 100 random numbers. The ramp( ) function generates an ordered array and delivers it to the randomize( ) function, which then generates random values between 0 and 1.

- **Time Stamp:** The now( ) function is used in the expression field of the I/O Transaction dialog box for transaction one in the To File object. When you change the format to TIME STAMP FORMAT, the dialog box gives you additional buttons to specify how the time will be stored.

- **Storing Two Values in a Line:** In both the third and fourth transactions in the To File object, we store a constant Text string, followed by a Real value. For example, in the third transaction you type **"Mean: ",B** in the expression field of the I/O Transaction box (assuming the mean value will be on the B input pin).

- **Extracting a Value From a File:** To get to the mean and standard deviation, you first have to send an EXECUTE REWIND to position the read pointer at the beginning. Then you use NULL with the proper format to READ past the time stamp and real array. Finally, you can read the last two lines in the file as strings.

- **Junction:** Use Flow => Junction when you want to connect more than one output to a single input -- the mean and sdev outputs to the Logging AlphaNumeric display for example.

- **Deselecting Show Title:** Notice that we've deselected Show Title in the object menu of the Logging AlphaNumeric display for a less cluttered appearance.

Records

Manipulating Records

Step 1

Build a record with three fields holding an integer, the time right now, and a four element array of reals. The fields should be named int, time, and ary, respectively. Merge this record with another that holds a random number between 0 and 1, and a waveform. Name these fields rand and wave. The resultant record should have five fields.

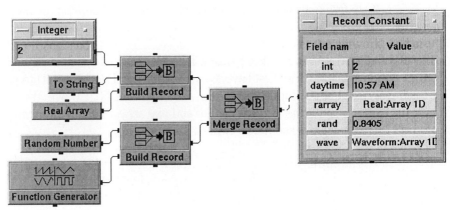

Fig. B-31. Manipulating Records, Step 1

Key Points

- **Time Stamp:** Use the now( ) function within the To String object to create your time stamp for this program.

- **Configuring a Data Constant as an Array:** Any data type in the Data => Constant menu can become an array by selecting Config... in its object menu, specifying the number of elements, and typing in the values.

Additional Lab Exercises

- **Naming Fields:** By renaming the input terminals on the Build Record object, you can give your record specific field names such as int, rand, and wave.

- **The Default Value Control Input:** A Record Constant makes an excellent interactive display object by adding a Default Value Control pin. The Record Constant will automatically configure itself for the record it receives.

Step 2

Use a triadic in a formula object to test the random value in the record, and display either the integer or a text string. If the value is less than 0.5, display the first field of the record; otherwise, output a text string "More than 0.5." Next, extract only the time and the waveform. (HINT: Do not use a Formula object.) Display this record with an AlphaNumeric object.

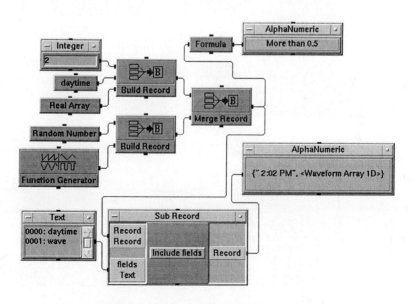

Fig. B-32. Manipulating Records, Step 2

CUTTING YOUR TEST DEVELOPMENT TIME WITH HP VEE

Step 3

Replace the integer input for the first field with a For Count object and step through 10 iterations. Be certain to "ping" the random number generator and the time function on each iteration. Send the complete record into a To DataSet object. In a separate thread, retrieve all records from the dataset where the random value is greater than 0.5. Put the resultant records into a record constant.

HINT: You'll need a control pin for a Default Value on the Record Constant object.

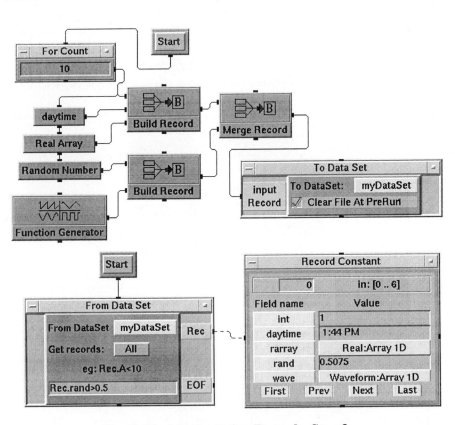

Fig. B-33. Manipulating Records, Step 3

Additional Lab Exercises

Key Points (Steps 2 and 3)

- **(Step 2) Using a Conditional Expression:** HP VEE supports a conditional expression, which provides an efficient way to implement an if-then-else action. For example, in this case we wrote the expression (A.rand < 0.5 ? A.int : "More than 0.5") in the Formula object. *If* A.rand is less than 0.5, *then* the condition is true and A.int becomes the result, *else* the string "More than 0.5" becomes the result.

- **(Step 2) The Sub Record Object:** Notice that we've put a Text array of the fields desired on the Sub Record input pin labeled *fields*. When you configure the Sub Record object to *include fields*, it will output a record that only contains the fields you have specified.

- **(Step 3) The To DataSet Object:** The *Clear File at PreRun* option only clears the file before data is sent the first time. Notice that the program sends 10 different records to the same file sequentially, and they are simply appended to the file.

- **(Step 3) The From DataSet Object:** This object is configured to retrieve all records where the *rand* field is greater than 0.5. In this case, seven out of ten records meet that criterion.

CUTTING YOUR TEST DEVELOPMENT TIME WITH HP VEE

Step 4

Create a panel display that allows you to edit the information from the dataset. Include a button that sends your changes back to the dataset. Run this program several times to see that your changes are being stored into the dataset.

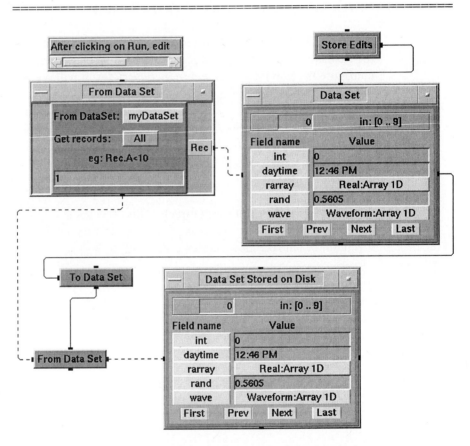

Fig. B-34. Manipulating Records, Step 4, Detail View

Additional Lab Exercises

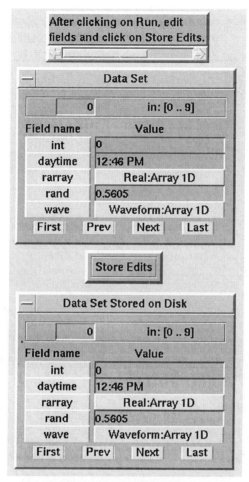

Fig. B-35. **Manipulating Records, Step 4, Panel View**

Key Points

- **Renaming the OK Object:** Note that the OK object has been renamed *Store Edits*. This is a useful technique for making your program readable.

- **Rewind Control Pin:** Use it on From Data Set to reset the read pointer.

Test Sequencing

Using the Test Sequencer

Step 1

Create a simple user function called UpperLimit that is a pop-up panel with a Real Slider and a Confirm (OK) object. Send the output of the slider to a Global variable called UL and also to an output terminal.

Test1 in the sequencer should be an EXEC transaction that calls UpperLimit.

Create another function called AddRand that simulates the test you might actually call. This function should add an input value to a random value (0 to 1). Hence, one input pin and one output pin.

From the sequencer, make a tests2 call AddRand and send in a 0. Test the return value to do a limit comparison < the global UL value. If it passes, then return "PASS " +test2.result. If it fails, then return "FAILED " +test2.result.

Put an AlphaNumeric display on the Return pin of the Sequencer.

After the Sequencer object, ping a Get Global object (UL) and another AlphaNumeric display.

Run the program several times.

Additional Lab Exercises

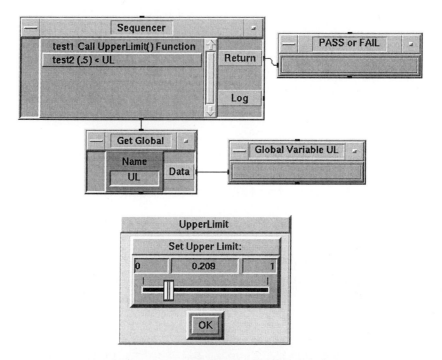

Fig. B-36. Using the Test Sequencer, Step 1

Key Points

- **Setting Global Variables with a User Function:** A typical use of the first Sequencer transaction is to call a User Function that sets Global Variables, as it does in this case. Then you can utilize these variables in any test that follows, as we have done here.

- **The Sequencer Return Pin:** We have used the Return pin in this example to deliver a pass or fail message plus the test value. You could use this pin to deliver any message or value from a particular test.

B - 41

CUTTING YOUR TEST DEVELOPMENT TIME WITH HP VEE

Step 2

Disable the first test step. Assuming you don't need the global anywhere else, you can call the UpperLimit function directly. Change test2 so that it compares the return value against the result of the UpperLimit function.

Extra Credit:

Load the example in the HP VEE subdirectory:
examples/mfgtest/mfgtest.ex

Look at the two sequencer objects in this example. The first, Login Control, checks the user's name and password. The second sequencer uses the EXEC TRANS control pin and accepts an array of text strings to call specific tests.

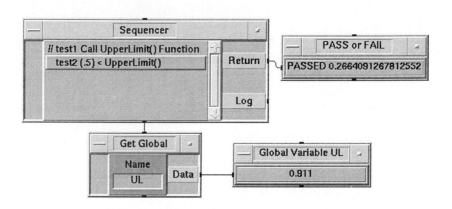

Fig. B-37. Using the Test Sequencer, Step 2

Key Points

- **The User Function in an Expression Field:** In this example, instead of comparing a test result to the UL variable, you can type the function name, UpperLimit(), in the expression field where the variable would go.

Additional Lab Exercises

Logging Sequencer Data

Edit a test1 Sequencer transaction that simply calls the HP VEE function random( ). Compare the result against a limit < 0.5. Cut the test1 transaction and paste it back several times. You should have a total of 4 tests.

Build a program to run the sequencer five times with each Sequencer Log record going into an array and a dataset. Using the array, find the minimum, the maximum, the mean, and the standard deviation of the results of the second test.

HINT: Use a Formula object with a <record>.<record>.<field> in the expression field.

In a separate thread, get all of the records from the dataset where the first test passed or the second test failed. Print the timestamp field from the records on a Logging AlphaNumeric display.

HINT: You may need to access the Logging Config menu in the object menu of the Sequencer.

==

CUTTING YOUR TEST DEVELOPMENT TIME WITH HP VEE

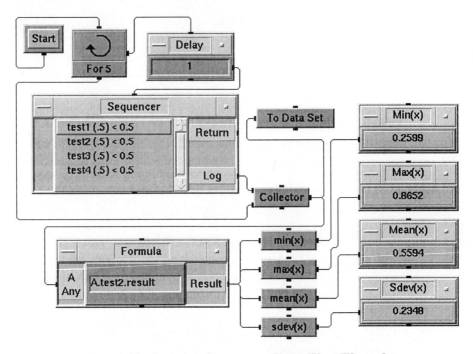

Fig. B-38. Logging Sequencer Data, First Thread

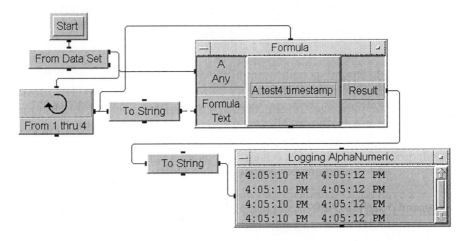

Fig. B-39. Logging Sequencer Data, Second Thread

B - 44

Additional Lab Exercises

Key Points

- **The Delay Object (First Thread):** This object simply holds execution flow for the specified number of seconds. Here we've used it to create time stamp values that varied between each run of the Sequencer.

- **The Data Format for Several Runs of the Sequencer (First Thread):** When the Sequencer executes once, it outputs a Record of Records -- the first record has field names that match the test names, then each field holds a record containing the different pieces of data for that particular test. When the Sequencer runs several times, each Record of Records can be added to an array, which can then be investigated. If you use the <record>.<record>.<field> format in the Formula object, you will get an array of data -- in this case, an array of real values giving the test results for five runs of test2. You then caluculated the minimum, maximum, mean, and standard deviation from this array. You could have specified a single run of test2 by indicating a particular element in your array of records of records. For example, to get the first run result of test2 you would use the expression: *A[0].test2.result*. If you don't specify a particular element in an array, HP VEE assumes you mean the whole array.

- **The EOF Pin on the From Data Set Object (Second Thread):** We've added the EOF pin, in case there are no records that fit the criteria. If this happens then the EOF pin will fire, instead of HP VEE halting the program with an error message.

- **The Conditional Expression in the From Data Set Object (Second Thread):** We have used the expression *(Rec.test1.pass==1) OR (Rec.test2.pass==0)*. Again we've used the <record>.<record>.<field> format. We use Rec, since that is the name of the array of records being returned. Test1 and test2 specify which tests HP VEE should examine, and the field name *pass* is the default name for the pass-fail indicator (1 or 0) assigned by HP VEE. (You enable or disable different fields for all tests by selecting Logging Config... in the Sequencer object menu.)

- **Formula Control Pin on the Formula Object (Second Thread):** Notice that you want to run the Formula object four times with a different formula each time accessing the runs of a particular test. The data output

B - 45

of the For Range object (labeled *From 1 thru 4*) is connected to the sequence input pins on the To String and Formula objects to make certain those objects execute after they have the new formula information. The For Range object will output the numbers 1 through 4 sequentially in this case. The general formula would look like this: *A.test<test number>.timestamp* (where *<test number>* is a number between 1 and 4). You can use the Formula control pin for this purpose. You use the To String and For Range objects to create the formula. The To String object holds the transaction *WRITE TEXT "A.test"+A+".timestamp"* (where A is the input terminal on To String that holds the test number from 1 to 4).

- **Converting Time Stamp Formats (Second Thread):** The To String object before Logging AlphaNumeric converts the time stamps from a Real format to a Time Stamp format for more clarity.

Instrument Drivers

Using HP Instrument Drivers

Step 1

Using the HP driver for the HP3314A Function Generator, change the Frequency from 0 to 100 kHz with a step of 1 kHz, and clock the performance.

Step2

Repeat step 1 using a Component driver and characterize the performance differences.

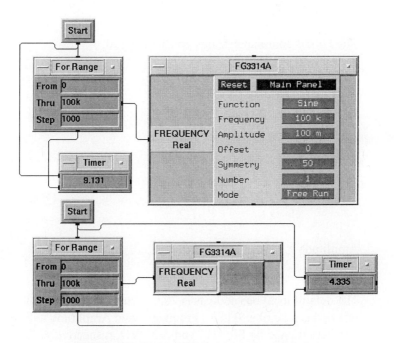

Fig. B-40. Using HP Instrument Drivers

CUTTING YOUR TEST DEVELOPMENT TIME WITH HP VEE

Key Points

- **Component Drivers:** The component driver uses relevant parts of the instrument driver file and ignores the rest, so it will execute much faster than a complete instrument driver. In this case, it's about twice as fast. You could increase performance more by deselecting error checking when you're configuring either type of driver.

Creating Customized Instrument Drivers

Assume there is no driver for the HP3314A Function Generator. Create a customized driver using the Driver Writer's Tool that allows user control of:

Function
Frequency
Amplitude

The HP-IB command strings you'll need are:

3314A Function	**Program**	**Query**
Function OFF	FU0	QFU
Sine	FU1	
Square	FU2	
Triangle	FU3	
Frequency	FR	QFR
Hertz	HZ	
Amplitude	AP	QAP
Volt p-p	VO	

The default local bus address is 707. Function will return the string "FUd", where d is a number 0 to 3. Frequency and Amplitude will return real numbers framed by FR - HZ and AP - VO, respectively. The Amplitude range is from 0.00 to 10.00V p-p. The Frequency range is from 0.001Hz to 19.99MHz.

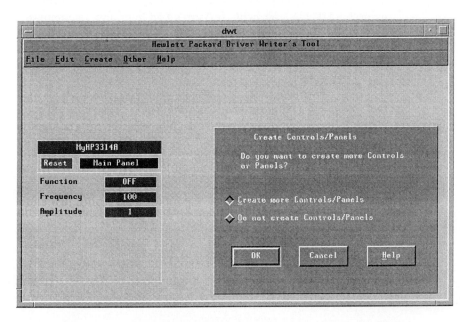

Fig. B-41. Customized Instrument Drivers Using the DWT

Compiled Functions (HP-UX)

This lab is to show you what is required from HP VEE to call C functions using the HP-UX platform. It does not address how to create the function in C or how to compile the function and build a shared library.

HP VEE includes an example C program designed to add the number 1 to a real array that is sent to the program. The C source code for the *myFunc* function is located in /usr/lib/veetest/examples/escapes/manual49.c.

> *Note: The example program in manual49.vee in the same directory performs a similar task, but the program is written so that it will work on HP-UX, MS Windows, MS Windows NT, or SunOS.*

Step 1

Import and call the function from the following shared library: /usr/lib/veetest/examples/escapes/manual49.sl.

The header file is stored in: /usr/lib/veetest/examples/escapes/manual49.h

The function expects two input pins and one output pin plus the Ret Value pin.

Use a five element array to send to the array data input pin. Use the totSize object for the array size input pin. Display the results.

===

Additional Lab Exercises

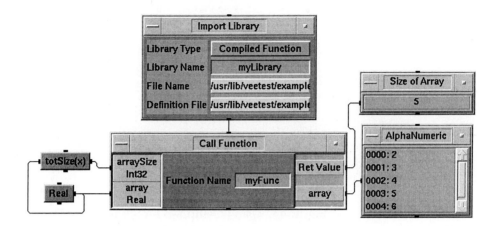

Fig. B-42. Using Compiled Functions, Step 1

Step2

Replace the totSize object with an integer value of 3. Subtract the array you sent to the Call Function object from the array you receive back from the function. Notice that this only adds 1 to the number of elements you specified.

Extra Credit:

WARNING...If you do this exercise, be prepared to kill your HP VEE process and re-start HP VEE.

Change the integer value on arraysize to 50. Press Run.

This is telling the C program that although HP VEE is giving it a five element array, it is OK to use enough memory for 50 elements. This allows the C program to overwrite HP VEE memory. If this happens, you should always re-start your HP VEE process. This is why it's a good idea to use the totSize object.

CUTTING YOUR TEST DEVELOPMENT TIME WITH HP VEE

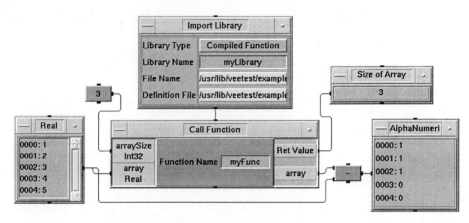

Fig. B-43. Using Compiled Functions, Step 2